C-3230   CAREER EXAMINATION SERIES

This is your
PASSBOOK for...

Clerk of the Works

Test Preparation Study Guide
Questions & Answers

COPYRIGHT NOTICE

This book is SOLELY intended for, is sold ONLY to, and its use is RESTRICTED to individual, bona fide applicants or candidates who qualify by virtue of having seriously filed applications for appropriate license, certificate, professional and/or promotional advancement, higher school matriculation, scholarship, or other legitimate requirements of education and/or governmental authorities.

This book is NOT intended for use, class instruction, tutoring, training, duplication, copying, reprinting, excerption, or adaptation, etc., by:

1) Other publishers
2) Proprietors and/or Instructors of "Coaching" and/or Preparatory Courses
3) Personnel and/or Training Divisions of commercial, industrial, and governmental organizations
4) Schools, colleges, or universities and/or their departments and staffs, including teachers and other personnel
5) Testing Agencies or Bureaus
6) Study groups which seek by the purchase of a single volume to copy and/or duplicate and/or adapt this material for use by the group as a whole without having purchased individual volumes for each of the members of the group
7) Et al.

Such persons would be in violation of appropriate Federal and State statutes.

PROVISION OF LICENSING AGREEMENTS – Recognized educational, commercial, industrial, and governmental institutions and organizations, and others legitimately engaged in educational pursuits, including training, testing, and measurement activities, may address request for a licensing agreement to the copyright owners, who will determine whether, and under what conditions, including fees and charges, the materials in this book may be used them. In other words, a licensing facility exists for the legitimate use of the material in this book on other than an individual basis. However, it is asseverated and affirmed here that the material in this book CANNOT be used without the receipt of the express permission of such a licensing agreement from the Publishers. Inquiries re licensing should be addressed to the company, attention rights and permissions department.

All rights reserved, including the right of reproduction in whole or in part, in any form or by any means, electronic or mechanical, including photocopying, recording, or by any information storage and retrieval system, without permission in writing from the Publisher.

Copyright © 2024 by
National Learning Corporation

212 Michael Drive, Syosset, NY 11791
(516) 921-8888 • www.passbooks.com
E-mail: info@passbooks.com

PASSBOOK® SERIES

THE *PASSBOOK® SERIES* has been created to prepare applicants and candidates for the ultimate academic battlefield – the examination room.

At some time in our lives, each and every one of us may be required to take an examination – for validation, matriculation, admission, qualification, registration, certification, or licensure.

Based on the assumption that every applicant or candidate has met the basic formal educational standards, has taken the required number of courses, and read the necessary texts, the *PASSBOOK® SERIES* furnishes the one special preparation which may assure passing with confidence, instead of failing with insecurity. Examination questions – together with answers – are furnished as the basic vehicle for study so that the mysteries of the examination and its compounding difficulties may be eliminated or diminished by a sure method.

This book is meant to help you pass your examination provided that you qualify and are serious in your objective.

The entire field is reviewed through the huge store of content information which is succinctly presented through a provocative and challenging approach – the question-and-answer method.

A climate of success is established by furnishing the correct answers at the end of each test.

You soon learn to recognize types of questions, forms of questions, and patterns of questioning. You may even begin to anticipate expected outcomes.

You perceive that many questions are repeated or adapted so that you can gain acute insights, which may enable you to score many sure points.

You learn how to confront new questions, or types of questions, and to attack them confidently and work out the correct answers.

You note objectives and emphases, and recognize pitfalls and dangers, so that you may make positive educational adjustments.

Moreover, you are kept fully informed in relation to new concepts, methods, practices, and directions in the field.

You discover that you are actually taking the examination all the time: you are preparing for the examination by "taking" an examination, not by reading extraneous and/or supererogatory textbooks.

In short, this PASSBOOK®, used directedly, should be an important factor in helping you to pass your test.

CLERK OF THE WORKS

DUTIES
Acts as a resident inspector of buildings being constructed, altered or repaired by contract forces. Confers with contractors and insures that county standards and specifications are being adhered to. Checks materials and arranges for laboratory tests. Keeps an accurate daily log of the work done and the equipment used by contractor. Provides written and oral reports of inspection results. Performs related work as required.

SCOPE OF THE EXAMINATION
The written test will cover knowledge, skills and/or abilities in such areas as:

1. Principles and practices of building construction;
2. Building construction materials, standards and their applications;
3. Mechanical systems and equipment in buildings;
4. Drawings, specifications and contract documents;
5. Inspection and supervision of building construction projects;
6. Understanding and interpreting written material; and
7. Preparing written material.

HOW TO TAKE A TEST

I. YOU MUST PASS AN EXAMINATION

A. WHAT EVERY CANDIDATE SHOULD KNOW

Examination applicants often ask us for help in preparing for the written test. What can I study in advance? What kinds of questions will be asked? How will the test be given? How will the papers be graded?

As an applicant for a civil service examination, you may be wondering about some of these things. Our purpose here is to suggest effective methods of advance study and to describe civil service examinations.

Your chances for success on this examination can be increased if you know how to prepare. Those "pre-examination jitters" can be reduced if you know what to expect. You can even experience an adventure in good citizenship if you know why civil service exams are given.

B. WHY ARE CIVIL SERVICE EXAMINATIONS GIVEN?

Civil service examinations are important to you in two ways. As a citizen, you want public jobs filled by employees who know how to do their work. As a job seeker, you want a fair chance to compete for that job on an equal footing with other candidates. The best-known means of accomplishing this two-fold goal is the competitive examination.

Exams are widely publicized throughout the nation. They may be administered for jobs in federal, state, city, municipal, town or village governments or agencies.

Any citizen may apply, with some limitations, such as the age or residence of applicants. Your experience and education may be reviewed to see whether you meet the requirements for the particular examination. When these requirements exist, they are reasonable and applied consistently to all applicants. Thus, a competitive examination may cause you some uneasiness now, but it is your privilege and safeguard.

C. HOW ARE CIVIL SERVICE EXAMS DEVELOPED?

Examinations are carefully written by trained technicians who are specialists in the field known as "psychological measurement," in consultation with recognized authorities in the field of work that the test will cover. These experts recommend the subject matter areas or skills to be tested; only those knowledges or skills important to your success on the job are included. The most reliable books and source materials available are used as references. Together, the experts and technicians judge the difficulty level of the questions.

Test technicians know how to phrase questions so that the problem is clearly stated. Their ethics do not permit "trick" or "catch" questions. Questions may have been tried out on sample groups, or subjected to statistical analysis, to determine their usefulness.

Written tests are often used in combination with performance tests, ratings of training and experience, and oral interviews. All of these measures combine to form the best-known means of finding the right person for the right job.

II. HOW TO PASS THE WRITTEN TEST

A. NATURE OF THE EXAMINATION

To prepare intelligently for civil service examinations, you should know how they differ from school examinations you have taken. In school you were assigned certain definite pages to read or subjects to cover. The examination questions were quite detailed and usually emphasized memory. Civil service exams, on the other hand, try to discover your present ability to perform the duties of a position, plus your potentiality to learn these duties. In other words, a civil service exam attempts to predict how successful you will be. Questions cover such a broad area that they cannot be as minute and detailed as school exam questions.

In the public service similar kinds of work, or positions, are grouped together in one "class." This process is known as *position-classification*. All the positions in a class are paid according to the salary range for that class. One class title covers all of these positions, and they are all tested by the same examination.

B. FOUR BASIC STEPS

1) Study the announcement

How, then, can you know what subjects to study? Our best answer is: "Learn as much as possible about the class of positions for which you've applied." The exam will test the knowledge, skills and abilities needed to do the work.

Your most valuable source of information about the position you want is the official exam announcement. This announcement lists the training and experience qualifications. Check these standards and apply only if you come reasonably close to meeting them.

The brief description of the position in the examination announcement offers some clues to the subjects which will be tested. Think about the job itself. Review the duties in your mind. Can you perform them, or are there some in which you are rusty? Fill in the blank spots in your preparation.

Many jurisdictions preview the written test in the exam announcement by including a section called "Knowledge and Abilities Required," "Scope of the Examination," or some similar heading. Here you will find out specifically what fields will be tested.

2) Review your own background

Once you learn in general what the position is all about, and what you need to know to do the work, ask yourself which subjects you already know fairly well and which need improvement. You may wonder whether to concentrate on improving your strong areas or on building some background in your fields of weakness. When the announcement has specified "some knowledge" or "considerable knowledge," or has used adjectives like "beginning principles of..." or "advanced ... methods," you can get a clue as to the number and difficulty of questions to be asked in any given field. More questions, and hence broader coverage, would be included for those subjects which are more important in the work. Now weigh your strengths and weaknesses against the job requirements and prepare accordingly.

3) Determine the level of the position

Another way to tell how intensively you should prepare is to understand the level of the job for which you are applying. Is it the entering level? In other words, is this the position in which beginners in a field of work are hired? Or is it an intermediate or advanced level? Sometimes this is indicated by such words as "Junior" or "Senior" in the class title. Other jurisdictions use Roman numerals to designate the level – Clerk I, Clerk II, for example. The word "Supervisor" sometimes appears in the title. If the level is not indicated by the title, check the description of duties. Will you be working under very close supervision, or will you have responsibility for independent decisions in this work?

4) Choose appropriate study materials

Now that you know the subjects to be examined and the relative amount of each subject to be covered, you can choose suitable study materials. For beginning level jobs, or even advanced ones, if you have a pronounced weakness in some aspect of your training, read a modern, standard textbook in that field. Be sure it is up to date and has general coverage. Such books are normally available at your library, and the librarian will be glad to help you locate one. For entry-level positions, questions of appropriate difficulty are chosen – neither highly advanced questions, nor those too simple. Such questions require careful thought but not advanced training.

If the position for which you are applying is technical or advanced, you will read more advanced, specialized material. If you are already familiar with the basic principles of your field, elementary textbooks would waste your time. Concentrate on advanced textbooks and technical periodicals. Think through the concepts and review difficult problems in your field.

These are all general sources. You can get more ideas on your own initiative, following these leads. For example, training manuals and publications of the government agency which employs workers in your field can be useful, particularly for technical and professional positions. A letter or visit to the government department involved may result in more specific study suggestions, and certainly will provide you with a more definite idea of the exact nature of the position you are seeking.

III. KINDS OF TESTS

Tests are used for purposes other than measuring knowledge and ability to perform specified duties. For some positions, it is equally important to test ability to make adjustments to new situations or to profit from training. In others, basic mental abilities not dependent on information are essential. Questions which test these things may not appear as pertinent to the duties of the position as those which test for knowledge and information. Yet they are often highly important parts of a fair examination. For very general questions, it is almost impossible to help you direct your study efforts. What we can do is to point out some of the more common of these general abilities needed in public service positions and describe some typical questions.

1) General information

Broad, general information has been found useful for predicting job success in some kinds of work. This is tested in a variety of ways, from vocabulary lists to questions about current events. Basic background in some field of work, such as sociology or economics, may be sampled in a group of questions. Often these are principles which have become familiar to most persons through exposure rather than through formal training. It is difficult to advise you how to study for these questions; being alert to the world around you is our best suggestion.

2) Verbal ability

An example of an ability needed in many positions is verbal or language ability. Verbal ability is, in brief, the ability to use and understand words. Vocabulary and grammar tests are typical measures of this ability. Reading comprehension or paragraph interpretation questions are common in many kinds of civil service tests. You are given a paragraph of written material and asked to find its central meaning.

3) Numerical ability
Number skills can be tested by the familiar arithmetic problem, by checking paired lists of numbers to see which are alike and which are different, or by interpreting charts and graphs. In the latter test, a graph may be printed in the test booklet which you are asked to use as the basis for answering questions.

4) Observation
A popular test for law-enforcement positions is the observation test. A picture is shown to you for several minutes, then taken away. Questions about the picture test your ability to observe both details and larger elements.

5) Following directions
In many positions in the public service, the employee must be able to carry out written instructions dependably and accurately. You may be given a chart with several columns, each column listing a variety of information. The questions require you to carry out directions involving the information given in the chart.

6) Skills and aptitudes
Performance tests effectively measure some manual skills and aptitudes. When the skill is one in which you are trained, such as typing or shorthand, you can practice. These tests are often very much like those given in business school or high school courses. For many of the other skills and aptitudes, however, no short-time preparation can be made. Skills and abilities natural to you or that you have developed throughout your lifetime are being tested.

Many of the general questions just described provide all the data needed to answer the questions and ask you to use your reasoning ability to find the answers. Your best preparation for these tests, as well as for tests of facts and ideas, is to be at your physical and mental best. You, no doubt, have your own methods of getting into an exam-taking mood and keeping "in shape." The next section lists some ideas on this subject.

IV. KINDS OF QUESTIONS

Only rarely is the "essay" question, which you answer in narrative form, used in civil service tests. Civil service tests are usually of the short-answer type. Full instructions for answering these questions will be given to you at the examination. But in case this is your first experience with short-answer questions and separate answer sheets, here is what you need to know:

1) Multiple-choice Questions
Most popular of the short-answer questions is the "multiple choice" or "best answer" question. It can be used, for example, to test for factual knowledge, ability to solve problems or judgment in meeting situations found at work.
A multiple-choice question is normally one of three types—
- It can begin with an incomplete statement followed by several possible endings. You are to find the one ending which *best* completes the statement, although some of the others may not be entirely wrong.
- It can also be a complete statement in the form of a question which is answered by choosing one of the statements listed.

- It can be in the form of a problem – again you select the best answer.

Here is an example of a multiple-choice question with a discussion which should give you some clues as to the method for choosing the right answer:

When an employee has a complaint about his assignment, the action which will *best* help him overcome his difficulty is to
- A. discuss his difficulty with his coworkers
- B. take the problem to the head of the organization
- C. take the problem to the person who gave him the assignment
- D. say nothing to anyone about his complaint

In answering this question, you should study each of the choices to find which is best. Consider choice "A" – Certainly an employee may discuss his complaint with fellow employees, but no change or improvement can result, and the complaint remains unresolved. Choice "B" is a poor choice since the head of the organization probably does not know what assignment you have been given, and taking your problem to him is known as "going over the head" of the supervisor. The supervisor, or person who made the assignment, is the person who can clarify it or correct any injustice. Choice "C" is, therefore, correct. To say nothing, as in choice "D," is unwise. Supervisors have and interest in knowing the problems employees are facing, and the employee is seeking a solution to his problem.

2) True/False Questions

The "true/false" or "right/wrong" form of question is sometimes used. Here a complete statement is given. Your job is to decide whether the statement is right or wrong.

SAMPLE: A roaming cell-phone call to a nearby city costs less than a non-roaming call to a distant city.

This statement is wrong, or false, since roaming calls are more expensive.

This is not a complete list of all possible question forms, although most of the others are variations of these common types. You will always get complete directions for answering questions. Be sure you understand *how* to mark your answers – ask questions until you do.

V. RECORDING YOUR ANSWERS

Computer terminals are used more and more today for many different kinds of exams.

For an examination with very few applicants, you may be told to record your answers in the test booklet itself. Separate answer sheets are much more common. If this separate answer sheet is to be scored by machine – and this is often the case – it is highly important that you mark your answers correctly in order to get credit.

An electronic scoring machine is often used in civil service offices because of the speed with which papers can be scored. Machine-scored answer sheets must be marked with a pencil, which will be given to you. This pencil has a high graphite content which responds to the electronic scoring machine. As a matter of fact, stray dots may register as answers, so do not let your pencil rest on the answer sheet while you are pondering the correct answer. Also, if your pencil lead breaks or is otherwise defective, ask for another.

Since the answer sheet will be dropped in a slot in the scoring machine, be careful not to bend the corners or get the paper crumpled.

The answer sheet normally has five vertical columns of numbers, with 30 numbers to a column. These numbers correspond to the question numbers in your test booklet. After each number, going across the page are four or five pairs of dotted lines. These short dotted lines have small letters or numbers above them. The first two pairs may also have a "T" or "F" above the letters. This indicates that the first two pairs only are to be used if the questions are of the true-false type. If the questions are multiple choice, disregard the "T" and "F" and pay attention only to the small letters or numbers.

Answer your questions in the manner of the sample that follows:

32. The largest city in the United States is
    A. Washington, D.C.
    B. New York City
    C. Chicago
    D. Detroit
    E. San Francisco

1) Choose the answer you think is best. (New York City is the largest, so "B" is correct.)
2) Find the row of dotted lines numbered the same as the question you are answering. (Find row number 32)
3) Find the pair of dotted lines corresponding to the answer. (Find the pair of lines under the mark "B.")
4) Make a solid black mark between the dotted lines.

VI. BEFORE THE TEST

Common sense will help you find procedures to follow to get ready for an examination. Too many of us, however, overlook these sensible measures. Indeed, nervousness and fatigue have been found to be the most serious reasons why applicants fail to do their best on civil service tests. Here is a list of reminders:

- Begin your preparation early – Don't wait until the last minute to go scurrying around for books and materials or to find out what the position is all about.
- Prepare continuously – An hour a night for a week is better than an all-night cram session. This has been definitely established. What is more, a night a week for a month will return better dividends than crowding your study into a shorter period of time.
- Locate the place of the exam – You have been sent a notice telling you when and where to report for the examination. If the location is in a different town or otherwise unfamiliar to you, it would be well to inquire the best route and learn something about the building.
- Relax the night before the test – Allow your mind to rest. Do not study at all that night. Plan some mild recreation or diversion; then go to bed early and get a good night's sleep.
- Get up early enough to make a leisurely trip to the place for the test – This way unforeseen events, traffic snarls, unfamiliar buildings, etc. will not upset you.
- Dress comfortably – A written test is not a fashion show. You will be known by number and not by name, so wear something comfortable.

- Leave excess paraphernalia at home – Shopping bags and odd bundles will get in your way. You need bring only the items mentioned in the official notice you received; usually everything you need is provided. Do not bring reference books to the exam. They will only confuse those last minutes and be taken away from you when in the test room.
- Arrive somewhat ahead of time – If because of transportation schedules you must get there very early, bring a newspaper or magazine to take your mind off yourself while waiting.
- Locate the examination room – When you have found the proper room, you will be directed to the seat or part of the room where you will sit. Sometimes you are given a sheet of instructions to read while you are waiting. Do not fill out any forms until you are told to do so; just read them and be prepared.
- Relax and prepare to listen to the instructions
- If you have any physical problem that may keep you from doing your best, be sure to tell the test administrator. If you are sick or in poor health, you really cannot do your best on the exam. You can come back and take the test some other time.

VII. AT THE TEST

The day of the test is here and you have the test booklet in your hand. The temptation to get going is very strong. Caution! There is more to success than knowing the right answers. You must know how to identify your papers and understand variations in the type of short-answer question used in this particular examination. Follow these suggestions for maximum results from your efforts:

1) Cooperate with the monitor

The test administrator has a duty to create a situation in which you can be as much at ease as possible. He will give instructions, tell you when to begin, check to see that you are marking your answer sheet correctly, and so on. He is not there to guard you, although he will see that your competitors do not take unfair advantage. He wants to help you do your best.

2) Listen to all instructions

Don't jump the gun! Wait until you understand all directions. In most civil service tests you get more time than you need to answer the questions. So don't be in a hurry. Read each word of instructions until you clearly understand the meaning. Study the examples, listen to all announcements and follow directions. Ask questions if you do not understand what to do.

3) Identify your papers

Civil service exams are usually identified by number only. You will be assigned a number; you must not put your name on your test papers. Be sure to copy your number correctly. Since more than one exam may be given, copy your exact examination title.

4) Plan your time

Unless you are told that a test is a "speed" or "rate of work" test, speed itself is usually not important. Time enough to answer all the questions will be provided, but this does not mean that you have all day. An overall time limit has been set. Divide the total time (in minutes) by the number of questions to determine the approximate time you have for each question.

5) Do not linger over difficult questions

If you come across a difficult question, mark it with a paper clip (useful to have along) and come back to it when you have been through the booklet. One caution if you do this – be sure to skip a number on your answer sheet as well. Check often to be sure that you have not lost your place and that you are marking in the row numbered the same as the question you are answering.

6) Read the questions

Be sure you know what the question asks! Many capable people are unsuccessful because they failed to *read* the questions correctly.

7) Answer all questions

Unless you have been instructed that a penalty will be deducted for incorrect answers, it is better to guess than to omit a question.

8) Speed tests

It is often better NOT to guess on speed tests. It has been found that on timed tests people are tempted to spend the last few seconds before time is called in marking answers at random – without even reading them – in the hope of picking up a few extra points. To discourage this practice, the instructions may warn you that your score will be "corrected" for guessing. That is, a penalty will be applied. The incorrect answers will be deducted from the correct ones, or some other penalty formula will be used.

9) Review your answers

If you finish before time is called, go back to the questions you guessed or omitted to give them further thought. Review other answers if you have time.

10) Return your test materials

If you are ready to leave before others have finished or time is called, take ALL your materials to the monitor and leave quietly. Never take any test material with you. The monitor can discover whose papers are not complete, and taking a test booklet may be grounds for disqualification.

VIII. EXAMINATION TECHNIQUES

1) Read the general instructions carefully. These are usually printed on the first page of the exam booklet. As a rule, these instructions refer to the timing of the examination; the fact that you should not start work until the signal and must stop work at a signal, etc. If there are any *special* instructions, such as a choice of questions to be answered, make sure that you note this instruction carefully.

2) When you are ready to start work on the examination, that is as soon as the signal has been given, read the instructions to each question booklet, underline any key words or phrases, such as *least, best, outline, describe* and the like. In this way you will tend to answer as requested rather than discover on reviewing your paper that you *listed without describing*, that you selected the *worst* choice rather than the *best* choice, etc.

3) If the examination is of the objective or multiple-choice type – that is, each question will also give a series of possible answers: A, B, C or D, and you are called upon to select the best answer and write the letter next to that answer on your answer paper – it is advisable to start answering each question in turn. There may be anywhere from 50 to 100 such questions in the three or four hours allotted and you can see how much time would be taken if you read through all the questions before beginning to answer any. Furthermore, if you come across a question or group of questions which you know would be difficult to answer, it would undoubtedly affect your handling of all the other questions.

4) If the examination is of the essay type and contains but a few questions, it is a moot point as to whether you should read all the questions before starting to answer any one. Of course, if you are given a choice – say five out of seven and the like – then it is essential to read all the questions so you can eliminate the two that are most difficult. If, however, you are asked to answer all the questions, there may be danger in trying to answer the easiest one first because you may find that you will spend too much time on it. The best technique is to answer the first question, then proceed to the second, etc.

5) Time your answers. Before the exam begins, write down the time it started, then add the time allowed for the examination and write down the time it must be completed, then divide the time available somewhat as follows:
    - If 3-1/2 hours are allowed, that would be 210 minutes. If you have 80 objective-type questions, that would be an average of 2-1/2 minutes per question. Allow yourself no more than 2 minutes per question, or a total of 160 minutes, which will permit about 50 minutes to review.
    - If for the time allotment of 210 minutes there are 7 essay questions to answer, that would average about 30 minutes a question. Give yourself only 25 minutes per question so that you have about 35 minutes to review.

6) The most important instruction is to *read each question* and make sure you know what is wanted. The second most important instruction is to *time yourself properly* so that you answer every question. The third most important instruction is to *answer every question*. Guess if you have to but include something for each question. Remember that you will receive no credit for a blank and will probably receive some credit if you write something in answer to an essay question. If you guess a letter – say "B" for a multiple-choice question – you may have guessed right. If you leave a blank as an answer to a multiple-choice question, the examiners may respect your feelings but it will not add a point to your score. Some exams may penalize you for wrong answers, so in such cases *only*, you may not want to guess unless you have some basis for your answer.

7) Suggestions
    a. Objective-type questions
        1. Examine the question booklet for proper sequence of pages and questions
        2. Read all instructions carefully
        3. Skip any question which seems too difficult; return to it after all other questions have been answered
        4. Apportion your time properly; do not spend too much time on any single question or group of questions

5. Note and underline key words – *all, most, fewest, least, best, worst, same, opposite,* etc.
6. Pay particular attention to negatives
7. Note unusual option, e.g., unduly long, short, complex, different or similar in content to the body of the question
8. Observe the use of "hedging" words – *probably, may, most likely,* etc.
9. Make sure that your answer is put next to the same number as the question
10. Do not second-guess unless you have good reason to believe the second answer is definitely more correct
11. Cross out original answer if you decide another answer is more accurate; do not erase until you are ready to hand your paper in
12. Answer all questions; guess unless instructed otherwise
13. Leave time for review

b. Essay questions
1. Read each question carefully
2. Determine exactly what is wanted. Underline key words or phrases.
3. Decide on outline or paragraph answer
4. Include many different points and elements unless asked to develop any one or two points or elements
5. Show impartiality by giving pros and cons unless directed to select one side only
6. Make and write down any assumptions you find necessary to answer the questions
7. Watch your English, grammar, punctuation and choice of words
8. Time your answers; don't crowd material

8) Answering the essay question

Most essay questions can be answered by framing the specific response around several key words or ideas. Here are a few such key words or ideas:

M's: manpower, materials, methods, money, management
P's: purpose, program, policy, plan, procedure, practice, problems, pitfalls, personnel, public relations

a. Six basic steps in handling problems:
1. Preliminary plan and background development
2. Collect information, data and facts
3. Analyze and interpret information, data and facts
4. Analyze and develop solutions as well as make recommendations
5. Prepare report and sell recommendations
6. Install recommendations and follow up effectiveness

b. Pitfalls to avoid
1. *Taking things for granted* – A statement of the situation does not necessarily imply that each of the elements is necessarily true; for example, a complaint may be invalid and biased so that all that can be taken for granted is that a complaint has been registered

2. *Considering only one side of a situation* – Wherever possible, indicate several alternatives and then point out the reasons you selected the best one
3. *Failing to indicate follow up* – Whenever your answer indicates action on your part, make certain that you will take proper follow-up action to see how successful your recommendations, procedures or actions turn out to be
4. *Taking too long in answering any single question* – Remember to time your answers properly

IX. AFTER THE TEST

Scoring procedures differ in detail among civil service jurisdictions although the general principles are the same. Whether the papers are hand-scored or graded by machine we have described, they are nearly always graded by number. That is, the person who marks the paper knows only the number – never the name – of the applicant. Not until all the papers have been graded will they be matched with names. If other tests, such as training and experience or oral interview ratings have been given, scores will be combined. Different parts of the examination usually have different weights. For example, the written test might count 60 percent of the final grade, and a rating of training and experience 40 percent. In many jurisdictions, veterans will have a certain number of points added to their grades.

After the final grade has been determined, the names are placed in grade order and an eligible list is established. There are various methods for resolving ties between those who get the same final grade – probably the most common is to place first the name of the person whose application was received first. Job offers are made from the eligible list in the order the names appear on it. You will be notified of your grade and your rank as soon as all these computations have been made. This will be done as rapidly as possible.

People who are found to meet the requirements in the announcement are called "eligibles." Their names are put on a list of eligible candidates. An eligible's chances of getting a job depend on how high he stands on this list and how fast agencies are filling jobs from the list.

When a job is to be filled from a list of eligibles, the agency asks for the names of people on the list of eligibles for that job. When the civil service commission receives this request, it sends to the agency the names of the three people highest on this list. Or, if the job to be filled has specialized requirements, the office sends the agency the names of the top three persons who meet these requirements from the general list.

The appointing officer makes a choice from among the three people whose names were sent to him. If the selected person accepts the appointment, the names of the others are put back on the list to be considered for future openings.

That is the rule in hiring from all kinds of eligible lists, whether they are for typist, carpenter, chemist, or something else. For every vacancy, the appointing officer has his choice of any one of the top three eligibles on the list. This explains why the person whose name is on top of the list sometimes does not get an appointment when some of the persons lower on the list do. If the appointing officer chooses the second or third eligible, the No. 1 eligible does not get a job at once, but stays on the list until he is appointed or the list is terminated.

X. HOW TO PASS THE INTERVIEW TEST

The examination for which you applied requires an oral interview test. You have already taken the written test and you are now being called for the interview test – the final part of the formal examination.

You may think that it is not possible to prepare for an interview test and that there are no procedures to follow during an interview. Our purpose is to point out some things you can do in advance that will help you and some good rules to follow and pitfalls to avoid while you are being interviewed.

What is an interview supposed to test?

The written examination is designed to test the technical knowledge and competence of the candidate; the oral is designed to evaluate intangible qualities, not readily measured otherwise, and to establish a list showing the relative fitness of each candidate – as measured against his competitors – for the position sought. Scoring is not on the basis of "right" and "wrong," but on a sliding scale of values ranging from "not passable" to "outstanding." As a matter of fact, it is possible to achieve a relatively low score without a single "incorrect" answer because of evident weakness in the qualities being measured.

Occasionally, an examination may consist entirely of an oral test – either an individual or a group oral. In such cases, information is sought concerning the technical knowledges and abilities of the candidate, since there has been no written examination for this purpose. More commonly, however, an oral test is used to supplement a written examination.

Who conducts interviews?

The composition of oral boards varies among different jurisdictions. In nearly all, a representative of the personnel department serves as chairman. One of the members of the board may be a representative of the department in which the candidate would work. In some cases, "outside experts" are used, and, frequently, a businessman or some other representative of the general public is asked to serve. Labor and management or other special groups may be represented. The aim is to secure the services of experts in the appropriate field.

However the board is composed, it is a good idea (and not at all improper or unethical) to ascertain in advance of the interview who the members are and what groups they represent. When you are introduced to them, you will have some idea of their backgrounds and interests, and at least you will not stutter and stammer over their names.

What should be done before the interview?

While knowledge about the board members is useful and takes some of the surprise element out of the interview, there is other preparation which is more substantive. It *is* possible to prepare for an oral interview – in several ways:

1) Keep a copy of your application and review it carefully before the interview

This may be the only document before the oral board, and the starting point of the interview. Know what education and experience you have listed there, and the sequence and dates of all of it. Sometimes the board will ask you to review the highlights of your experience for them; you should not have to hem and haw doing it.

2) Study the class specification and the examination announcement

Usually, the oral board has one or both of these to guide them. The qualities, characteristics or knowledges required by the position sought are stated in these documents. They offer valuable clues as to the nature of the oral interview. For example, if the job involves supervisory responsibilities, the announcement will usually indicate that knowledge of modern supervisory methods and the qualifications of the candidate as a supervisor will be tested. If so, you can expect such questions, frequently in the form of a hypothetical situation which you are expected to solve. NEVER go into an oral without knowledge of the duties and responsibilities of the job you seek.

3) Think through each qualification required

Try to visualize the kind of questions you would ask if you were a board member. How well could you answer them? Try especially to appraise your own knowledge and background in each area, *measured against the job sought*, and identify any areas in which you are weak. Be critical and realistic – do not flatter yourself.

4) Do some general reading in areas in which you feel you may be weak

For example, if the job involves supervision and your past experience has NOT, some general reading in supervisory methods and practices, particularly in the field of human relations, might be useful. Do NOT study agency procedures or detailed manuals. The oral board will be testing your understanding and capacity, not your memory.

5) Get a good night's sleep and watch your general health and mental attitude

You will want a clear head at the interview. Take care of a cold or any other minor ailment, and of course, no hangovers.

What should be done on the day of the interview?

Now comes the day of the interview itself. Give yourself plenty of time to get there. Plan to arrive somewhat ahead of the scheduled time, particularly if your appointment is in the fore part of the day. If a previous candidate fails to appear, the board might be ready for you a bit early. By early afternoon an oral board is almost invariably behind schedule if there are many candidates, and you may have to wait. Take along a book or magazine to read, or your application to review, but leave any extraneous material in the waiting room when you go in for your interview. In any event, relax and compose yourself.

The matter of dress is important. The board is forming impressions about you – from your experience, your manners, your attitude, and your appearance. Give your personal appearance careful attention. Dress your best, but not your flashiest. Choose conservative, appropriate clothing, and be sure it is immaculate. This is a business interview, and your appearance should indicate that you regard it as such. Besides, being well groomed and properly dressed will help boost your confidence.

Sooner or later, someone will call your name and escort you into the interview room. *This is it.* From here on you are on your own. It is too late for any more preparation. But remember, you asked for this opportunity to prove your fitness, and you are here because your request was granted.

What happens when you go in?

The usual sequence of events will be as follows: The clerk (who is often the board stenographer) will introduce you to the chairman of the oral board, who will introduce you to the other members of the board. Acknowledge the introductions before you sit down. Do not be surprised if you find a microphone facing you or a stenotypist sitting by. Oral interviews are usually recorded in the event of an appeal or other review.

Usually the chairman of the board will open the interview by reviewing the highlights of your education and work experience from your application – primarily for the benefit of the other members of the board, as well as to get the material into the record. Do not interrupt or comment unless there is an error or significant misinterpretation; if that is the case, do not hesitate. But do not quibble about insignificant matters. Also, he will usually ask you some question about your education, experience or your present job – partly to get you to start talking and to establish the interviewing "rapport." He may start the actual questioning, or turn it over to one of the other members. Frequently, each member undertakes the questioning on a particular area, one in which he is perhaps most competent, so you can expect each member to participate in the examination. Because time is limited, you may also expect some rather abrupt switches in the direction the questioning takes, so do not be upset by it. Normally, a board member will not pursue a single line of questioning unless he discovers a particular strength or weakness.

After each member has participated, the chairman will usually ask whether any member has any further questions, then will ask you if you have anything you wish to add. Unless you are expecting this question, it may floor you. Worse, it may start you off on an extended, extemporaneous speech. The board is not usually seeking more information. The question is principally to offer you a last opportunity to present further qualifications or to indicate that you have nothing to add. So, if you feel that a significant qualification or characteristic has been overlooked, it is proper to point it out in a sentence or so. Do not compliment the board on the thoroughness of their examination – they have been sketchy, and you know it. If you wish, merely say, "No thank you, I have nothing further to add." This is a point where you can "talk yourself out" of a good impression or fail to present an important bit of information. Remember, *you close the interview yourself.*

The chairman will then say, "That is all, Mr. _____, thank you." Do not be startled; the interview is over, and quicker than you think. Thank him, gather your belongings and take your leave. Save your sigh of relief for the other side of the door.

How to put your best foot forward

Throughout this entire process, you may feel that the board individually and collectively is trying to pierce your defenses, seek out your hidden weaknesses and embarrass and confuse you. Actually, this is not true. They are obliged to make an appraisal of your qualifications for the job you are seeking, and they want to see you in your best light. Remember, they must interview all candidates and a non-cooperative candidate may become a failure in spite of their best efforts to bring out his qualifications. Here are 15 suggestions that will help you:

1) Be natural – Keep your attitude confident, not cocky

If you are not confident that you can do the job, do not expect the board to be. Do not apologize for your weaknesses, try to bring out your strong points. The board is interested in a positive, not negative, presentation. Cockiness will antagonize any board member and make him wonder if you are covering up a weakness by a false show of strength.

2) Get comfortable, but don't lounge or sprawl

Sit erectly but not stiffly. A careless posture may lead the board to conclude that you are careless in other things, or at least that you are not impressed by the importance of the occasion. Either conclusion is natural, even if incorrect. Do not fuss with your clothing, a pencil or an ashtray. Your hands may occasionally be useful to emphasize a point; do not let them become a point of distraction.

3) Do not wisecrack or make small talk

This is a serious situation, and your attitude should show that you consider it as such. Further, the time of the board is limited – they do not want to waste it, and neither should you.

4) Do not exaggerate your experience or abilities

In the first place, from information in the application or other interviews and sources, the board may know more about you than you think. Secondly, you probably will not get away with it. An experienced board is rather adept at spotting such a situation, so do not take the chance.

5) If you know a board member, do not make a point of it, yet do not hide it

Certainly you are not fooling him, and probably not the other members of the board. Do not try to take advantage of your acquaintanceship – it will probably do you little good.

6) Do not dominate the interview

Let the board do that. They will give you the clues – do not assume that you have to do all the talking. Realize that the board has a number of questions to ask you, and do not try to take up all the interview time by showing off your extensive knowledge of the answer to the first one.

7) Be attentive

You only have 20 minutes or so, and you should keep your attention at its sharpest throughout. When a member is addressing a problem or question to you, give him your undivided attention. Address your reply principally to him, but do not exclude the other board members.

8) Do not interrupt

A board member may be stating a problem for you to analyze. He will ask you a question when the time comes. Let him state the problem, and wait for the question.

9) Make sure you understand the question

Do not try to answer until you are sure what the question is. If it is not clear, restate it in your own words or ask the board member to clarify it for you. However, do not haggle about minor elements.

10) Reply promptly but not hastily

A common entry on oral board rating sheets is "candidate responded readily," or "candidate hesitated in replies." Respond as promptly and quickly as you can, but do not jump to a hasty, ill-considered answer.

11) Do not be peremptory in your answers

A brief answer is proper – but do not fire your answer back. That is a losing game from your point of view. The board member can probably ask questions much faster than you can answer them.

12) Do not try to create the answer you think the board member wants

He is interested in what kind of mind you have and how it works – not in playing games. Furthermore, he can usually spot this practice and will actually grade you down on it.

13) Do not switch sides in your reply merely to agree with a board member

Frequently, a member will take a contrary position merely to draw you out and to see if you are willing and able to defend your point of view. Do not start a debate, yet do not surrender a good position. If a position is worth taking, it is worth defending.

14) Do not be afraid to admit an error in judgment if you are shown to be wrong

The board knows that you are forced to reply without any opportunity for careful consideration. Your answer may be demonstrably wrong. If so, admit it and get on with the interview.

15) Do not dwell at length on your present job

The opening question may relate to your present assignment. Answer the question but do not go into an extended discussion. You are being examined for a *new* job, not your present one. As a matter of fact, try to phrase ALL your answers in terms of the job for which you are being examined.

Basis of Rating

Probably you will forget most of these "do's" and "don'ts" when you walk into the oral interview room. Even remembering them all will not ensure you a passing grade. Perhaps you did not have the qualifications in the first place. But remembering them will help you to put your best foot forward, without treading on the toes of the board members.

Rumor and popular opinion to the contrary notwithstanding, an oral board wants you to make the best appearance possible. They know you are under pressure – but they also want to see how you respond to it as a guide to what your reaction would be under the pressures of the job you seek. They will be influenced by the degree of poise you display, the personal traits you show and the manner in which you respond.

ABOUT THIS BOOK

This book contains tests divided into Examination Sections. Go through each test, answering every question in the margin. We have also attached a sample answer sheet at the back of the book that can be removed and used. At the end of each test look at the answer key and check your answers. On the ones you got wrong, look at the right answer choice and learn. Do not fill in the answers first. Do not memorize the questions and answers, but understand the answer and principles involved. On your test, the questions will likely be different from the samples. Questions are changed and new ones added. If you understand these past questions you should have success with any changes that arise. Tests may consist of several types of questions. We have additional books on each subject should more study be advisable or necessary for you. Finally, the more you study, the better prepared you will be. This book is intended to be the last thing you study before you walk into the examination room. Prior study of relevant texts is also recommended. NLC publishes some of these in our Fundamental Series. Knowledge and good sense are important factors in passing your exam. Good luck also helps. So now study this Passbook, absorb the material contained within and take that knowledge into the examination. Then do your best to pass that exam.

EXAMINATION SECTION

EXAMINATION SECTION
TEST 1

DIRECTIONS: Each question or incomplete statement is followed by several suggested answers or completions. Select the one that BEST answers the question or completes the statement. *PRINT THE LETTER OF THE CORRECT ANSWER IN THE SPACE AT THE RIGHT.*

1. A percentage of the payment for a contract is held back until the job is completed for one year.
   The MAIN reason for this practice is to insure that the

   A. city doesn't overpay the contractor for the job
   B. contractor will return to correct defective work after the job is completed
   C. contractor will not make unwarranted claims against the city
   D. contractor will pay all his subcontractors

2. There are four separate major contracts on a certain building construction project.
   The MAJOR disadvantage of this practice, as compared to the practice of having a single contract, is

   A. the difficulty in coordinating the work
   B. the low level of productivity of the tradesman
   C. cost of the material going into the building is greater
   D. the difficulty in finding competent bidders on the contracts

3. Of the following, the PREFERRED way to authorize a contractor to perform work other than required by the contract is by a

   A. T & M order   B. unit price order
   C. lump sum modification D. change order

4. A contract requires that the prime contractor do a certain minimum percentage of the work with his own forces.
   Of the following, the BEST reason for this requirement is to

   A. insure good work
   B. discourage bidders who may not have the ability to do the job
   C. encourage more people to bid the job, thus lowering the bid price
   D. freeze out incompetent subcontractors

5. In computing an extra based on the actual cost of work done, the THREE MAJOR items that go into the cost are

   A. taxes, labor, and material
   B. time, taxes, and material
   C. labor, material, and equipment
   D. taxes, labor, and equipment

6. A contractor is to be penalized if he exceeds a certain completion date. There is a major strike lasting a month that shuts down all construction.
   Under these conditions, the completion date should be

A. held unchanged
B. made two weeks later than the original date
C. made one month later than the original date
D. made six weeks later than the original completion date

7. The one of the following that refers to a Federal safety program in construction is 7.____

   A. OSHA   B. AISC   C. AIEE   D. UL

8. With regard to the placing of concrete, the contractor is GENERALLY 8.____

   A. limited to a specific method by the contract
   B. not permitted to rent equipment to place the concrete
   C. not permitted to pump the concrete into place
   D. permitted to choose his own method of placing the concrete

9. The MOST practical control the inspector or resident engineer has over the contractor when the inspector is not satisfied with the quality of the work is to 9.____

   A. discuss withholding payment on that part of the work that is unsatisfactory
   B. threaten to have the contractor thrown off the job
   C. request that the contractor fire the men responsible for the unsatisfactory work
   D. call the owner of the company and explain the situation to him

10. The MOST practical method of being sure that the architect will be satisfied with the appearance of the exterior brick work for a building is to 10.____

    A. build a sample wall section, for the architect's approval, with the brick that is delivered to the job site
    B. send the architect to the plant supplying the brick to insure that the color and tone of the brick is satisfactory
    C. have the architect's representative on the job while the brick work is being erected to be sure the finished product is satisfactory
    D. put a damage clause in the contract penalizing the contractor if the brick work is not satisfactory to the architect

11. Of the following, the MOST frequent problem that will arise during the construction of a building is 11.____

    A. inability to fit all the reinforcing steel in the space allotted to it
    B. interference in piping and ductwork
    C. inability to keep walls level
    D. settling of the foundation as the load comes on the building

12. To find the number of reinforcing bars that should be in a slab, the inspector SHOULD refer to the 12.____

    A. architect's plan
    B. reinforcing steel design drawings
    C. standard detail drawings
    D. reinforcing steel detail drawings

13. The specifications for a building state that a certain brick type shall be *Stark Brick type XX or equal.*
    The BEST reason for inserting the *or equal* clause is to

    A. permit other companies to compete in supplying the brick
    B. allow other companies to submit their product to determine which is best
    C. limit the suppliers only to those companies whose product is superior to that produced by Stark
    D. allow Stark Brick Company to set the standard for the industry

    13._____

14. In the absence of a formal training program for inspectors, the BEST of the following ways to train a new man who is to do inspection work is to

    A. give him the literature on the subject so that he can learn what he has to know
    B. have him accompany an inspector as the inspector does his work so that he can learn by observing
    C. assign him the job and let him learn on his own
    D. tell him to go to a school at night that specializes in this field so that he will gain the necessary background

    14._____

15. Of the following, the safety practice that is REQUIRED on the construction job site is

    A. safety shoes must be worn by all workers
    B. safety goggles must be worn by all workers
    C. safety helmets must be worn by all workers
    D. all workers must have a safety kit in their possession

    15._____

16. Safety on the job is the concern of

    A. the individual workman only
    B. the contractor only
    C. all parties on the job
    D. the insuring company only

    16._____

17. Frequently, payments due the contractor are delayed many months because of a backlog of work in the agency.
    This practice is considered

    A. *good* because the city saves money by delaying payment
    B. *poor* because the contractors will raise their bids in the future to compensate for the added cost
    C. *poor* because it becomes difficult to compute payments
    D. *good* because it forces the contractor to do good work in order to be sure that he will receive payment

    17._____

18. Provisions are made in a contract for payment for certain items when delivered to the job before installation.
    The MAIN reason for this practice is to

    A. enable better inspection of the items
    B. prevent bottlenecks during construction
    C. give the contractor a quick profit on the items
    D. allow the contractor more time to shop for the items

    18._____

19. The agency that approves payments to building contractors is the

    A. Corporation Counsel
    B. Comptroller's Office
    C. Board of Estimate
    D. City Planning Commission

20. The bond that the contractor puts up to insure that he will start work is the

    A. Bid Bond
    B. Payment Bond
    C. Performance Bond
    D. Liability Insurance

21. Of the following, the BEST practice to follow in order to minimize claims of damage to adjacent buildings during the construction of a building is to

    A. take out special insurance against such claims
    B. make a detailed survey of the condition of the nearby buildings before construction begins
    C. make a payment to adjacent property owners in advance so that they waive claims of damage to their property
    D. have the buildings underpinned

22. The four MAJOR contracts on a building project are:

    A. General Construction, Electrical, Plumbing and Drainage, Heating, Ventilating and Air Conditioning
    B. Plumbing, Heating and Ventilating, Air Conditioning, and General Construction
    C. Foundations, Superstructure, Mechanical, and Electrical
    D. Air Conditioning, Electrical, Mechanical, and Structural

23. Oil tanks, when set in place inside a building, are frequently filled with water.
    The BEST reason for this practice is

    A. to prevent them from floating off their foundation if water fills the room
    B. to enable them to be lifted up more easily
    C. to prevent them from becoming rusted
    D. for emergency use in case of fire

24. The filing system used in the field for correspondence is required to be uniform for all jobs.
    The BEST reason for this requirement is that

    A. there is only one good way of setting up the filing system
    B. the standardized system is compact, thereby saving space
    C. other interested parties such as engineers from the main office will be able to use the files
    D. the contractor's forces will understand the filing system and will be able to extract necessary correspondence

25. Upon excavation to the subgrade of a footing to be placed on piles, the inspector finds that the soil is very poor.
    Of the following, the PROPER action for the inspector to take is to

    A. do nothing
    B. add 20% to the number of piles
    C. notify the engineer's office of this condition
    D. order the contractor to keep excavating until he hits better soil

26. The general contractor is required to submit a progress schedule before starting work. Of the following, the BEST reason for this requirement is to

    A. determine if the contractor intends to complete the job
    B. enable the inspector to determine whether the contractor is on schedule
    C. enable the inspector to estimate monthly payments
    D. check minority hiring

27. If a contractor is falling behind schedule, the FIRST thing to check if the inspector is looking for the cause of this condition is the

    A. number of men he has on the job
    B. efficiency of his crew
    C. availability of equipment needed to do the job
    D. availability of the latest drawings needed by the contractor

28. The critical path method is a method for

    A. finding the best material needed for a specific use
    B. determining the best arrangement of equipment
    C. determining the best time to replace a piece of machinery
    D. scheduling work

29. The contractor states to the inspector that a given structural detail is undersized and unsafe.
    Of the following, the BEST action for the inspector to take in this situation is to

    A. ignore the complaint since the contractor is not an engineer
    B. change the detail by issuing a change order
    C. notify your superiors of the contractor's statements
    D. allow the contractor to modify the detail since it is his responsibility

30. The contractor proposes to use an additive to the concrete to accelerate its set. He asks you, the inspector, for permission to use it.
    Of the following, the FIRST action to take in response to his request is to

    A. check if the use of the additive is permitted by the specifications
    B. tell him to put the request in writing
    C. ask your superior if the use of the additive is acceptable
    D. deny him permission since additives to concrete are not permitted

KEY (CORRECT ANSWERS)

1.	B	16.	C
2.	A	17.	B
3.	D	18.	B
4.	B	19.	B
5.	C	20.	A
6.	C	21.	B
7.	A	22.	A
8.	D	23.	A
9.	A	24.	C
10.	A	25.	A
11.	B	26.	B
12.	D	27.	A
13.	A	28.	D
14.	B	29.	C
15.	C	30.	A

EXAMINATION SECTION
TEST 1

DIRECTIONS: Each question or incomplete statement is followed by several suggested answers or completions. Select the one that BEST answers the question or completes the statement. *PRINT THE LETTER OF THE CORRECT ANSWER IN THE SPACE AT THE RIGHT.*

Questions 1-3.

DIRECTIONS: Questions 1 through 3, inclusive, are to be answered in accordance with the American Standard Graphical Symbols for Pipe Fittings, Valves, and Piping and American Standard Graphical Symbols for Heating, Ventilating and Air Conditioning.

1. The symbol ⊙┼ shown on a piping drawing represents a _____ elbow.

    A. turned down
    B. reducing
    C. long radius
    D. turned up

2. The symbol ⊐─⊏ shown on a heating drawing represents a(n)

    A. expansion joint
    B. hanger or support
    C. heat exchanger
    D. air eliminator

3. The symbol ─┤⋈├─ shown on a piping drawing represents a _____ gate valve.

    A. welded
    B. flanged
    C. screwed
    D. bell and spigot

4. The MAIN purpose for the inspection of plant equipment, buildings, and facilities is to

    A. determine the quality of maintenance work of all the trades
    B. prevent the overstocking of equipment and materials used in maintenance work
    C. forecast normal maintenance jobs for existing equipment, buildings, and facilities
    D. prevent unscheduled interruptions of operating equipment and excessive deterioration of buildings and facilities

5. Of the following devices, the one that is used to determine the rating, in cubic feet per minute, of a unit ventilator is a(n)

    A. psychrometer
    B. pyrometer
    C. anemometer
    D. manometer

6. A number of 4' x 6' skids loaded with material are to be stored. Assume that the total weight of each loaded skid is 1200 pounds and that the maximum allowable floor load is 280 lbs. per sq. ft.
   The MAXIMUM number of skids that can be stacked vertically without exceeding the MAXIMUM allowable floor load is

    A. 4   B. 5   C. 6   D. 7

2 (#1)

7. Specifications which contain the term *slump test* would MOST likely refer to

   A. lumber   B. paint   C. concrete   D. water

8. Of the following sizes of copper conductors, the one which has the LEAST current-carrying capacity is _____ AWG.

   A. 000   B. 0   C. 8   D. 12

9. The size of a steel beam is shown on a steel drawing as W 8 x 15.
   In accordance with the latest edition of the Steel Construction Manual of the American Institute of Steel Construction, the number 8 in W 8 x 15 represents the beam's *approximate*

   A. depth   B. flange thickness
   C. width   D. web thickness

10. For expediting control functions such as work methods, planning, scheduling, and work measurement, EQUIPMENT RECORDS must contain specific data.
    Of the following, the data which is NOT usually indicated on an EQUIPMENT RECORD card is

    A. machinery and parts specifications numbers
    B. a breakdown history
    C. a preventive maintenance history
    D. salvage value on the open market

11. Refrigeration piping, valves, fittings, and related parts used in the construction and installation of refrigeration systems shall conform to the

    A. American Society of Mechanical Engineers Boiler and Pressure Vessel Code
    B. American Standards Association Code for Pressure Piping
    C. Pipe Fabrication Institute Standards
    D. Underwriters Laboratory Standards

12. The maintenance term *downtime* means MOST NEARLY the

    A. period of time in which a machine is out of service
    B. routine replacement of parts or materials to a piece of equipment
    C. labor required for clean-up of equipment to insure its proper operation
    D. maintenance work which is confined to checking, adjusting, and lubrication of equipment

13. A supplier quotes a list price of $172.00 less 15 and 10 percent for twelve tools.
    The ACTUAL cost for these twelve tools is MOST NEARLY

    A. $146   B. $132   C. $129   D. $112

14. Of the following colors of electrical conductor coverings, the one which indicates a conductor used SOLELY for grounding portable or fixed electrical equipment is

    A. blue   B. green   C. red   D. black

15. A *medium duty* type of scaffold is one on which the working load on the platform surface must NOT exceed _____ pounds per square foot.

    A. 50   B. 70   C. 90   D. 110

16. Assume that a mechanic is using a powder-actuated tool and the cartridge misfires. According to recommended safe practices regarding a misfired cartridge, the FIRST course of action the mechanic should take is to

    A. place the misfired cartridge carefully into a metal container filled with water
    B. carefully reload the tool with the misfired cartridge and try it again
    C. immediately bury the misfired cartridge at least two feet in the ground
    D. remove the wadding from the misfired cartridge and empty the powder into a pail of sand

17. The ratings used in classifying fire resistant building construction materials are MOST frequently expressed in

    A. Btu's   B. hours   C. temperatures   D. pounds

18. The only legible portion of the nameplate on a piece of equipment reads: *208 volts, 3 phase, 10 H.P.*
    This data would MOST NEARLY indicate that the piece of equipment is a(n)

    A. amplifier   B. fixture ballast
    C. motor   D. rectifier

19. Of the following items relating to the maintenance of roofs, the one which is of the LEAST value in a preventive maintenance program for roofs is knowledge of the

    A. roofing specifications   B. application procedures
    C. process of deterioration   D. frequency of rainstorms

20. In an oxyacetylene cutting outfit, the color of the hose that is connected to the oxygen cylinder is USUALLY

    A. white   B. yellow   C. red   D. green

21. Assume that a welding generator is to be used to weld partitions made of 18 gauge steel. Of the following settings, the BEST one to use would be a _____ setting of voltage and a _____ setting of amperage.

    A. high; high   B. high; low   C. low; high   D. low; low

22. According to the administrative code, when color marking is used, potable water lines shall be painted

    A. yellow   B. blue   C. red   D. green

23. A set of mechanical plan drawings is drawn to a scale of 1/8" = 1 foot.
    If a length of pipe measures 15 7/16" on the drawing, the ACTUAL length of the pipe is _____ feet.

    A. 121.5   B. 122.5   C. 123.5   D. 124.5

24. A portion of a specification states: *Concrete, other than that placed under water, should be compacted and worked into place by spading or puddling.*
    The MAIN reason why *spading and puddling* is required is to

    A. insure that all water in the concrete mix is brought to the surface
    B. eliminate stone pockets and large bubbles of air

C. provide a means to obtain a spade full of concrete for test purposes
D. make allowances for *bleeding and segregation* of the concrete

25. Assume that the following statement appears in a construction contract: *Payment will be made for the number of pounds of bar reinforcement incorporated in the work as shown on the plans.*
    This type of contract is MOST likely

    A. cost plus   B. lump sum   C. subcontract   D. unit price

26. Partial payments to outside contractors are USUALLY based on the

    A. breakdown estimate submitted after the contract was signed
    B. actual cost of labor and material plus overhead and profit
    C. estimate of work completed which is generally submitted periodically
    D. estimate of material delivered to the job

27. Building contracts usually require that estimates for changes made in the field be submitted for approval before the work can start.
    The MAIN reason for this requirement is to

    A. make sure that the contractor understands the change
    B. discourage such changes
    C. keep the contractor honest
    D. enable the department to control its expenses

28. An *addendum* to contract specifications means MOST NEARLY

    A. a substantial completion payment to the contractor for work almost completed
    B. final acceptance of the work by authorities of all contract work still to be done
    C. additional contract provisions issued in writing by authorities prior to receipt of bids
    D. work other than that required by the contract at the time of its execution

29. Of the following terms, the one which is usually NOT used to describe the types of payments to outside contractors for work done is the _____ payment.

    A. partial payment   B. substantial completion
    C. final   D. surety

30. Of the following metals, the one which is a ferrous metal is

    A. cast iron   B. brass   C. bronze   D. babbit

31. Assume that you have assigned six mechanics to do a job that must be finished in four days. At the end of three days, your men have completed only two-thirds of the job. In order to complete the job on time and because the job is such that it cannot be speeded up, you should assign a MINIMUM of _____ extra men.

    A. 3   B. 4   C. 5   D. 6

32. Of the following traps, the one which is NORMALLY used to retain steam in a heating unit or piping is the _____ trap.

    A. P   B. running   C. float   D. bell

33. Of the following materials, the one which is a convenient and powerful adhesive for cementing tears in canvas jackets that are wrapped around warm pipe insulation is

    A. cylinder oil
    B. wheat paste
    C. water glass
    D. latex paint

34. Pipe chases should be provided with an access door PRIMARILY to provide means to

    A. replace piping lines
    B. either inspect or manipulate valves
    C. prevent condensate from forming on the pipes
    D. check the chase for possible structural defects

35. Electric power is measured in

    A. volts   B. amperes   C. watts   D. ohms

KEY (CORRECT ANSWERS)

1. D		16. A	
2. A		17. B	
3. B		18. C	
4. D		19. D	
5. C		20. D	
6. B		21. B	
7. C		22. D	
8. D		23. C	
9. A		24. B	
10. D		25. D	
11. B		26. C	
12. A		27. D	
13. B		28. C	
14. B		29. D	
15. A		30. A	

31. A
32. C
33. C
34. B
35. C

TEST 2

DIRECTIONS: Each question or incomplete statement is followed by several suggested answers or completions. Select the one that BEST answers the question or completes the statement. *PRINT THE LETTER OF THE CORRECT ANSWER IN THE SPACE AT THE RIGHT.*

1. The HIGHEST quality tools should

   A. always be bought
   B. never be bought
   C. be bought when they offer an overall advantage
   D. be bought only for foreman

2. Master keys should have no markings that will identify them as such.
   This statement is

   A. *false;* it would be impossible to keep records about them without such markings
   B. *true;* markings are subject to alteration and vandalization
   C. *false;* without such markings, they would be too lightly regarded by those to whom issued
   D. *true;* markings would only highlight their value to a potential wrongdoer

3. For a foreman to usually delay for a few weeks handling grievances his men make is a

   A. *poor* practice; it can affect the morale of the men
   B. *good* practice; it will discourage grievances
   C. *poor* practice; the causes of grievances usually disappear if action is delayed
   D. *good* practice; most employee grievances are not justified

4. Whenever an important change in procedure is contemplated, some foremen make a point of discussing the matter with their subordinates in order to get their viewpoint on the proposed change.
   In general, this practice is advisable MAINLY for the reason that

   A. subordinates can often see the effects of procedural changes more clearly than foremen
   B. the foreman has an opportunity to explain the advantages of the new procedure
   C. future changes will be welcomed if subordinates are kept informed
   D. participation in work planning helps to build a spirit of cooperation among employees

5. An estimate of employee morale could LEAST effectively be appraised by

   A. checking accident and absenteeism records
   B. determining the attitudes of employees toward their job
   C. examining the number of requests for emergency leaves of absence
   D. reviewing the number and nature of employee suggestions

6. Assume that you are a foreman and that a visitor at the job site asks you what your crew is doing.
   You should

A. respectfully decline to answer since all questions must be answered by the proper authority
B. answer as concisely as possible but discourage undue conversation
C. refer the man to your superiors
D. give the person complete details of the job

7. Cooperation can BEST be obtained from the general public by

   A. siding with them whenever they have a complaint
   B. sticking carefully to your work and ignoring everything else
   C. explaining the department's objectives and why the public must occasionally be temporarily inconvenienced
   D. listening politely to their complaints and telling them that the complaints will be forwarded to the main office

7._____

8. While you are working for the city, a man says to you that one of the rules of your job doesn't make sense and he gets mad.
   You should say to him

   A. Leave me alone so I can get my work done
   B. Everyone must follow the rules
   C. Let me tell you the reason for the rule
   D. I'm only doing my job so don't get mad at me

8._____

9. One approach to preparing written reports to superiors is to present first the conclusions and recommendations and then the data on which the conclusions and recommendations are based.
   The use of this approach is BEST justified when the

   A. data completely support the conclusions and recommendations
   B. superiors lack the specific training and experience required to understand and interpret the data
   C. data contain more information than is required for making the conclusions and recommendations
   D. superiors are more interested in the conclusions and recommendations than in the data

9._____

10. The MOST important reason why separate paragraphs might be used in writing a report is that this

    A. makes it easier to understand the report
    B. permits the report to be condensed
    C. gives a better appearance to the report
    D. prevents accidental elimination of important facts

10._____

11. On a drawing, the following standard cross-section represents MOST NEARLY

    A. sand   B. concrete   C. earth   D. rock

11._____

12. On a drawing, the following standard cross-section represents MOST NEARLY

    A. malleable iron   B. steel
    C. bronze   D. lead

13. On a piping plan drawing, the symbol represents a 90° _____ elbow.

    A. flanged   B. screwed
    C. bell and spigot   D. welded

14. On a drawing, the symbol represents

    A. stone   B. steel   C. glass   D. wood

15. On a heating piping drawing, the symbol _____ represents piping.

    A. high-pressure steam   B. medium-pressure steam
    C. low-pressure   D. hot water supply

16. Of the following devices, the one that is LEAST frequently used to attach a piece of equipment to concrete or masonry walls is a(n)

    A. carriage bolt   B. through bolt
    C. lag screw   D. expansion bolt

17. A vapor barrier is usually installed in conjunction with

    A. drainage piping   B. roof flashing
    C. building insulation   D. wood sheathing

Questions 18-20.

DIRECTIONS: Questions 18 through 20 are to be answered in accordance with the following table

	Man Days Borough 1 Oct. Nov.	Man Days Borough 2 Oct. Nov.	Man Days Borough 3 Oct. Nov.	Man Days Borough 4 Oct. Nov.
Carpenter	70 100	35 180	145 205	120 85
Plumber	95 135	195 100	70 130	135 80
House Painter	90 90	120 80	85 85	95 195
Electrician	120 110	135 155	120 95	70 205
Blacksmith	125 145	60 180	205 145	80 125

18. In accordance with the above table, if the average daily pay of the five trades listed above is $47.50, the approximate labor cost of work done by the five trades during the month of October for Borough 1 is MOST NEARLY

    A. $22,800   B. $23,450   C. $23,750   D. $26,125

19. In accordance with the above table, the Borough which MOST NEARLY made up 22.4% of the total plumbing work force for the month of November is Borough

    A. 1 B. 2 C. 3 D. 4

20. In accordance with the above table, the average man days per month per Borough spent on electrical work for all Boroughs combined is MOST NEARLY

    A. 120 B. 126 C. 130 D. 136

21. Of the following percentages of carbon, the one that would indicate a medium carbon steel is

    A. 0.2% B. 0.4% C. 0.8% D. 1.2%

22. A *screw pitch gage* measures only the

    A. looseness of threads
    B. tightness of threads
    C. number of threads per inch
    D. gage number

23. Assume that you are to make an inspection of a building to determine the need for painting.
    Of the following tools, the one which is LEAST needed to aid you in your inspection is a

    A. sharp penknife   B. putty knife
    C. lightweight tack hammer D. six-foot rule

24. A *slump test* for concrete is used MAINLY to measure the concrete's

    A. strength B. consistency C. flexibility D. porosity

25. Specifications which contain the term *kiln dried* would MOST likely refer to

    A. asphalt shingles B. brick veneer
    C. paint lacquer   D. lumber

26. In accordance with established jurisdictional work procedures among the trades, the person you would assign to replace a malfunctioning fire sprinkler head would be a

    A. plumber B. laborer C. housesmith D. steamfitter

27. Of the following types of union shops, the one which is illegal under the Taft-Hartley Law is the _____ shop.

    A. closed B. open
    C. union   D. union representative

28. Of the following types of contracts, the one that in city work would MOST likely be limited to emergency work *only* is

    A. lump-sum
    B. unit-price
    C. cost-plus
    D. partial cost-plus and lump-sum

29. Of the following qualifications of outside work contractors, the one which is the LEAST important requirement for determining eligible contractors is

    A. availability
    B. size of work force
    C. experience
    D. location of business

30. Of the following piping materials, the one that combines the physical strength of mild steel with the corrosion resistance of gray iron is

    A. grade A steel
    B. grey cast iron
    C. welded wrought iron
    D. ductile iron

31. Assume that a can of red lead paint needs to be thinned slightly. Of the following, the one that should be used is

    A. turpentine
    B. lacquer thinner
    C. water
    D. alcohol

32. Assume that a trench is 42" wide, 5' deep, and 100' long. If the unit price of excavating the trench is $35 per cubic yard, the cost of excavating the trench is MOST NEARLY

    A. $2,275   B. $5,110   C. $7,000   D. $21,000

33. Of the following uses, the one for which a bituminous compound would usually be used is to

    A. prevent corrosion of burled steel tanks
    B. increase the strength of concrete
    C. caulk water pipes
    D. paint inside wood columns

34. An electrical drawing is drawn to a scale of 1/4" = 1'.
    If a length of conduit on the drawing measures 7 3/8", the actual length of the conduit, in feet, is MOST NEARLY

    A. 7.5'   B. 15.5'   C. 22.5'   D. 29.5'

35. Of the following steam heating systems, the one that operates under both vacuum and low pressure conditions, without using a vacuum pump, is generally known as a _____ system.

    A. one pipe low pressure
    B. vacuum
    C. vapor
    D. high pressure

36. Of the following valve trim symbols, the one which designates a valve trim made of monel material is

    A. 8-18   B. NI-CU   C. SM   D. MI

37. A replacement part for a piece of equipment is to be made of S.A.E. 4047 steel. This material is MOST likely a _____ steel.

    A. wrought
    B. nickel
    C. chrome-vanadium
    D. molybdenum

38. A metallic underground water piping system is to be used as a means of grounding. Of the following statements concerning use of this system, the one that is MOST NEARLY CORRECT is that this use is

   A. not permitted
   B. permitted where available
   C. absolutely required
   D. permitted only in certain cases

39. For pipe sizes up to 8", schedule 40 pipe is identical to _____ pipe.

   A. standard
   B. extra strong
   C. double extra strong
   D. type M copper

40. Assume that a shop is undergoing a general housecleaning, and all excess unused materials have been removed. *Clean-up work,* as pertains to painting in this case, means MOST NEARLY

   A. a thorough two-coat paint job
   B. only that surface which was marred to be painted
   C. a one-coat job to *freshen things up*
   D. only that iron work is to be painted

41. The *United States Standard Gage* is used to measure sheet metal thicknesses of

   A. iron and steel
   B. aluminum
   C. copper
   D. tin

42. Headers and stretchers are used in the construction of

   A. floors   B. walls   C. ceilings   D. roofs

Questions 43-44.

DIRECTIONS: Questions 43 and 44, inclusive, are to be answered in accordance with the following paragraph.

For cast iron pipe lines, the middle ring or sleeve shall have beveled ends and shall be high quality cast iron. The middle ring shall have a minimum wall thickness of 3/8" for pipe up to 8", 7/16" for pipe 10" to 30", and 1/2" for pipe over 30", nominal diameter. Minimum length of middle ring shall be 5" for pipe up to 10", 6" for pipe 10" to 30", and 10" for pipe 30" nominal diameter and larger. The middle ring shall not have a center pipe stop, unless otherwise specified.

43. As used in the above paragraph, the word *beveled* means MOST NEARLY

   A. straight   B. slanted   C. curved   D. rounded

44. In accordance with the above paragraph, the middle ring of a 24" nominal diameter pipe would have a minimum wall thickness and length of _____ thick and _____ long.

   A. 3/8"; 5"   B. 3/8"; 6"   C. 7/16"; 6"   D. 1/2"; 6"

45. A work order is NOT usually issued for which one of the following jobs: 45.___

    A. Repairing wood door frames
    B. Taking daily inventory
    C. Installing electric switches in maintenance shop
    D. Repairing a number of valves in boiler room

46. Of the following statements, the one which usually does NOT pertain to preventative maintenance programs is 46.___

    A. periodic inspection of facilities
    B. lubrication of equipment
    C. minor repair of equipment
    D. complete replacement of deteriorated equipment

Questions 47-50.

DIRECTIONS: Questions 47 through 50, inclusive, are based on the sketch of metal sheet shown below. (Sketch not to scale.)

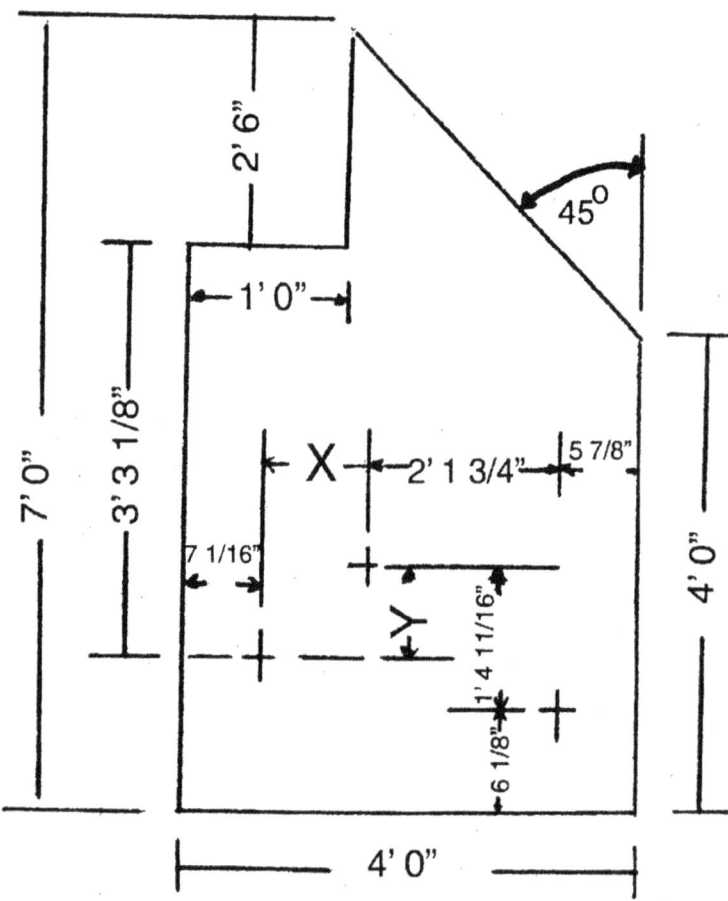

47. From the above sketch, the distance marked X is MOST NEARLY 47.___

    A. 5 1/4"   B. 6 5/16"   C. 7 1/8"   D. 9 5/16"

48. From the above sketch, the distance marked Y is MOST NEARLY　　48.____

    A. 5 11/16"　　　B. 6 3/16"　　　C. 7 5/16"　　　D. 8 11/16"

49. In reference to the above sketch, if each piece is made from a rectangular piece of metal   49.____
    measuring 4' x 7', the percent of waste material is MOST NEARLY

    A. 10%　　　B. 15%　　　C. 25%　　　D. 30%

50. In reference to the above sketch, if the metal is 1/4" thick and weighs 144 pounds per   50.____
    cubic foot, the net weight of one piece would be MOST NEARLY _____ pounds.

    A. 51　　　B. 63　　　C. 75　　　D. 749

KEY (CORRECT ANSWERS)

1. C	11. A	21. B	31. A	41. A
2. D	12. C	22. C	32. A	42. B
3. A	13. A	23. D	33. A	43. B
4. D	14. D	24. B	34. D	44. C
5. C	15. B	25. D	35. C	45. B
6. B	16. A	26. D	36. B	46. D
7. C	17. C	27. A	37. D	47. D
8. C	18. C	28. C	38. B	48. D
9. D	19. B	29. D	39. A	49. C
10. A	20. B	30. D	40. C	50. B

EXAMINATION SECTION
TEST 1

DIRECTIONS: Each question or incomplete statement is followed by several suggested answers or completions. Select the one that BEST answers the question or completes the statement. *PRINT THE LETTER OF THE CORRECT ANSWER IN THE SPACE AT THE RIGHT.*

1. The combustion efficiency of a boiler can be determined with a CO_2 indicator and the

    A. under fire draft
    B. boiler room humidity
    C. flue gas temperature
    D. outside air temperature

2. A quick, practical method of determining if the cast-iron waste pipe delivered to a job has been damaged in transit is to

    A. hydraulically test it
    B. "ring" each length with a hammer
    C. drop each length to see whether it breaks
    D. visually examine the pipe for cracks

3. An electrostatic precipitator is used to

    A. filter the air supply
    B. remove sludge from the fuel oil
    C. remove particles from the fuel gas
    D. supply samples for an Orsat analysis

4. The PRIMARY cause of cracking and spalling of refractory lining in the furnace of a steam generator is *most likely* due to

    A. continuous over-firing of boiler
    B. slag accumulation on furnace walls
    C. change in fuel from solid to liquid
    D. uneven heating and cooling within the refractory brick

5. The term "effective temperature" in air conditioning means

    A. the dry bulb temperature
    B. the average of the wet and dry bulb temperatures
    C. the square root of the product of wet and dry bulb temperatures
    D. an arbitrary index combining the effects of temperature, humidity, and movement

6. The piping in all buildings having dual water distribution systems should be identified by a color coding of _____ for potable water lines and _____ for non-potable water lines.

    A. green; red
    B. green; yellow
    C. yellow; green
    D. yellow; red

7. The breaking of a component of a machine subjected to excessive vibration is called

    A. tensile failure
    B. fatigue failure
    C. caustic embrittlement
    D. amplitude failure

8. The TWO MOST important factors to be considered in selecting fans for ventilating systems are

   A. noise and efficiency
   B. space available and weight
   C. first cost and dimensional bulk
   D. construction and arrangement of drive

9. In the modern power plant deaerator, air is removed from water to

   A. reduce heat losses in the heaters
   B. reduce corrosion of boiler steel due to the air
   C. reduce the load of the main condenser air pumps
   D. prevent pumps from becoming vapor bound

10. The abbreviations BOD, COD, and DO are associated with

    A. flue gas analysis
    B. air pollution control
    C. boiler water treatment
    D. water pollution control

11. The piping of a newly installed drainage system should be tested upon completion of the rough plumbing with a head of water of NOT LESS THAN _____ feet.

    A. 10   B. 15   C. 20   D. 25

12. Of the following statements concerning aquastats, the one which is CORRECT is:

    A. Aquastats may be obtained with either a narrow or wide range of settings
    B. Aquastats have a mercury tube switch which is controlled by the stack switch
    C. An aquastat is a device used to shut down the burner in the event of low water in the boiler
    D. An aquastat should be located about 4 inches above the normal water line of the boiler

13. The SAFEST way to protect the domestic water supply from contamination by sewage or non-potable water is to insert

    A. air gaps
    B. swing connections
    C. double check valves
    D. tanks with overhead discharge

14. The MAIN function of a back-pressure valve which is sometimes found in the connection between a water drain pipe and the sewer system is to

    A. equalize the pressure between the drain pipe and the sewer
    B. prevent sewer water from flowing into the drain pipe
    C. provide pressure to enable waste to reach the sewer
    D. make sure that there is not too much water pressure in the sewer line

15. Boiler water is neutral if its pH value is

    A. 0   B. 1   C. 7   D. 14

16. A domestic hot water mixing or tempering valve should be preceded in the hot water line by a

    A. strainer
    B. foot valve
    C. check valve
    D. steam trap

17. Between a steam boiler and its safety valve there should be

    A. no valve of any type
    B. a gate valve of the same size as the safety valve
    C. a swing check valve of at least the same size as the safety valve
    D. a cock having a clear opening equal in area to the pipe connecting the boiler and safety valve

18. A diagram of horizontal plumbing drainage lines should have cleanouts shown

    A. at least every 25 feet
    B. at least every 100 feet
    C. wherever a basin is located
    D. wherever a change in direction occurs

19. When a Bourdon gauge is used to measure steam pressures, some form of siphon or water seal must be maintained.
    The reason for this is to

    A. obtain "absolute" pressure readings
    B. prevent steam from entering the gage
    C. prevent condensate from entering the gage
    D. obtain readings below atmospheric pressure

20. In a closed heat exchanger, oil is cooled by condensate which is to be returned to a boiler. In order to avoid the possibility of contaminating the condensate with oil should a tube fail in the oil cooler, it would be good practice to

    A. cool the oil by air instead of water
    B. treat the condensate with an oil solvent
    C. keep the oil pressure in the exchanger higher than the water pressure
    D. keep the water pressure in the exchanger higher than the oil pressure

21. A radiator thermostatic trap is used on a vacuum return type of heating system to

    A. release the pocketed air only
    B. reduce the amount of condensate
    C. maintain a predetermined radiator water level
    D. prevent the return of live steam to the return line

22. According to the color coding of piping, fire protection piping should be painted

    A. green   B. yellow   C. purple   D. red

23. The MAIN purpose of a standpipe system is to

    A. supply the roof water tank
    B. provide water for firefighting

C. circulate water for the heating system
D. provide adequate pressure for the water supply

24. The name "Saybolt" is associated with the measurement of

    A. viscosity
    B. Btu content
    C. octane rating
    D. temperature

25. Recirculation of conditioned air in an air-conditioned building is done MAINLY to

    A. reduce refrigeration tonnage required
    B. increase room entrophy
    C. increase air specific humidity
    D. reduce room temperature below the dewpoint

26. In a plumbing installation, vent pipes are GENERALLY used to

    A. prevent the loss of water seal from traps by evaporation
    B. prevent the loss of water seal due to several causes other than evaporation
    C. act as an additional path for liquids to flow through during normal use of a plumbing fixture
    D. prevent the backflow of water in a cross-connection between a drinking water line and a sewage line

27. The designation "150 W" cast on the bonnet of a gate valve is an indication of the

    A. water working temperature
    B. water working pressure
    C. area of the opening in square inches
    D. weight of the valve in pounds

28. In the city, the size soil pipe necessary in a sewage drainage system is determined by the

    A. legal occupancy of the building
    B. vertical height of the soil line
    C. number of restrooms connected to the soil line
    D. number of "fixture units" connected to the soil line

29. Fins or other extended surfaces are used on heat exchanger tubes when

    A. the exchanger is a water-to-water exchanger
    B. water is on one side of the tube and condensing steam on the other side
    C. the surface coefficient of heat transfer on both sides of the tube is high
    D. the surface coefficient of heat transfer on one side of the tube is low compared to the coefficient on the other side of the tube

30. A fusible plug may be put in a fire tube boiler as an emergency device to indicate low water level. The fusible plug is installed so that under normal operating conditions,

    A. both sides are exposed to steam
    B. one side is exposed to water and the other side to steam
    C. one side is exposed to steam and the other side to hot gases
    D. one side is exposed to the water and the other side to hot gases

31. Extra strong wrought-iron pipe, as compared to standard wrought-iron pipe of the same nominal size, has

    A. the same outside diameter but a smaller inside diameter
    B. the same inside diameter but a larger outside diameter
    C. a larger outside diameter and a smaller inside diameter
    D. larger inside and outside diameters

31.____

32. Fans may be rated on a dynamic or a static efficiency basis. The dynamic efficiency would *probably* be

    A. lower in value because of the energy absorbed by the air velocity
    B. the same as the static in the case of centrifugal blowers running at various speeds
    C. the same as the static in the case of axial flow blowers running at various speeds
    D. higher in value than the static

32.____

33. The function of the stack relay in an oil burner installation is to

    A. regulate the draft over the fire
    B. regulate the flow of fuel oil to the burner
    C. stop the motor if the oil has not ignited
    D. stop the motor if the water or steam pressure is too high

33.____

34. The type of centrifugal pump which is inherently balanced for hydraulic thrust is the

    A. double suction impeller type
    B. single suction impeller type
    C. single stage type
    D. multistage type

34.____

35. The specifications for a job using sheet lead calls for "4-lb. sheet lead."
    This means that each sheet should weigh

    A. 4 lbs.
    B. 4 lbs. per square
    C. 4 lbs. per square foot
    D. 4 lbs. per cubic inch

35.____

36. The total cooling load design conditions for a building are divided for convenience into two components.
    These are:

    A. infiltration and radiation
    B. sensible heat and latent heat
    C. wet and dry bulb temperatures
    D. solar heat gain and moisture transfer

36.____

37. The function of a Hartford loop used on some steam boilers is to

    A. limit boiler steam pressure
    B. limit temperature of the steam
    C. prevent high water levels in the boiler
    D. prevent back flow of water from the boiler into the return main

37.____

38. Vibration from a ventilating blower can be prevented from being transmitted to the duct work by

    A. installing straighteners in the duct
    B. throttling the air supply to the blower
    C. bolting the blower tightly to the duct
    D. installing a canvas sleeve at the blower outlet

39. A specification states that access panels to suspended ceiling will be of metal. The MAIN reason for providing access panels is to

    A. improve the insulation of the ceiling
    B. improve the appearance of the ceiling
    C. make it easier to construct the building
    D. make it easier to maintain the building

40. A plumber on a job reports that the steamfitter has installed a 3" steam line in a location at which the plans show the house trap. On inspecting the job, you should

    A. tell the steamfitter to remove the steam line
    B. study the condition to see if the house trap can be relocated
    C. tell the plumber and steamfitter to work it out between themselves and then report to you
    D. tell the plumber to find another location for the trap because the steamfitter has already completed his work

41. In the installation of any heating system, the MOST important consideration is that

    A. all elements be made of a good grade of cast iron
    B. all radiators and connectors be mounted horizontally
    C. the smallest velocity of flow of heating medium be used
    D. there be proper clearance between hot surfaces and surrounding combustible material

42. Which one of the following is the PRIMARY object in drawing up a set of specifications for materials to be purchased?

    A. Control of quality
    B. Outline of intended use
    C. Establishment of standard sizes
    D. Location and method of inspection.

43. The drawing which should be used as a LEGAL reference when checking completed construction work is the _____ drawing.

    A. contract   B. assembly
    C. working or shop   D. preliminary

Questions 44-50.

DIRECTIONS: Questions 44 through 50 refer to the plumbing drawing shown below.

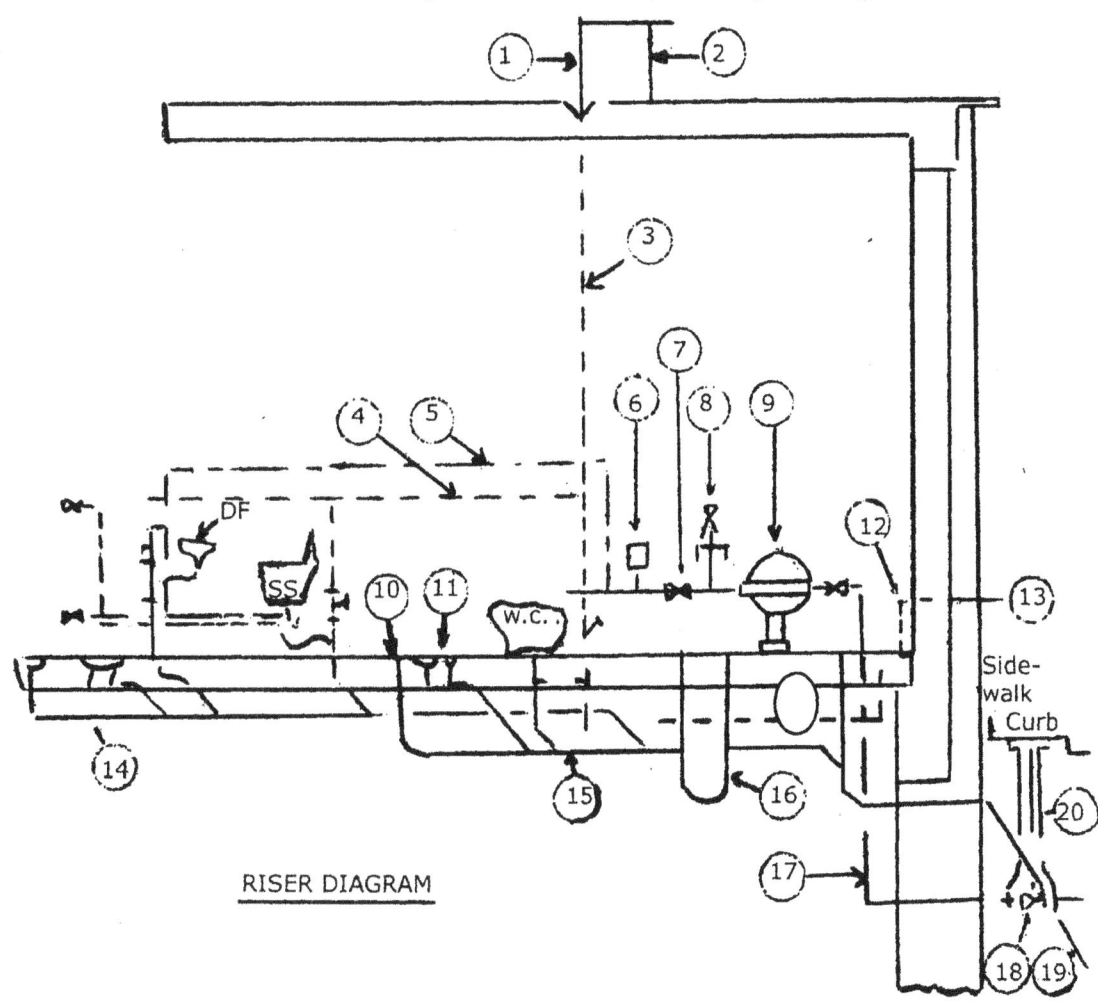

RISER DIAGRAM

44. According to the building code, the MINIMUM diameter of No. 1 and its minimum height, No. 2 respectively, are

    A. 2" and 12"   B. 3" and 18"
    C. 4" and 24"   D. 6" and 36"

44.____

45. No. 6 is a

    A. relief valve   B. shock absorber
    C. testing connection   D. drain

45.____

46. No. 9 is a

    A. strainer   B. float valve
    C. meter   D. pedestal

46.____

47. No. 11 is a

    A. floor drain   B. cleanout
    C. trap   D. vent connection

47.____

48. No. ⑬ is a

    A. standpipe
    C. sprinkler head
    B. air inlet
    D. cleanout

49. The size of No. ⑯ is

    A. 2" x 2"
    C. 3" x 3"
    B. 2" x 3"
    D. 4" x 4"

50. No. ⑱ is a

    A. pressure reducing valve
    B. butterfly valve
    C. curb cock
    D. sprinkler head

KEY (CORRECT ANSWERS)

1. C	11. A	21. D	31. A	41. D
2. B	12. C	22. D	32. D	42. A
3. C	13. A	23. B	33. C	43. A
4. D	14. B	24. A	34. A	44. C
5. D	15. C	25. A	35. C	45. B
6. B	16. A	26. B	36. B	46. C
7. B	17. A	27. B	37. D	47. A
8. A	18. D	28. D	38. D	48. B
9. B	19. B	29. D	39. D	49. D
10. D	20. D	30. D	40. B	50. C

EXAMINATION SECTION
TEST 1

DIRECTIONS: Each question or incomplete statement is followed by several suggested answers or completions. Select the one that BEST answers the question or completes the statement. *PRINT THE LETTER OF THE CORRECT ANSWER IN THE SPACE AT THE RIGHT.*

1. The dial of a water meter shall be a MAXIMUM height above the floor of _____ ft.   1.____

   A. 1   B. 2   C. 3   D. 4

2. A stop-and-waste cock is GENERALLY used on   2.____

   A. soil lines
   B. gas supply lines
   C. water supply lines subjected to low temperatures
   D. refrigerant lines connected to compressors

3. Assume that your superior has directed you to make certain changes in your established inspection procedure. After using this modified procedure on several inspections, you find that the original procedure was distinctly superior and you wish to return to it.   3.____
You should

   A. let your superior find this out for himself
   B. simply change back to the original procedure
   C. compile definite data and information to prove your case to your superior
   D. persuade one of the more experienced inspectors to take this matter up with your superior

4. When automatic sprinklers are attached to a piping system containing air under pressure, the sprinkler system is called a _____ system.   4.____

   A. wet-pipe   B. dry-pipe
   C. deluge   D. compressed air

5. When making an inspection of one of the buildings under your supervision, the BEST procedure to follow in making a record of the inspection is to   5.____

   A. return immediately to the office and write a report from memory
   B. write down all the important facts during or as soon as you complete the inspection
   C. fix in your mind all important facts so that you can repeat them from memory if necessary
   D. fix in your mind all important facts so that you can make out your report at the end of the day

6. The MAIN reason for pitching a steam pipe in a heating system is to   6.____

   A. reduce friction in the pipe
   B. prevent the formation of scale
   C. facilitate repairs
   D. prevent accumulation of condensate

7. Nozzles on 2 1/2" diameter hose for standpipe systems must GENERALLY have a minimum length of _____ inches.

    A. 3 B. 6 C. 10 D. 15

8. An inspector visited a large building under construction. He inspected the soil lines at 9 A.M., water lines at 10 A.M., fixtures at 11 A.M., and did his office work in the afternoon. He followed the same pattern daily for weeks.
    This procedure was

    A. *good,* because it was methodical and he did not miss anything
    B. *good,* because it gave equal time to all phases of the plumbing
    C. *bad,* because not enough time was devoted to fixtures
    D. *bad,* because the tradesmen knew when the inspection would occur

9. When an unusually long run of supply pipe for sprinklers is needed, an increase in pipe size over that called for in the schedules may be required to

    A. compensate for increased friction
    B. provide enough water if the pipe diameter decreases due to corrosion deposits
    C. adequately protect areas which are separated by fire walls
    D. provide enough water in case more than one fire occurs at the same time

10. Roof drainage downspouts or leaders should be sized according to the

    A. type of sewer connection
    B. type of building occupancy
    C. size of cold water risers
    D. area of the roof to be drained

11. The type of pipe which is GENERALLY advantageous to use where corrosion is severe is

    A. cast iron   B. wrought iron
    C. steel   D. galvanized iron

12. A contractor has made an unjustified complaint against an inspector to the inspector's superior.
    In future contacts with this contractor, the inspector should be

    A. very careful in what he says
    B. courteous and fair in enforcing the law
    C. cool and distant to avoid more trouble
    D. exceptionally friendly in order to ease matters

13. A tank is filled with fresh water to a height of 20 ft. The pressure at the bottom of the tank is _____ pounds per square foot.

    A. 1168 B. 1248 C. 1322 D. 1404

14. The one of the following terms which is NOT used to classify buildings for purposes of sprinkler installations is _____ hazard.

    A. light B. ordinary C. regular D. extra

15. The PROPER type of fitting to use in a horizontal hot water heating main, when changing pipe size, is a(n)   15._____

    A. concentric reducer   B. eccentric reducer
    C. hexagon bushing   D. face bushing

16. Fire pumps shall be tested after installation to ascertain that the pump is supplying its rated capacity at   16._____

    A. the lowest required hose outlet
    B. the highest required hose outlet
    C. every hose outlet in the building
    D. one hose outlet which has been selected for testing

17. A pipe chase is a   17._____

    A. wire brush for cleaning the inside of pipes
    B. wire brush used for cleaning the outside of pipes
    C. continuous space in a building through which pipes run
    D. thimble through a wall to allow a pipe to pierce the wall

18. The utility line that USUALLY enters or leaves the building at the lowest elevation is the   18._____

    A. water inlet   B. gas line
    C. electric supply   D. building drain

19. The standpipe system shall be zoned by use of gravity tanks, automatic fire pumps, pressure tanks, and street pressure so that the MAXIMUM pressure at the inlet of any hose valve in the zone is _____ psig.   19._____

    A. 40   B. 60   C. 80   D. 100

20. Yard hydrant systems which are connected to city water mains shall be provided with post indicator valves located in an accessible position.
    Such post indicator valves shall be locked _____ and painted _____ .   20._____

    A. shut; green   B. shut; red
    C. open; green   D. open; red

21. A practice which is likely to cause some confusion when dealing with contractors is for an inspector to   21._____

    A. issue detailed instruction only in writing
    B. relay instructions to the contractor through one or two of the contractor's men
    C. transmit simple instructions orally
    D. follow up all his instructions after issuing them

22. Small commercial sizes of steel pipe are GENERALLY designated by their _____ diameter.   22._____

    A. exact inside   B. exact outside
    C. nominal inside   D. nominal outside

23. A head of water of 50 feet is equivalent to a pressure of MOST NEARLY _____ psi.   23._____

    A. 16   B. 22   C. 28   D. 34

24. A contractor demands to see your supervisor after accusing you of being prejudiced against him.
    The BEST course of action for you to follow is to

    A. convince him that you are not prejudiced
    B. remind him that you can make trouble for him if he fails to show you proper respect
    C. take him to your superior as he requests
    D. do nothing if you feel that you are not prejudiced

25. The water supply pipe which extends from the street main to the house control valve is GENERALLY called the _____ pipe.

    A. main   B. intake   C. service   D. gooseneck

26. The number of threads per inch on standard steel pipe threads GENERALLY

    A. decreases as the diameter of the pipe increases
    B. increases as the diameter of the pipe increases
    C. does not vary with the diameter of the pipe
    D. depends solely on the pressure the pipe must withstand

27. A specification requires that sewer pipe be laid with a smooth and uniform invert.
    The term *invert* refers to the _____ of the pipe, _____.

    A. inside; all around   B. outside; all around
    C. inside; at the bottom   D. outside; at the bottom

Questions 28-40.

DIRECTIONS: Questions 28 through 40 refer to the Riser Diagram shown below.

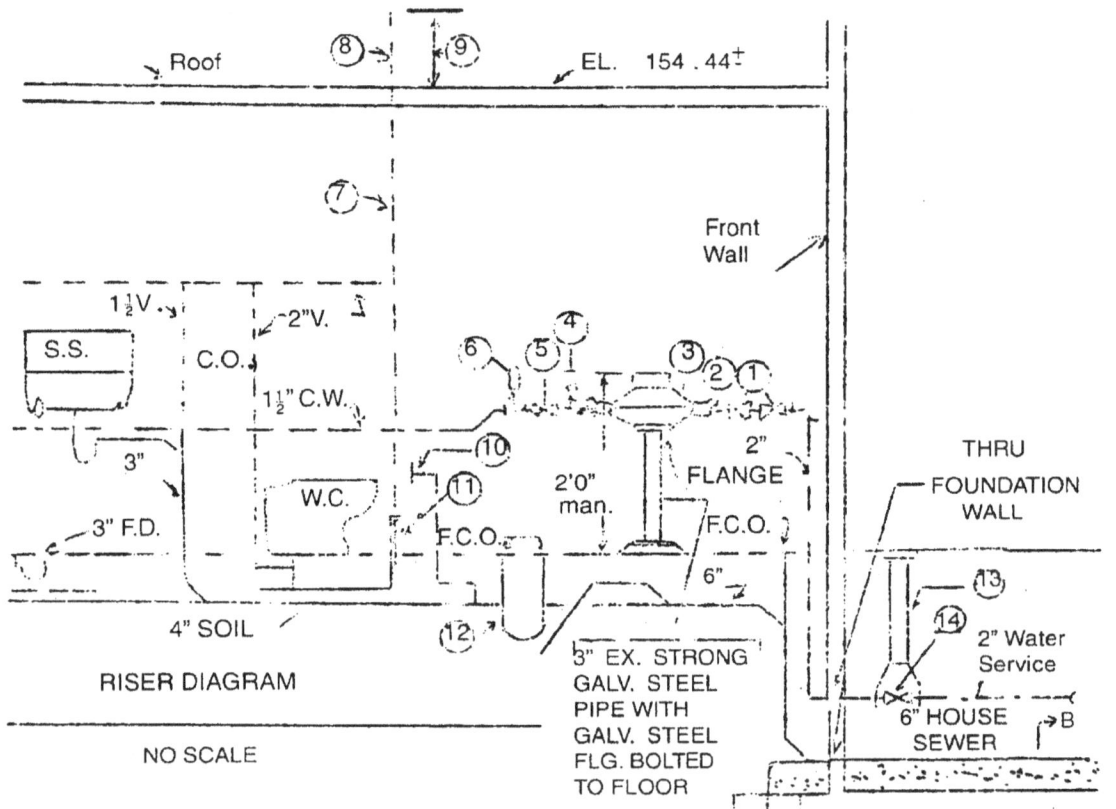

28. Item *1* is a _____ valve.

   A. check B. globe C. gate D. pressure

29. Item *2* is a

   A. valve B. union C. reducer D. flange

30. Item *3* is a

   A. meter
   C. water fountain
   B. sink
   D. reducing valve

31. Item *4* is a

   A. pressure valve
   C. relief fitting
   B. test connection
   D. supply valve

32. Item *6* is

   A. meter
   C. water indicator
   B. pressure gauge
   D. shock absorber

33. Item *7* is a

   A. soil line
   C. water supply line
   B. vent line
   D. heater exhaust

34. Item *8* should have a minimum diameter of _____ inches.

   A. 2 B. 3 C. 4 D. 6

35. Distance *9* should be a minimum of _____ ft.

   A. 1 B. 2 C. 4 D. 6

36. Item *10* is a

   A. sprinkler connection
   C. fresh air inlet
   B. clean-out plug
   D. floor drain

37. Item *11* is a

   A. hot water connection
   C. flushometer fitting
   B. clean-out plug
   D. floor drain

38. Item *12* is a

   A. trap
   C. floor drain
   B. running trap
   D. return bend

39. Item *13* is a

   A. curb box
   C. metering point
   B. sewer access
   D. pressure gage location

40. Item *14* has the main purpose of
    A. permitting water supply to be turned off
    B. reducing water supply pressure
    C. checking backflow
    D. permitting a pressure check

KEY (CORRECT ANSWERS)

1. C	11. A	21. B	31. B
2. C	12. B	22. C	32. D
3. C	13. B	23. B	33. B
4. B	14. C	24. C	34. C
5. B	15. B	25. C	35. B
6. D	16. B	26. A	36. C
7. D	17. C	27. C	37. B
8. D	18. D	28. C	38. B
9. A	19. B	29. C	39. A
10. D	20. D	30. A	40. A

TEST 2

DIRECTIONS: Each question or incomplete statement is followed by several suggested answers or completions. Select the one that BEST answers the question or completes the statement. *PRINT THE LETTER OF THE CORRECT ANSWER IN THE SPACE AT THE RIGHT.*

1. Two full lengths of black standard steel gas pipe in a continuous run should be connected together by a   1.____

    A. running thread coupling
    B. right and left coupling
    C. gasketed union
    D. tee with side outlet plugged

2. The factor which is NOT generally considered to be a major cause of accidents is   2.____

    A. failure to use personal protective devices
    B. working at a very rapid speed
    C. using inoperative safety devices
    D. lack of familiarity with a particular job

3. Underground mains and lead-in connections to system risers shall be flushed thoroughly before any connection is made to sprinkler piping in order to   3.____

    A. make sure that there are no leaks in the mains
    B. check that the pressure meets building code requirements
    C. make sure that the proper number of gpm can flow through the pipes
    D. remove foreign materials which may have entered during the course of installation

4. A plumbing specification states: *Each pipe shall have clearly impressed on its outer surface the name of the manufacturer and of the factory in which it was made.* The BEST reason for this requirement is that this   4.____

    A. identifies the grade of the pipe
    B. helps locate the pipe in the field
    C. insures that approved material is used
    D. shows who is responsible for defective material

5. A plumbing system should be tested at a water pressure which is determined by multiplying the working pressure of the system by a factor of   5.____

    A. 1.0   B. 1.25   C. 1.5   D. 2.0

6. A *by-pass loop* in a piping system   6.____

    A. tends to eliminate pulsations of fluid flow
    B. provides a method for increasing the capacity of the piping system
    C. prevents excessive piping stresses by providing for expansion and contraction
    D. provides emergency routing of flow if the primary system is shut down

7. In an accident report, the information which may be MOST useful in decreasing the recurrence of similar type accidents is the

   A. time the accident happened
   B. cause of the accident
   C. extent of injuries sustained
   D. number of people involved

8. Joints in glass pipe used for chemical waste should NOT be made by use of

   A. compression couplings   B. adapter couplings
   C. caulking   D. adjustable joints

9. Assume that 90 gallons per minute flow through a certain 3-inch pipe which is tapped into a street main.
   The amount of water which would flow through a 1-inch pipe tapped into the same street main is MOST NEARLY _____ gpm

   A. 90   B. 45   C. 30   D. 10

10. Accessible cleanouts in drainage piping shall be installed at each change of direction GREATER than _____ °.

    A. 20   B. 45   C. 90   D. 135

11. The kitchen sink in a dwelling may be used to receive the discharge of an indirect waste pipe from a

    A. clothes washer   B. dishwasher
    C. refrigerator   D. drinking fountain

12. The material which should NOT generally be used for roof drains is

    A. wrought iron   B. lead
    C. stainless steel   D. copper

13. The time required to pump 2500 gallons of water out of a sump at the rate of 12 1/2 gallons per minute would be _____ hour(s), _____ minutes.

    A. 1; 40   B. 2; 30   C. 3; 20   D. 6; 40

14. Copper tubing which has an inside diameter of 1 1/16 inches and a wall thickness of .095 inches has an outside diameter which is MOST NEARLY _____ inches.

    A. 1 5/32   B. 1 3/16   C. 1 7/32   D. 1 1/4

15. Valves used to control a standpipe system shall have the name of the manufacturer

    A. on a tag which is permanently attached to each valve by means of a chain
    B. cast on or in each valve
    C. on a tag which is welded to each valve
    D. readily available in the records kept by the building custodian

16. The PREFERRED type of feed to sprinklers, especially where there are over six sprinklers on a branch line is _____ feed.

    A. center central   B. central end
    C. side end   D. cross main

17. A *branch interval* is defined as 17.____
   A. the length along the center line of pipe and fittings both horizontal and vertical
   B. a distance along a soil or waste stack corresponding in general to a story height, but in no case less than 8 feet, within which the horizontal branches from one floor or story of a building are connected to the stack
   C. a vent connecting one or more individual vents with a vent stack or stack vent
   D. that part of a piping system other than a main riser or stack that extends to fixtures on two or less consecutive floors

18. The distance which is measured along the center line of pipes and fittings is called the _____ length. 18.____
   A. system   B. effective
   C. equivalent   D. developed

19. The HEAVIEST commercially obtainable steel and wrought iron pipe is called 19.____
   A. extra strong   B. double extra strong
   C. heavy duty   D. high strength

20. Pressure tanks for sprinkler systems should be located 20.____
   A. in the basement of the building
   B. at or above the top level of sprinklers
   C. at any convenient location in the building
   D. on any floor where they will be easily accessible

21. Fire pumps in standpipe systems should be 21.____
   A. in sump pits below the pump room floor level
   B. mounted directly on the pump room floor
   C. on concrete foundations at least 1 foot above the pump room floor level
   D. on concrete platforms at least 3 feet above the pump room floor level

22. A *street ell* is a fitting which has 22.____
   A. threads on the inside of one end and on the outside of the other end
   B. threads on the inside of both ends
   C. threads on the outside of both ends
   D. non-tapered threads on both ends

23. The MAIN difference between schedule-80 pipe and schedule-40 pipe is that schedule-80 pipe 23.____
   A. weighs more per foot
   B. has a smaller wall thickness
   C. has a larger inside diameter
   D. has more threads per inch.

24. If a 4-inch pipe is directly coupled to a 2-inch pipe and 16 gallons per minute are flowing through the 4-inch pipe, then the flow through the 2-inch pipe will be _____ gallons per minute. 24.____
   A. 4   B. 8   C. 16   D. 32

25. A contractor is always complaining that he is being treated too harshly by an inspector. The BEST action for the inspector to take is to

    A. consider the complaints on their merit
    B. tell the contractor that he will not listen to any of his complaints
    C. *ride* the contractor until he stops complaining
    D. ignore the contractor's complaints

26. Each standpipe system control valve shall have a metal disk at least 3 inches in diameter securely attached to the valve.
    The disk shall have white markings with a red background and should ALWAYS indicate

    A. the number assigned to it on the riser diagram for the standpipe system
    B. the direction to turn the valve to open and shut
    C. whether the water is good for drinking
    D. whether the valve is in the open or closed position

27. Riser control valves for standpipe systems shall, where practicable, be located

    A. outside the building in an easily accessible location
    B. as near as possible to the main control valves in the basement
    C. in the lobby of the building
    D. within a required stair enclosure serving the entrance floor

28. The BEST method to use to determine whether a large cast iron fitting is cracked is to

    A. visually examine the fitting for cracks
    B. put a water test on the fitting
    C. bang the fitting on concrete to see if it breaks
    D. *ring* the fitting with a hammer

29. Hydrostatic pressure tests for standpipe systems shall NORMALLY be performed for a period of at least

    A. 15 minutes   B. 1 hour
    C. 12 hours   D. 24 hours

30. The weight of a 6 foot length of 8-inch pipe which weighs 24.70 pounds per foot is _____ lbs.

    A. 148.2   B. 176.8   C. 197.6   D. 212.4

31. A *dresser* is MOST frequently used on _____ pipe.

    A. chrome-plated   B. brass
    C. lead   D. wrought iron

32. The cast iron fitting which is called a l/8th bend changes the direction of flow by an angle of

    A. 12 1/2°   B. 22 1/2°   C. 45°   D. 30°

33. Each service directly supplying a standpipe system or a fire pump shall be equipped with a control valve located

   A. in an exposed location within 1 ft. above the sidewalk
   B. in an exposed location within 2 ft. above the sidewalk
   C. under the sidewalk in a flush sidewalk box located within 1 ft. of the street line
   D. under the sidewalk in a flush sidewalk box located within 2 ft. of the street line

34. The MOST important requirement of a well-written report is that it should

   A. be very long and detailed
   B. have a proper heading
   C. be clear and brief
   D. have good punctuation

35. Gas service connections which supply gas to small residential buildings shall be provided with a regulator that will reduce the pressure of the gas to _____ psi.

   A. 4   B. 1   C. 2   D. 3

36. Each fixture trap in abuilding shall have a liquid seal of AT LEAST _____ inch(es).

   A. 4   B. 3   C. 2   D. 1

37. A pneumatic water supply system supplies water to the fixtures by means of _____ pressure.

   A. street   B. air   C. pump   D. steam

38. The opening pressure of the pressure relief valve on a boiler should be AT LEAST _____ pounds above the _____.

   A. 10; rated pressure of the boiler
   B. 25; rated pressure of the boiler
   C. 10; normal working pressure
   D. 25; normal working pressure

39. The plumbing term *pot piece* is GENERALLY used in connection with work involving the

   A. installation of water closets
   B. soldering of a lead cap
   C. caulking of a cast iron joint
   D. storing of fixtures and trim

40. The one of the following which is MOST likely to influence the minimum required size of a soil or waste stack is the

   A. number of offsets needed in the stack
   B. slope of the house drain
   C. height of the stack
   D. number and type of fixtures serviced by the stack

KEY (CORRECT ANSWERS)

1.	B	11.	B	21.	C	31.	C
2.	D	12.	A	22.	A	32.	C
3.	D	13.	C	23.	A	33.	D
4.	C	14.	D	24.	C	34.	C
5.	B	15.	B	25.	A	35.	A
6.	D	16.	A	26.	A	36.	C
7.	B	17.	B	27.	D	37.	B
8.	C	18.	D	28.	D	38.	D
9.	D	19.	B	29.	B	39.	C
10.	B	20.	B	30.	A	40.	D

EXAMINATION SECTION
TEST 1

DIRECTIONS: Each question or incomplete statement is followed by several suggested answers or completions. Select the one that BEST answers the question or completes the statement. *PRINT THE LETTER OF THE CORRECT ANSWER IN THE SPACE AT THE RIGHT.*

Questions 1-16.

DIRECTIONS: Questions 1 through 16 deal with graphical symbols of electrical items as recommended by the ANSI (ex-ASA). For each item, select the proper graphical symbol and print the letter corresponding to it.

1. Telephone switchboard

   A. 6   B. 16   C. 17   D. 18

2. Exit light wall outlet

   A. 5   B. 12   C. 15   D. 16

3. City fire alarm station

   A. 19   B. 21   C. 22   D. 23

4. Electric door opener

   A. 9   B. 10   C. 11   D. 15

5. Duplex convenience outlet

   A. 9   B. 10   C. 15   D. 24

6. Range outlet

   A. 3   B. 6   C. 13   D. 14

7. Push button

   A. 5   B. 8   C. 11   D. 12

8. Power panel

   A. 1   B. 2   C. 3   D. 4

1. ▭
2. ▨
3. ⊟⊦
4. ⊠
5. ▭✓
6. Ⓣ
7. Ⓑ
8. ▣ (O)
9. Ⓓ
10. ▣ (D)
11. ⊗
12. -⊗
13. ≡◉R
14. ⊖◯ R̄
15. Ⓔ
16. S_4
17. ◁

9. Four-way switch

   A. 4   B. 13   C. 14   D. 16

10. Controller

    A. 3   B. 4   C. 5   D. 9

11. Lighting panel

    A. 1   B. 2   C. 3   D. 4

12. Buzzer

    A. 3   B. 5   C. 8   D. 11

13. Isolating switch

    A. 3   B. 5   C. 9   D. 10

14. Interconnecting telephone

    A. 13   B. 14   C. 17   D. 18

15. Fire alarm central station

    A. 21   B. 22   C. 23   D. 26

16. Clock outlet

    A. 9   B. 10   C. 15   D. 26

18. ▷

19. S_F

20. S_{MC}

21. [FA]

22. [F]

23. ⊠

24. ─◯

25. ≡◯ 3

26. Ⓒ

9. ____

10. ____

11. ____

12. ____

13. ____

14. ____

15. ____

16. ____

17. A riser diagram is an electrical drawing which would give information about the   17.____

    A. voltage drop in feeders
    B. size of feeders and panel loads
    C. external connections to equipment
    D. sequence of operation of devices and equipment

18. When a contractor fails to adhere to an approved progress schedule, he should   18.____

    A. revise the schedule without delay
    B. ask for an extension of time on account of delays
    C. adopt such additional means and methods of construction as will make up for the time lost
    D. take no immediate action with the hope that sufficient time will be available later on that will assure the completion in accordance with the schedule

19. The usual contract for work includes a section entitled, *Instructions to Bidders,* which states that the   19.____

    A. contractor agrees that he has made his own examination and will make no claims for damages on account of errors or omissions
    B. contractor shall not make claims for damages of any discrepancy, error or omission in any plans
    C. estimates of quantities and calculations are guaranteed by the Board to be correct and are deemed to be a representation of the conditions affecting the work
    D. plans, measurements, dimensions, and conditions under which the work is to be performed are guaranteed by the Board

20. The purpose of performing a dielectric test on a sample of oil taken from the casing of an oil-filled power transformer is to determine the   20.____

    A. viscosity   B. insulating quality
    C. flashpoint   D. extent of contamination

21. A neon test lamp can be used to test   21.____

    A. the field intensity of a relay magnet
    B. the phase rotation of a source of supply
    C. whether a supply source is A.C. or D.C.
    D. the power factor of a source of supply

22. The size, in circular mils, of a wire whose diameter is known can be calculated by   22.____

    A. multiplying the diameter in mils by $\pi/4$
    B. squaring the diameter in mils
    C. squaring the diameter in mils and multiplying the product by $\pi/4$
    D. squaring the diameter in inches

23. The short time rating and the continuous rating of a given piece of electrical machinery differ, but both are based on the   23.____

    A. cost of energy
    B. line potential

C. power factor of the machine
D. temperature rise of the machine

24. A lump sum type of contract may require the contractor to submit a schedule of unit prices.
   The BEST reason for this is that it

   A. prevents the lump sum from being too high
   B. simplifies the selection of the lowest bidder
   C. enables the estimators to check the total cost
   D. provides a means of making equitable partial payments

24.____

25. In assigning his men to various jobs, the BEST principle for a supervisor to follow is to

   A. study the men's abilities and assign them accordingly
   B. rotate a man from job to job until you find one which he can do well
   C. assign each of them a job and let them adjust to it in their own way
   D. assume that men appointed to the position can do all parts of the work equally well

25.____

KEY (CORRECT ANSWERS)

1.	D	11.	A
2.	B	12.	B
3.	D	13.	A
4.	B	14.	C
5.	D	15.	A
6.	C	16.	D
7.	B	17.	B
8.	B	18.	C
9.	D	19.	A
10.	B	20.	C

21. C
22. B
23. D
24. D
25. A

TEST 2

DIRECTIONS: Each question or incomplete statement is followed by several suggested answers or completions. Select the one that BEST answers the question or completes the statement. *PRINT THE LETTER OF THE CORRECT ANSWER IN THE SPACE AT THE RIGHT.*

Questions 1-8.

DIRECTIONS: Questions 1 through 8 are to be answered in accordance with the requirements of the electrical code, assuming normal procedures. Do NOT consider exceptions which are granted by special permission.

1. The MINIMUM size of A.W.G. wire which may be used on a 15-ampere branch circuit is

   A. 10   B. 12   C. 14   D. 16

2. Conductors supplying an individual motor whose full-load current is 100 amperes should have a MINIMUM carrying capacity of _____ amperes.

   A. 100   B. 115   C. 125   D. 150

3. The MINIMUM rating of a service switch is _____ amperes.

   A. 30   B. 60   C. 100   D. 200

4. In the installation of fluorescent fixtures, the MAXIMUM number of single or two-lamp type auxiliaries which can be placed on any single fifteen-ampere branch circuit is

   A. 10   B. 12   C. 15   D. 18

5. Where rubber-covered conductors are used in a conduit, the MINIMUM radius of the curve of the inner edge of any field bend, in terms of the internal diameter of the conduit, shall not be less than _____ times.

   A. 4   B. 6   C. 8   D. 10

6. Except for fixture wire of MI cable, single conductors of No. 6 A.W.G. or smaller intended for use as identified conductors of circuits shall have an outer identification of

   A. green
   B. black
   C. white or natural gray
   D. gray with a yellow marker throughout its length

7. Motor running protective devices, other than fuses, should have a continuous current-carrying capacity, in terms of the full load current rating of the motor, of AT LEAST

   A. 100%   B. 115%   C. 120%   D. 125%

8. The one of the following which should ALWAYS be used as the grounding electrode, where available, is a

   A. driven non-ferrous metallic rod
   B. buried plate with an area of 2 sq.ft.
   C. driven iron rod with a resistance of 25 ohms
   D. continuous metallic underground water piping system

9. The MAIN reason for requiring written job reports is to

   A. avoid the necessity of oral orders
   B. develop better methods of doing the work
   C. provide a permanent record of what was done
   D. increase the amount of work that can be done

10. Of the following items, the one which should NOT be included in a proposed work schedule is

    A. a schedule of hourly wage rates and supplementary benefits
    B. an estimated time required for delivery of materials and equipment
    C. the anticipated commencement and completion of the various operations
    D. the sequence and inter-relationship of various operations with those of related contracts

11. The closed circuit is used primarily in communication and fire alarm systems to indicate, by various or audible means, which of the following abnormal circuit conditions?

    A. Open
    B. Ground
    C. Overload
    D. Direct short

12. A Board specification states that access panels to suspended ceiling will be of metal. The MAIN reason for providing access panels is to

    A. improve the insulation of the ceiling
    B. improve the appearance of the building
    C. make it easier to construct the building
    D. make it easier to maintain the building

13. The one of the following which is a successful means of decreasing electrolysis in underground metal pipes is to

    A. use galvanized pipe
    B. insert occasional insulating joints in the pipes
    C. keep the voltage drop in the ground return circuit over 15 volts
    D. coat the pipe with tar for 6 inches above and 6 inches below the point where it enters the ground

14. The abbreviation *MCM* placed next to a feeder cable in a wiring diagram would indicate the

    A. microamperes per circular mil
    B. area of the cable in millions of circular mils
    C. area of the cable in thousands of circular mils
    D. resistance of the cable in microhms per circular-mil-ft.

15. Which one of the following is the PRIMARY object in drawing up a set of specifications for materials to be purchased?

    A. Control of quality
    B. Outline of intended use
    C. Establishment of standard sizes
    D. Location and method of inspection

16. The marking or lettering that indicates a conductor having moisture-and-heat resistance thermoplastic covering and which may be used in both dry and wet locations is

    A. RHW B. SB C. THW D. TW

17. In performing field inspectional work, an inspector is the contact man between the public and the authority, and it is his job to secure compliance through the maximum utilization of persuasion and education and the minimum application of coercion.
    According to the above statement, an inspector performing inspectional duties should

    A. seek to obtain voluntary compliance and use coercion only as a last resort
    B. be conciliatory on all issues of non-compliance and not take an attitude of firmness and authority
    C. maintain a strictly impersonal attitude in the exercise of his duties at all times
    D. use the threat of legal action to secure conformance with specified requirements

18. In a polarized interior lighting system, the

    A. base of the lamp sockets is connected to the identified wire
    B. branch circuit light switch is connected to the identifying wire
    C. screwshells of the lamp sockets are connected to the identified wire
    D. branch circuit light switch is connected to the screwshell of the lamp socket

19. If a supervisor finds a discrepancy between the plans and specifications, he should

    A. always follow the plans
    B. ask for an interpretation
    C. always follow the specifications
    D. follow the plans if the difference is in dimensions

20. The BEST way to evaluate the overall state of completion of a construction project is to check the progress estimate against the

    A. inspection work sheet
    B. construction schedule
    C. inspector's checklist
    D. equipment maintenance schedule

21. Two-phase power may be converted to 3-phase power, or vice versa, by using which of the following transformer connections?

    A. Scott   B. Delta-wye
    C. Open delta   D. Autotransformer

22. The CHIEF purpose in preparing an outline for a report is usually to insure that

    A. the report will be grammatically correct
    B. every point will be given equal emphasis
    C. principal and secondary points will be properly integrated
    D. the language of the report will be of the same level and include the same technical terms

23. A contractor on a large construction project USUALLY receives partial payments based on

    A. estimates of completed work
    B. actual cost of materials delivered and work completed
    C. estimates of material delivered and not paid for by the contractor
    D. the breakdown estimate submitted after the contract was signed and prorated over the estimated duration of the contract

24. In testing insulation resistance, the MAIN reason that the use of a megger is *preferable* to the use of an ordinary ohmmeter is that a megger

    A. is more rugged
    B. does not require constant care
    C. has a lower internal resistance
    D. usually operates at the proper voltage

25. In order to avoid disputes over payments for extra work in a contract for construction, the BEST procedure to follow would be to

    A. have contractor submit work progress reports daily
    B. insert a special clause in the contract specifications
    C. have a representative on the job at all times to verify conditions
    D. allocate a certain percentage of the cost of the job to cover such expenses

KEY (CORRECT ANSWERS)

1. B		11. A	
2. C		12. D	
3. C		13. B	
4. C		14. C	
5. B		15. A	
6. C		16. C	
7. B		17. A	
8. D		18. C	
9. C		19. B	
10. A		20. B	

21. A
22. C
23. A
24. D
25. C

TEST 3

DIRECTIONS: Each question or incomplete statement is followed by several suggested answers or completions. Select the one that BEST answers the question or completes the statement. *PRINT THE LETTER OF THE CORRECT ANSWER IN THE SPACE AT THE RIGHT.*

1. During the actual construction work, the CHIEF value of a construction schedule is to   1.____

    A. insure that the work will be done on time
    B. reveal whether production is falling behind
    C. show how much equipment and material is required for the project
    D. furnish data as to the methods and techniques of construction operations

2. Prior to the installation of equipment called for in the specifications, the contractor is usually required to submit for approval   2.____

    A. sets of shop drawings
    B. a set of revised specifications
    C. a detailed description of the methods of work to be used
    D. a complete list of skilled and unskilled tradesmen he proposes to use

3. An inspector inspecting a large building under construction inspected lighting fixtures at 9 A.M. and electrical feeders at 10 A.M., machine connections at 11 A.M., and did his office work in the afternoon. He followed the same pattern daily for months.
   This procedure is   3.____

    A. *bad,* because not enough time is devoted to important electrical feeders
    B. *bad,* because the tradesmen know when the inspections occur
    C. *good,* because it is methodical and he does not miss any of the trades
    D. *good,* because it gives equal amount of time to the important trades

4. A rule of thumb for calculating the area of copper conductors in C.M. as given in the AWG tables is that for every _____ size, the wire cross section _____.   4.____

    A. second gage of larger; doubles
    B. second gage of larger; increases four times
    C. third gage of smaller; is halved
    D. third gage of smaller; is one-third

5. The drawing which should be used as a legal reference when checking completed construction work is the _____ drawing(s).   5.____

    A. contract   B. assembly
    C. working or shop   D. preliminary

6. The motor starting device commonly called a compensator is actually a(n)   6.____

    A. rheostat   B. potentiometer
    C. auto-transformer   D. capacitor

7. The BEST way for a supervisor to determine whether a new employee is learning his work properly is to   7.____

A. ask the other men how this man is making out
B. question him directly on details of the work
C. assume that if he asks no questions he knows the work
D. inspect and follow up on the work which is assigned to him

Questions 8-13.

DIRECTIONS: Questions 8 through 13 refer to the circuit drawn below.

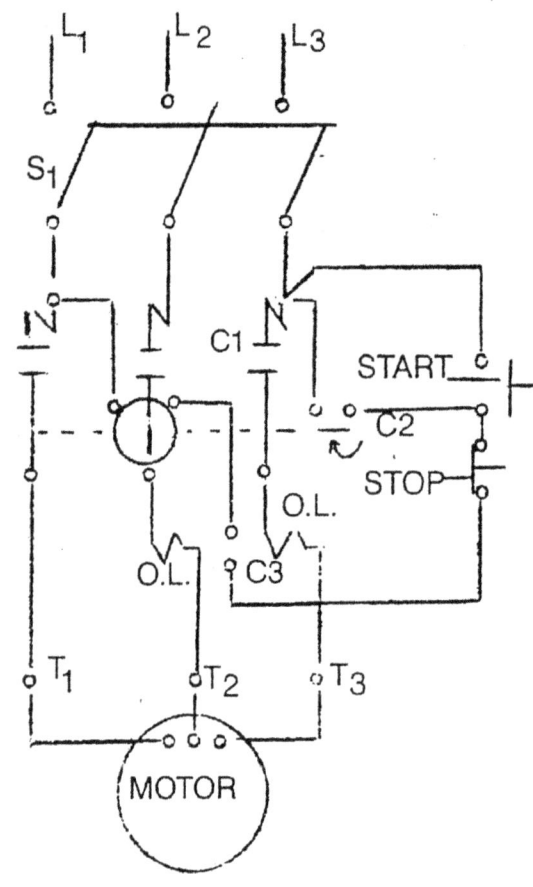

8. The circuitry shown is called a(n)

   A. D.C. motor controller
   B. reduced voltage starter
   C. two-speed motor control
   D. across-the-line starter

9. The circuit element indicated by C_1 is a

   A. capacitor
   B. circuit breaker
   C. pair of contacts which is normally open
   D. pair of start button contacts

10. If the motor is of the three-phase induction type, the incoming power is MOST likely   10.____

    A. plus and minus 115 volts D.C.
    B. 115 volts A.C. with neutral
    C. 208 volts A.C. line-to-line
    D. 230 volts D.C. with neutral

11. The PROPER designation for line switch S_1 is   11.____

    A. SPST   B. 3PDT   C. 3TSP   D. 3TDP

12. The O.L. relays are in the circuitry to   12.____

    A. protect the motor from overvoltages
    B. keep the stop button in after it has been depressed
    C. allow the motor to be operated on two lines if desired
    D. interrupt the contactor holding circuit on sustained overloads

13. The purpose of contact C_2 is to   13.____

    A. hold the start button in after it has been depressed
    B. hold the contactor in when the line voltages drop too low
    C. hold the contactor in after the start button has been depressed
    D. de-energize the contactor solenoid when the stop button is depressed

14. One ADVANTAGE of fluorescent lamps over incandescent lamps is that they   14.____

    A. are easier to handle
    B. are more efficient
    C. have simpler wiring circuits
    D. are not affected by temperature changes

15. To control a light fixture from three different locations, it is necessary to use _____ switches.   15.____

    A. one 4-way and two 3-way   B. three 3-way
    C. three 2-way   D. three single-pole

16. Good inspection methods require that the inspector   16.____

    A. be observant and check all details
    B. constantly check with the engineer who designed the school
    C. apply specifications according to his interpretations
    D. permit slight job violations to establish good public relations

17. Assume you are recommending in a report to your superior that a radical change in a standard maintenance procedure should be adopted.   17.____
    Of the following, the MOST important information to be included in this report is

    A. a list of the reasons for making this change
    B. the names of the other supervisors who favor the change
    C. a complete description of the present procedure
    D. amount of training time needed for the new procedure

18. A fixed amount of money is generally withheld from the contractor for a definite period after the completion of construction.
The BEST reason for this is

    A. that the money will be available for taxes due
    B. to penalize the contractor for poor work
    C. that it is a security for the repair of any defective work
    D. that the money will be available for modifications in the design of the structure

19. The frequency with which job reports are submitted should depend MAINLY on

    A. how comprehensive the report has to be
    B. the amount of information in the report
    C. the availability of an experienced man to write the report
    D. the importance of changes in the information included in the report

20. The use of groups of combinations of conductors in the same conduit will

    A. decrease conductor resistance
    B. be allowed for circuit voltages not exceeding 250V
    C. upgrade the current-carrying capacity of the conductors
    D. downgrade the current-carrying capacity of the conductors

KEY (CORRECT ANSWERS)

1.	B	11.	A
2.	A	12.	D
3.	B	13.	C
4.	C	14.	B
5.	A	15.	A
6.	C	16.	A
7.	B	17.	A
8.	D	18.	C
9.	C	19.	D
10.	C	20.	D

EXAMINATION SECTION
TEST 1

DIRECTIONS: Each question or incomplete statement is followed by several suggested answers or completions. Select the one that BEST answers the question or completes the statement. *PRINT THE LETTER OF THE CORRECT ANSWER IN THE SPACE AT THE RIGHT.*

QUESTIONS 1-16.

Questions 1 to 16, inclusive, refer to the drawings appearing on page 2.

1. The structural support of the flooring is provided by

   A. a concrete slab
   B. timber joists
   C. steel beams
   D. piles

2. The floor area of the plan and conference room measures, most nearly

   A. 18' x 28'
   B. 21' x 30'
   C. 15' x 30'
   D. 17' x 22'

3. The TOTAL number of windows in the building is

   A. 12   B. 11   C. 10   D. 9

4. The CORRECT number of coats of plaster required for this building is

   A. 0   B. 1   C. 2   D. 3

5. The number of doors that measure 2'8" wide is

   A. 1   B. 2   C. 3   D. 4

6. The number of convenience outlets in the superintendent's office is

   A. 0   B. 1   C. 2   D. 3

7. The thickness of the partitions is, in inches, most nearly,

   A. 1 1/2   B. 2   C. 4   D. 6

8. On the plan, just inside the entrance, is a notation 0'-0". This MOST LIKELY represents

   A. the tolerance for the width of the door
   B. the elevation above or below the floor
   C. information relative to the radiator
   D. information relative to the desk

9. The height from floor to ceiling in the superintendent's office is, most nearly,

   A. 8' 0"   B. 9' 0"   C. 7' 0"   D. 8' 6"

10. The height of the tops of the windows from the floor in the inspector's room is, most nearly,

    A. 6' 0"   B. 8' 0"   C. 7' 6"   D. 7' 0"

11. The height of the floor above the ground is, most nearly,

    A. 6' 0"   B. 4' 8"   C. 3' 4"   D. 2' 8"

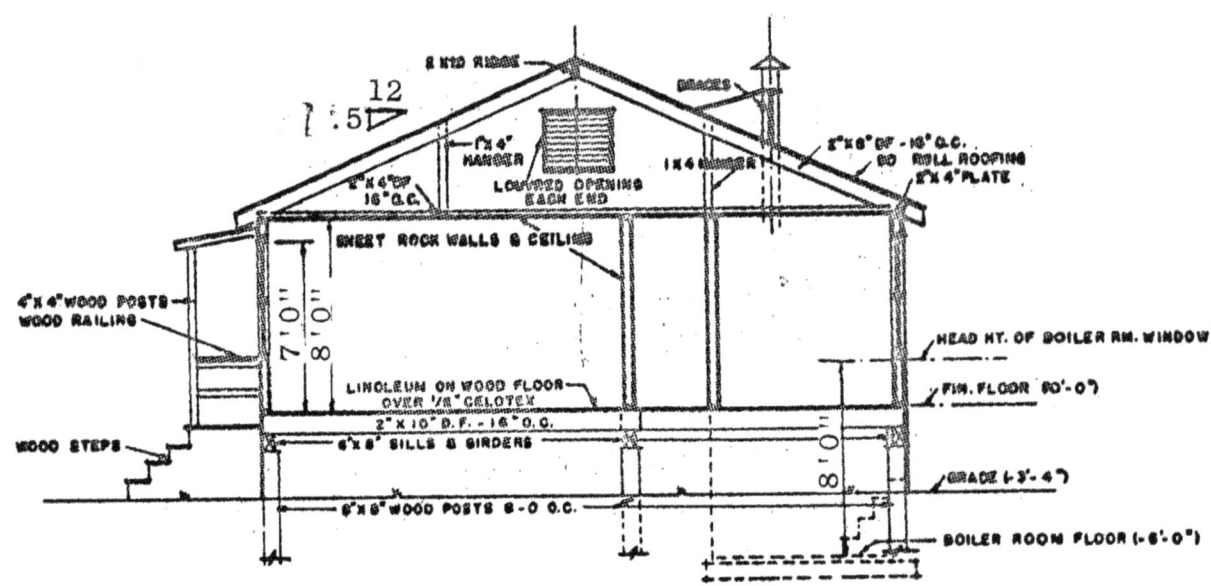

SECTION A-A

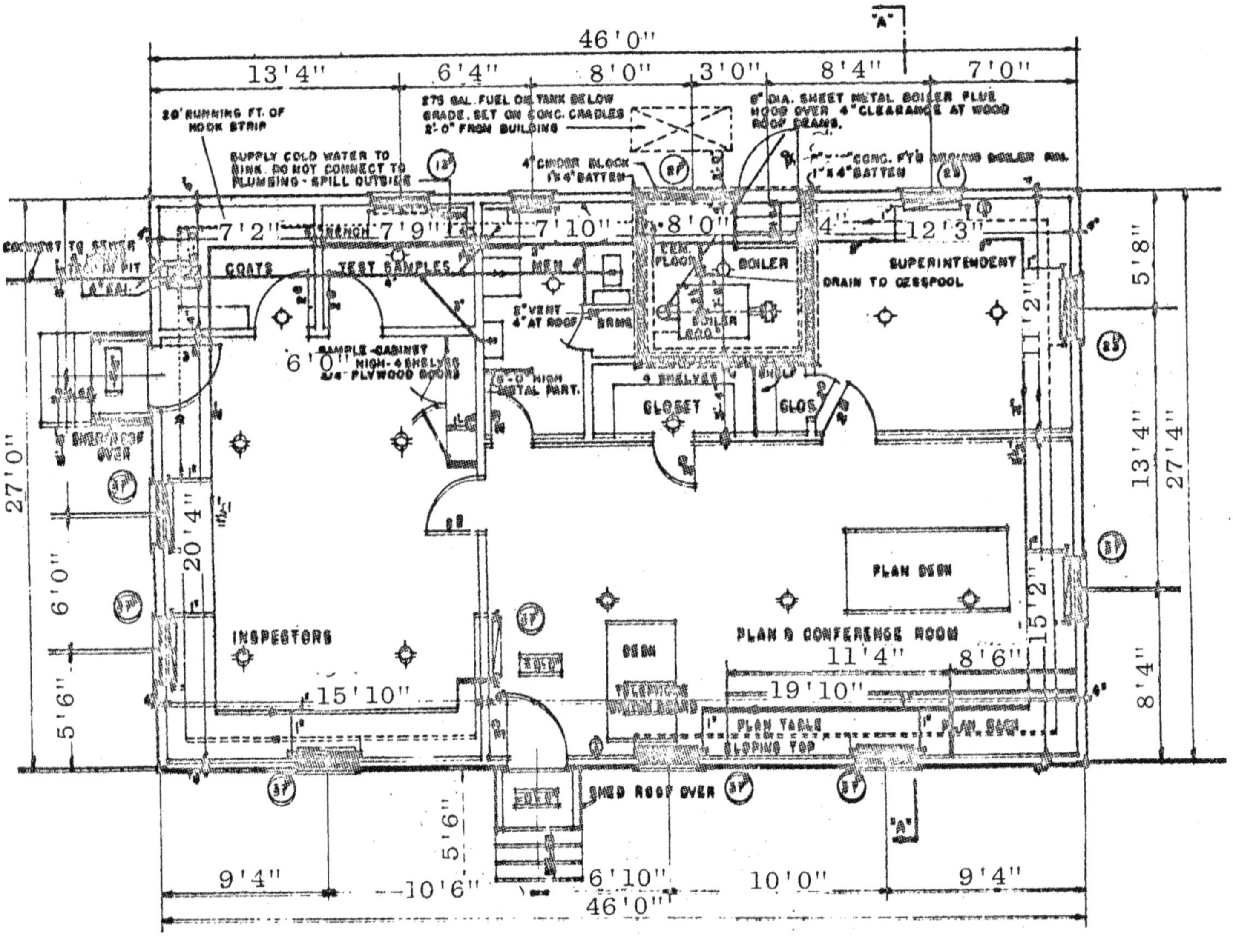

PLAN

12. Section A-A shows 8" x 8" wood posts supporting the sills and girders. The number of such posts required is, most nearly, 12.____

    A. 7 B. 14 C. 21 D. 28

13. Assume the roof rafters extend 1' 0" beyond the outside of the wall. The length of each rafter measures, most nearly, 13.____

    A. 14' 8" B. 13' 8" C. 16' 11" D. 15' 11"

14. The wearing surface on the floor is to be 14.____

    A. linoleum B. hardwood C. celotex D. asphalt tile

15. Referring to the stairway entrance to the building, if the treads are 10" each, then the distance from the edge of the landing to the entrance measures, most nearly, 15.____

    A. 2' 6" B. 3' 0" C. 3' 6" D. 4' 0"

16. From the information shown on the plan and section, the height of each riser in the stairway measures, most nearly, 16.____

    A. 10" B. 7 1/2" C. 8" D. 9"

17. The document known as the invitation to bidders does NOT have to include 17.____

    A. a description of the job
    B. the location of the job
    C. the plans and specifications for the job
    D. the name and address of the agency to which the bids are to be sent

18. The type of contract generally used on housing or school projects is 18.____

    A. unit price   B. cost plus
    C. fixed fee   D. lump sum

19. A lump-sum type of contract may require the contractor to submit a schedule of unit prices. Of the following, the BEST reason for this is that it 19.____

    A. prevents the lump sum from being too high
    B. provides a means of making equitable partial payments
    C. enables the estimators to check the total cost
    D. simplifies the selection of the lowest bidder

20. Instructions to bidders for a city housing project may require a bidder to submit a form of non-collusive affidavit. 20.____
    The purpose of this is to

    A. bind the contractor to comply with the specifications
    B. obtain an honest bid
    C. make the contractor responsible for collusion with sub-contractors
    D. prevent a contractor from subletting the contract at a lower cost

QUESTIONS 21-23.

The following specification refers to questions 21 to 23, inclusive:
The minimum time of mixing shall be one minute per cubic yard after all the material, including the water, has been placed in the drum, and the drum shall be reversed for an additional two minutes. Mixing water shall be added only in the presence of the inspector.

21. From the above specifications, it is REASONABLE to conclude that

    A. the total mixing time of all the material, including the water, shall be at least 3 minutes for a one-yard batch
    B. the total mixing time of all the material, including the water, shall not be more than 3 minutes
    C. after the material has been mixed for 1 minute, the drum should be discharged and reversed for 2 minutes
    D. the material is mixed for one minute, the water is then added, and mixing continues for 2 more minutes

22. The above specification requires the presence of the inspector at the time the mixing water is added. The PRIMARY reason for this is that he should

    A. see the permit from the water department
    B. obtain the truck number
    C. check the amount of water added
    D. check the quality of water added

23. The above specification MOST LIKELY refers to

    A. transit mix concrete
    B. mortar for brick masonry
    C. plaster for scratch coat
    D. plaster for finish coat

QUESTIONS 24-25.

The following specification applies to questions 24 and 25:
Rough grading shall consist of cutting or filling to the elevation herein established with a permissible tolerance of two inches plus or minus. This tolerance shall be so used that, within any area of 100 feet, it will not be necessary for a later contractor performing fine grading to remove excess or bring additional fill to meet the required elevations.

24. From the above specification, it is REASONABLE to conclude that

    A. the total amount of excavation removed in rough grading should equal the total volume of excavation needed to meet the required elevations
    B. rough grading may end at an elevation 2 inches too high over an area 100' x 100'
    C. rough grading may end at an elevation 2 inches too low over an area 100' x 100'
    D. the contractor performing fine grading will not be permitted to remove excess material

25. Of the following, the BEST reason for specifying the above paragraph is that

    A. a stronger foundation is assured
    B. a savings in concrete will result
    C. by keeping above the water table a dry foundation is assured
    D. it establishes limits for the rough grading contractor

QUESTIONS 26-28.

The following specification applies to questions 26 to 28 inclusive:

All present walls, cellar floors, foundations, footings, and other existing structural items shall be removed as follows: Within 3 feet of all new building walls, areas and ramp walls, the above work shall be removed to the depth of new construction. Under new footings the above work shall be entirely removed.

26. From the above specification, it is REASONABLE to conclude that

    A. present walls must be entirely removed if they are located directly under new walls
    B. old footings may be left in place if they are located within three feet of new building walls
    C. an existing foundation must be conpletely removed if located under a new footing
    D. the depth of construction may reach a maximum within 3 feet of new walls

27. The above specification MOST LIKELY refers to removal of

    A. walls and footings that were located off line
    B. walls and footings located at incorrect grade
    C. walls and footings of demolished buildings
    D. defective foundations as determined by test

28. Of the following titles, the one that is MOST appropriate for the section in which the above specification appears is:

    A. Work Not in Contract
    B. Removal of City Property
    C. Protection of Excavation
    D. Preparation of Site

QUESTIONS 29-30.

The following specification applies to questions 29 and 30:
All exterior concrete exposed to view and interior walls in rooms to be finished shall be formed of plywood, composition, or steel forms. Finish of remainder may be equivalent to that obtained by use of matched 6-inch roofers.

29. From the above specification, it is REASONABLE to conclude that

    A. matched 6-inch roofers give a better finish than composition or steel forms
    B. interiors of exterior walls that are to be finished need not be carefully formed
    C. formwork made up of 6-inch roofers may cause honeycombing
    D. exterior concrete exposed to view should be more
    E. carefully formed than other exterior concrete

30. The above specification is MOST LIKELY to be found in a section of the specifications titled:

    A. Forms and Finish
    B. Exterior Concrete
    C. Unfinished Concrete Surfaces
    D. Reinforcement for Concrete

31. If an acid wash is used on a new concrete surface, it will, MOST LIKELY,

    A. glaze the surface
    B. harden the surface
    C. make the surface soft and spongy
    D. disintegrate the surface

32. Of the following admixtures, the one that is MOST LIKELY to speed the setting of concrete is

    A. lamp black   B. calcium chloride
    C. hydrated lime   D. fly ash

33. The specifications state: Coarse aggregate shall consist of clean hard gravel or crushed stone and shall be graded from 1/8 inch to 3/8 inch with not less than 95% passing a 3/8 inch mesh sieve and not more than 10% passing a No. 8 sieve.
    Of the following, the coarse aggregate that would NOT meet the above specification is:

    A. All of the aggregate is between 1/8 inch and 3/8 inch in size
    B. 50% of the aggregate is 1/8 inch in diameter
    C. 5% of the aggregate is sand
    D. 15% of the aggregate is 1/2 inch in diameter

34. In the concrete for reinforced concrete, coarse agg-regate greater than a specified size is not permitted PRIMARILY because

    A. it is more economical since less water is required in the mix
    B. large sized coarse aggregate may not pass between the reinforced bars
    C. smaller sized coarse aggregate makes a denser concrete
    D. this makes a lighter concrete

35. The specification for formwork for concrete states: Formwork for all slabs shall be set with a camber of 1/4 inch for each 10 ft. of span.
    The BEST reason for this is that the

    A. underside of the finished slab will be level
    B. formwork will have additional strength to resist construction stresses
    C. concrete will flow more easily into the forms
    D. bracing normally required to support the wood formwork will be eliminated

36. Cinder concrete is useful in building construction PRIMARILY because of its

    A. high density   B. imperviousness
    C. frost resistance   D. light weight

37. A tie bar in a cavity wall has a crimp in the center. The purpose of the crimp is to

    A. make the bar more rigid
    B. prevent water from passing across the bar
    C. provide a better bond in the masonry
    D. provide a means of hanging a board to catch surplus mortar

38. Cored brick may sometimes be specified for use as face brick. The minimum thickness between the core and the face of the brick SHALL NOT BE LESS THAN

    A. 1/4"   B. 3/8"   C. 1/2"   D. 3/4"

39. Assume the specifications allow the substitution of sand-lime brick for common brick in certain locations. Of the following, the location at which it is LEAST likely that such substitution would be permitted is

    A. backing-up
    B. chimney flues
    C. piers
    D. walls

40. Of the following, the ONE that may MOST LIKELY be the cause of map cracking in the finish coat of plaster is

    A. a weak brown coat
    B. too much moisture present
    C. a warm dry draft blowing on fresh plaster
    D. too much retarder in the mix

41. An inspector reports a dryout in a room that has just been plastered. The MOST appropriate course of action to take is to

    A. wait until the plaster sets and determine the extent of the damage
    B. order the dryout removed and replastered
    C. order an increase in the amount of retarder used in the mix
    D. allow the contractor to spray water on the dry spot so that setting action may start again

42. The temperature below which it is NOT good practice to do plastering is, in degrees F, most nearly,

    A. 72   B. 65   C. 50   D. 36

43. Gaging plaster that is used to accelerate the setting time of finish coat plaster is, generally,

    A. plaster of Paris
    B. hydrated lime
    C. keene's cement
    D. dolomitic lime

44. Where bond plaster is specified for the scratch coat, it is generally required that the bond plaster be

    A. mixed with lime putty
    B. mixed neat without the addition of sand
    C. slaked at least 24 hours before use
    D. mixed with gypsum gaging plaster

45. For the finish coat of a three-coat plaster job, it is MOST LIKELY that the specifications would call for

    A. vermiculite
    B. silicon
    C. perlite
    D. gypsum

46. Good practice in laying asphalt tile requires that the temperature of the room, in degrees F, be *NOT LESS THAN*

    A. 32 B. 50 C. 70 D. 80

47. The joints in 2" face wood flooring are *MOST LIKELY* to be

    A. mortise and tenon
    B. tongue and groove
    C. butt
    D. dove-tail

48. Of the following species of wood, the *ONE* that is *MOST LIKELY* to be specified for finish flooring in a school or housing project is

    A. Douglas Fir
    B. Sitka Spruce
    C. Northern Hard Maple
    D. Hickory

49. Of the following, the *ONE* that is *MOST LIKELY* to be specified for fastening wood flooring in concrete is

    A. dowels in the concrete
    B. sleepers in the concrete
    C. set flooring in fresh concrete
    D. spread thin layer of grout and set flooring therein

50. After asphalt tile is cemented in place, the specifications generally require that it shall be

    A. cleaned only
    B. cleaned and waxed
    C. cleaned and stained
    D. cleaned and shellacked

KEY (CORRECT ANSWERS)

1. B	11. C	21. A	31. D	41. D
2. C	12. C	22. C	32. B	42. C
3. B	13. D	23. A	33. D	43. A
4. A	14. A	24. A	34. B	44. B
5. D	15. B	25. D	35. A	45. D
6. B	16. C	26. C	36. D	46. C
7. C	17. C	27. C	37. B	47. B
8. B	18. D	28. D	38. D	48. C
9. A	19. B	29. D	39. B	49. B
10. D	20. B	30. A	40. A	50. A

EXAMINATION SECTION
TEST 1

DIRECTIONS: Each question or incomplete statement is followed by several suggested answers or completions. Select the one that BEST answers the question or completes the statement. *PRINT THE LETTER OF THE CORRECT ANSWER IN THE SPACE AT THE RIGHT.*

1. One reason for specifying back-puttying in glazed work is that

    A. it seals the window against air and rain leaks
    B. less putty is required in this method
    C. the use of glazing clips is not required
    D. it is easier to apply putty on the inside of the glass than on the outside

2. A specification on finished hardware refers to Roses and Escutcheon plates. These are MOST LIKELY to be installed on

    A. desks   B. blackboards   C. windows   D. doors

3. Of the following statements, the one that *MOST CLOSELY* identifies the term "house sewer" is: The house sewer is

    A. located outside the building area and connects to the public sewer in the street
    B. located inside the building area and ends at the outside of the front wall of the building
    C. the pipe which carries the discharge from the plumbing fixtures to the house drain
    D. the house drain

4. A concrete level roof is to receive 4-ply composition slag roofing with insulation. The *FIRST* item to cover the concrete is

    A. the insulation   B. the slag
    C. a layer of felt   D. a bed of hot pitch

5. A common example of a paint thinner is usually

    A. tung oil   B. chinawood oil
    C. lead oxide   D. turpentine

6. In the painting of rooms in a housing project or school by the contractor, the superintendent representing the city is LEAST concerned with

    A. the area covered per man per day
    B. whether the paint is being used at the required spreading rate
    C. the moisture content of the plaster
    D. the condition of the surfaces to be painted

QUESTIONS 7-9.

Questions 7 to 9, inclusive, refer to the diagram shown below:

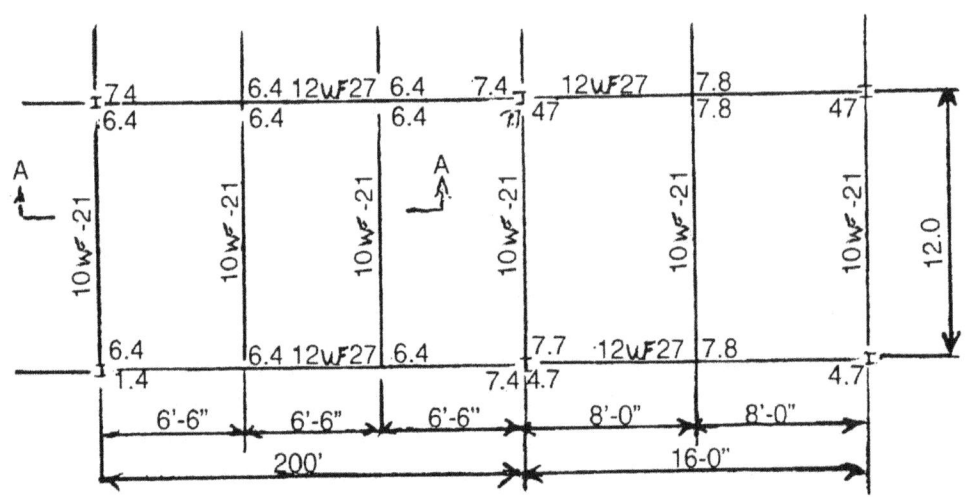

FLOOR PLAN

TOP OF BEAM 3 1/2" BELOW FINISHED FLOOR LEVEL

LIVE LOAD = 100#/SQ.FT.

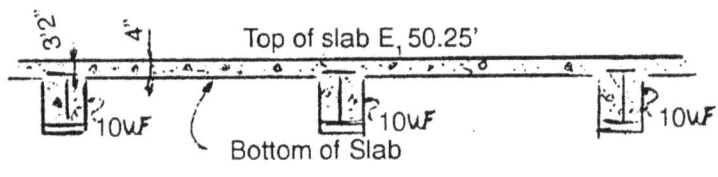

SECTION A-A

7. The elevation of the underside of the 4" slab is most nearly,

    A. 49.92   B. 50.00   C. 50.12   D. 50.25

8. The figures such as 6.4 and 4.7 represent, most nearly, the

    A. deadweight reactions of the slab
    B. distances to the points of 0 shear
    C. maximum moments that the beams carry
    D. end reactions of the beams

9. Of the following, the BEST reason for encasing the steel beams in concrete is to

    A. increase their resistance to corrosion
    B. simplify the formwork
    C. increase the deadweight of the floor
    D. increase their fire resistance

10. Splices in the steel columns of a tall steel frame building are usually located approximately

    A. 2' above the floor
    B. 2' below the floor

    C. halfway between floors
    D. at the level the floor beams frame into the column

11. Rivets that are to be driven in the field are usually heated until the color is

    A. white   B. light blue   C. cherry red   D. dull black

12. Reinforcing steel is USUALLY bent to its final shape

    A. on the jobsite   B. at the mill
    C. at the warehouse   D. in the shop

13. Copper sheet is USUALLY specified

    A. Birmingham Gage   B. United States Steel Gage
    C. in ounces per square foot   D. in pounds per square yard

14. The thickness of a 16-gage plate is, in inches, most nearly,

    A. 1/16   B. 1/8   C. 3/16   D. 1/4

15. A loose lintel is a lintel that

    A. has less than 4 inches of bearing on the masonry
    B. is not connected to the structural steel work
    C. is used over doors but not over windows
    D. should have a minimum bearing of 8" on the surface on which it rests

16. The diameter of a #6 reinforcing bar is, in inches, most nearly,

    A. 3/8   B. 1/2   C. 5/8   D. 3/4

17. The bent bar marked "A" is USUALLY called a

    A. tylag
    B. government anchor
    C. dead man
    D. strap bar

18. "Legal Curb Level", according to the code, means, most nearly,

    A. the curb level established by the county
    B. the curb level established by the department of public works
    C. that it is 6" above the crown of the road
    D. that it is the elevation established by the law department of the city

19. Of the following soils, the ONE that is MOST compressible is usually

    A. hardpan   B. sand   C. gravel   D. clay

20. The specifications state: Excavated material shall only be considered as rock when the Superintendent agrees that because of its density the most practical and economical method of removing same is by means of explosives. When rock is disintegrated to such an extent that it can readily be loosened by steam shovels or manually by tools not requiring fuel or power, then such material shall be regarded as earth excavation. Referring to the specification above, the MOST NEARLY correct statement is:

    A. A cubic yard boulder is considered rock excavation
    B. Material that can be economically removed only by explosives shall be classified as rock
    C. All disintegrated rock is to be classified under earth excavation
    D. If any material requires a steam shovel for its removal, it shall be classified as rock

21. Of the following, the ONE that is of LEAST importance to the inspector on timber pile driving is the

    A. plumbing of mandrel befroe driving
    B. condition of the pile before driving
    C. plumbness of pile
    D. final position of the pile

22. Of the following, the MOST important advantage in the use of steel shell piles is the

    A. savings in concrete
    B. opportunity for better inspection
    C. simplified pile cap construction
    D. elimination of pile caps

23. The Engineering News-Record formula for piles is $P = \dfrac{2Wh}{s+c}$

    The letter s represents, MOST NEARLY, the

    A. factor of safety used
    B. number of the hammer used
    C. average penetration of the last 5 blows in inches
    D. distance the pile has travelled vertically in feet

24. In the Engineering News-Record formula, the term "Wh" represents, MOST NEARLY, the

    A. weight of pile multiplied by height of hammer falls
    B. bearing energy of the pile
    C. weight of hammer multiplied by the height of fall
    D. speed at which the pile goes inth the ground

25. In the Engineering News-Record formula, the term c represents, MOST NEARLY,

    A. a constant depending upon the type of hammer used
    B. a correction factor that corrects for rebound
    C. the factor that allows a suitable factor of safety
    D. the penetration caused by the last blow

26. If steel weighs 490 #/cu. ft., the weight of a 1-inch square steel bar 1 foot long is, in pounds, MOST NEARLY,

   A. .434   B. 3.4   C. 42   D. 49

27. The invert elevation of a sewer is 18.54 at Manhole 1 and 18.22 at Manhole 2, 250 feet from Manhole 1. The slope of the sewer per foot is, MOST NEARLY,

   A. .0013   B. .32   C. .01   D. 0.1

QUESTIONS 28-31.
   Questions 28 to 31, inclusive, refer to the diagram shown below.

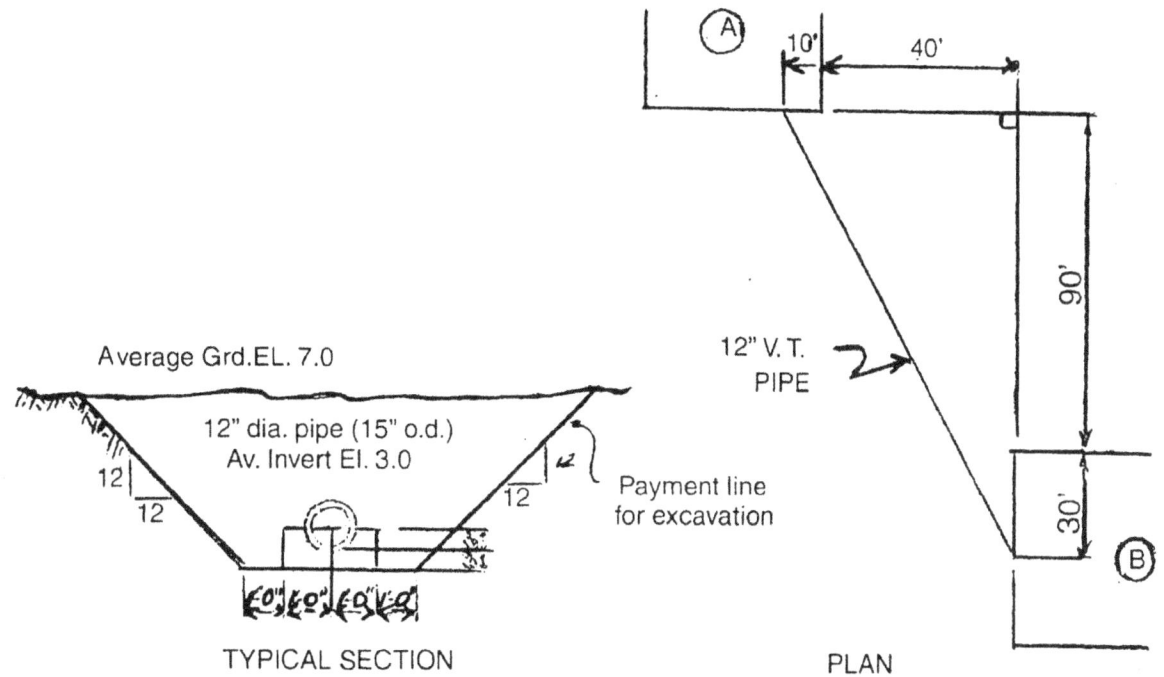

28. The length of the 12" vitrified pipe between Building A and Building B is, in feet, MOST NEARLY,

   A. 120   B. 130   C. 140   D. 150

29. For 100 feet of pipe, the volume of concrete in the concrete cradle under the pipe, is, in cubic yards, MOST NEARLY,

   A. 5.0   B. 6.0   C. 7.0   D. 9.0

30. The volume of payment excavation for 100 feet of trench is, in cubic yards, MOST NEARLY,

   A. 95   B. 120   C. 140   D. 165

31. The method of excavation shown in the typical section is USUALLY called

   A. skeleton sheeted   B. open cut
   C. lined   D. wellpointed

32. Shown below is a section through a concrete retaining wall. The volume of concrete per foot of retaining wall is, in cubic feet, *MOST NEARLY,* 32.___

A. 23.2
B. 25.0
C. 26.8
D. 28.8

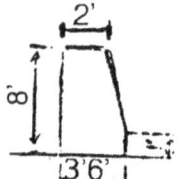

QUESTIONS 33-39.

Questions 33 to 39, inclusive, refer to the diagram shown below.

SECOND FLOOR FRAMING PLAN

SECTION C-C

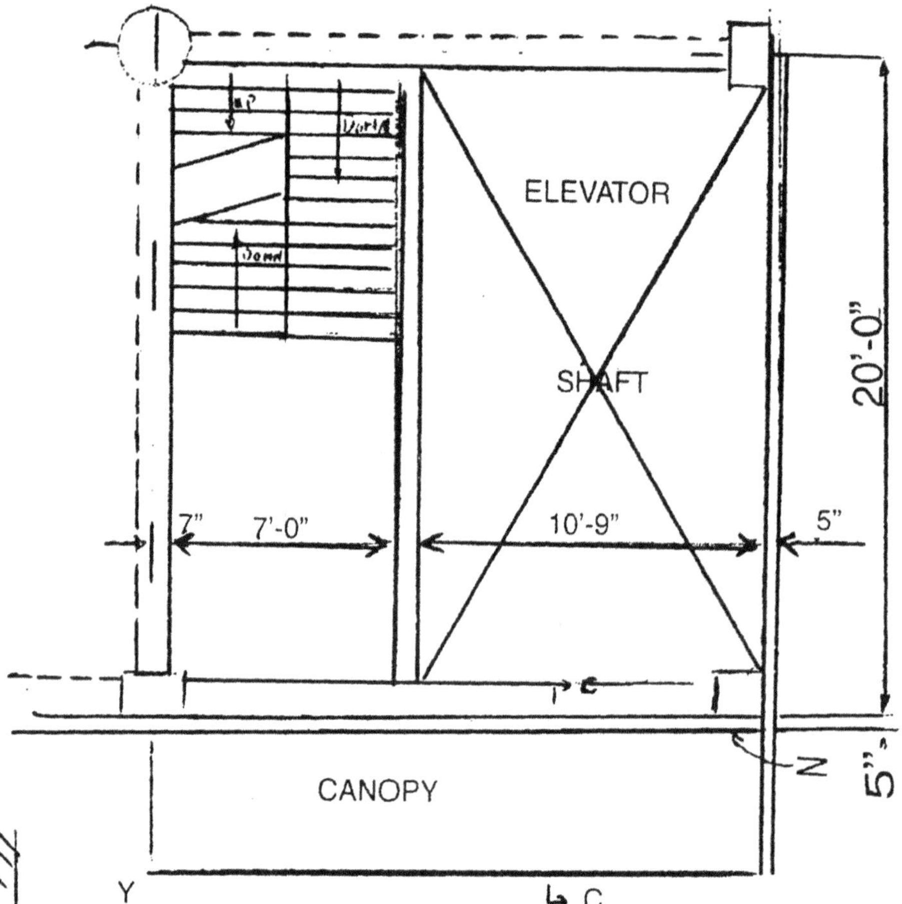

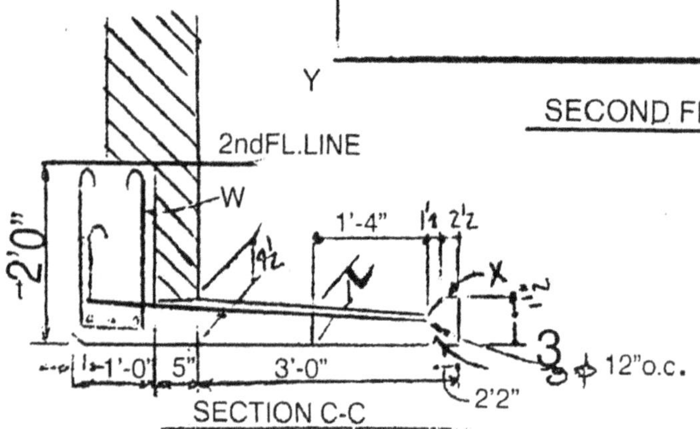

33. The elevation of the top of the outer edge of the canopy marked "X" is, *MOST NEARLY,* 33.___

A. 20.46 B. 20.42 C. 20.38 D. 20.34

34. The triangular inset on the bottom of the canopy marked "Y" is USUALLY called a   34.____

   A. raggle   B. reglet   C. drip   D. setback

35. Assuming the reinforcing steel is to be stopped 3 inches from the edge of the concrete   35.____
    and the bars marked 3/8" round at 12" o.c. are straight bars, the ordered length of the
    above mentioned bars should be, MOST NEARLY,

   A. 3' 11"   B. 19' 6"   C. 18' 6"   D. 19' 0"

36. In the plan, the line marked "Z" is the   36.____

   A. outside face of the canopy
   B. outside face of the masonry wall
   C. inside face of the reinforced concrete beam
   D. outside face of the reinforced concrete beam

37. The canopy is considered   37.____

   A. pre-stressed concrete
   B. a simply supported beam
   C. a cantilever
   D. pre-cast concrete

38. The bar marked "W" is usually called a   38.____

   A. chair   B. tie bar   C. stirrup   D. spacer

39. The dimension "V" is, in inches, MOST NEARLY,   39.____

   A. 4 1/8   B. 4 1/4   C. 4 3/8   D. 4 1/2

40. Of the following, the BEST way to measure a distance on a map with a scale of 1" =20' is   40.____
    to use a(n)

   A. planimeter set to the correct scale
   B. 50 foot tape
   C. engineer's scale
   D. architect's scale

41. The following appears on a floor plan The   41.____
    3'0" MOST LIKELY represents a

   A. double acting door 3'0" wide
   B. fire door
   C. door, 3'0" wide
   D. masonry opening, 3'0" wide

42. The following symbol on a plumbing plan   42.____
    MOST LIKELY represents a

   A. check valve
   B. vent
   C. sump
   D. trap

43. In the wall section shown below, the dimension that would MOST LIKELY represent the story height is

   A. A
   B. B
   C. C
   D. D

44. According to the section shown in the previous problem, the type of floor construction is, MOST LIKELY,

   A. reinforced concrete
   B. timber joist and wood flooring
   C. steel joist and wood flooring
   D. steel joist and cement flooring

45. A fixed amount of money is held from the contractor for a period of a year after the completion of construction. The BEST reason for this is

   A. that it acts as a security for the repair of defective work after completion of the construction
   B. to penalize the contractor for poor work
   C. the money will be available for modifications in the design of the structure
   D. the money will be available for taxes due

46. A "punch list" is usually a list

   A. showing the checkoff of union dues
   B. showing inspector's attendance
   C. of defects requiring correction by the contractor
   D. of injuries to the contractor's personnel kept for purpose of protecting the city against suit

47. The part of the structure that is MOST LIKELY to be affected by unforeseen existing conditions is the

   A. steel framework   B. plumbing
   C. electrical   D. foundation

48. The specifications state that no live load be placed on a concrete structure immediately following the stripping of its formwork.
    The BEST reason for this is

   A. the design of the structure may be wrong
   B. the concrete will not cure properly

C. to allow the easy removal of the formwork
D. to prevent overstressing of the concrete

49. A superintendent should have sufficient confidence in himself and his judgment to take a positive stand when the occasion arises and requires it. A man who changes his mind frequently, reversing his rulings under pressure, does not belong in such a position. However, if he has made a mistake, he should not be obstinate and refuse to alter his position. But too many such mistakes will demonstrate that he is unfit for the job.
From the above statement, it is *REASONABLE* to conclude that a

49._____

A. superintendent should stick to his decision, right or wrong
B. good superintendent will never make mistakes
C. superintendent should not be so bull-headed as to refuse to back down where he is manifestly wrong
D. man who changes his mind frequently is merely trying to avoid mistakes

50. Assume that a contractor disagrees with a ruling of the general superintendent and you, as a superintendent, believe the contractor is correct. You should

50._____

A. tell him to disregard the ruling until you discuss it with the general superintendent
B. tell him to stop talking about it since the general superintendent is not going to change his mind
C. ignore the criticism on the theory that the contractor will oppose any ruling of the general superintendent
D. tell him you will bring his criticism to the attention of the general superintendent

KEY (CORRECT ANSWERS)

1.	A	11.	C	21.	A	31.	B	41.	C
2.	D	12.	A	22.	B	32.	A	42.	D
3.	A	13.	C	23.	C	33.	A	43.	B
4.	D	14.	A	24.	C	34.	C	44.	A
5.	D	15.	B	25.	A	35.	C	45.	A
6.	A	16.	D	26.	B	36.	B	46.	C
7.	A	17.	B	27.	A	37.	C	47.	D
8.	D	18.	A	28.	B	38.	C	48.	D
9.	D	19.	D	29.	A	39.	B	49.	C
10.	A	20.	B	30.	C	40.	C	50.	D

EXAMINATION SECTION
TEST 1

DIRECTIONS: Each question or incomplete statement is followed by several suggested answers or completions. Select the one that BEST answers the question or completes the statement. *PRINT THE LETTER OF THE CORRECT ANSWER IN THE SPACE AT THE RIGHT.*

1. The most common approach used by a prime contractor to hold its subcontractors to their initial bids is the doctrine of promissory estoppel. In order to bind a subcontractor to its bid price, the prime contractor must prove each of the following EXCEPT that the

    A. prime contractor relied on the subcontractor's offer when making its own bid
    B. subcontractor submitted a clear and definite offer
    C. subcontractor's bid was formally accepted by the prime contractor
    D. subcontractor could have expected the prime contractor to rely on the subcontractor's offer when making its own bid

    1._____

2. Which type of specification in a construction contract is intended to invite the greatest amount of competition?

    A. Base bid   B. Closed
    C. Open   D. Bidder's choice

    2._____

3. Written or graphic instruments issued prior to the execution of a contract, which modify or interpret the bidding documents by additions, deletions, clarifications, or corrections, are generally referred to as

    A. contract modifications   B. addenda
    C. reference documents   D. supplementary conditions

    3._____

4. What type of warranty is used to limit the manufacturer's responsibility in a construction contract?

    A. Service agreement   B. Correction of work
    C. Limited term   D. Material-only

    4._____

5. Which of the following statements represents the most important difference between drawings and specifications?

    A. Specifications constitute one of the contract documents.
    B. Specifications segregate information in order to aid in forming subcontracts.
    C. Drawings are used to show which materials are to be used.
    D. Drawings name the quantity of materials to be used.

    5._____

6. The usual fidelity bond arrangement used in construction contracts is used to protect the contractor against

    A. loss, damage or excessive wear of rented equipment
    B. catastrophic damage to completed elements of the construction project
    C. dishonest acts of an employee such as theft, forgery or embezzlement
    D. bid stability of subcontractors

    6._____

7. Each of the following is a common purpose of an agreement in construction contract documents EXCEPT to

   A. state the work to be done and the price to be paid for it
   B. specifically formalize the construction contract
   C. act as a single instrument that brings together all of the contract segments by reference
   D. list the technical specifications that must be adhered to in the construction project

8. Which of the following is an attribute that might be considered for the ceiling subsystem in a performance specification?

   A. Maximum claim spread 25
   B. Fire safety
   C. Smoke development shall not exceed 75
   D. ASTM E84

9. Of the following types of hold-harmless clauses, _____ indemnification used in construction contracts indemnifies the owner and/or architect engineer even when the party indemnified is solely responsible for the loss.

   A. limited-form   B. intermediate-form
   C. broad-form   D. omnibus

10. Unit kitchens are an item that would be described under the _____ Division heading in the CSI Masterformat of specifications.

    A. Equipment   B. Special Construction
    C. Furnishings   D. Specialties

11. Which of the following information is usually described in contract specifications?

    A. Test and code requirements
    B. Size of component parts
    C. Overall dimensions
    D. Schedules of finishes, windows, and doors

12. The PRIMARY advantage associated with unit-price construction contracts is

    A. open competition on projects involving quantities of work that cannot be accurately forecast at the time of bidding or negotiation
    B. fully completed drawings and specifications at the time of bidding or negotiation
    C. greater-than-usual flexibility with regard to special reimbursable costs
    D. flexibility in negotiating a unit price for agreed-upon work items

13. Which of the following information is typically shown by drawings?

    A. Methods of fabrication, installation, and erection
    B. Alternates and unit prices
    C. Interrelation of materials, equipment, and space
    D. Gages of manufacturer's equipment

14. Which of the following is/are typical purposes of a changed-condition clause in a construction contract?
    I. To protect the owner from unforeseen increases in project costs
    II. To reduce the contractor's liability for the unexpected
    III. To alleviate the need for including large contingency sums in the bid
    The CORRECT answer is:

    A. I only   B. II only   C. I, II   D. II, III

15. In construction contracts, a special warranty most frequently applies to the work of a(n)

    A. architect   B. subcontractor
    C. engineer   D. contractor

16. The MAIN advantage associated with the use of bid bonds as security for submitted proposals is that they

    A. will hold subcontractors accountable for their subbids
    B. don't require an annual service charge
    C. are estimated according to the minimum bid price
    D. don't immobilize appreciable sums of a contractor's money

17. Under most statutes governing construction contract law, a prime contractor may be relieved from its bid at any time after the opening of bids by the *doctrine of mistake.* Which of the following are conditions that would support an argument for applying the doctrine of mistake?
    The
    I. mistake relates to a material feature of the contract
    II. mistake is one of judgment, rather than fact
    III. owner is put in a status quo position, to the extent that he suffers no serious prejudice except the loss of his bargain
    IV. mistake is of a mechanical or clerical nature
    The CORRECT answer is:

    A. I only   B. III only   C. II, IV   D. I, III, IV

18. Which of the following is NOT typically a disadvantage associated with the use of retainage arrangements in construction contracts?

    A. Reduced bidding competition
    B. Higher construction costs for owners
    C. Tends to sacrifice workmanship for speed of completion
    D. Cash-flow problems for contractors

19. What is the term for a detailed compilation of the quantity of each elementary work item that is called for on the project?

    A. Specification   B. Takeoff
    C. Bid invitation   D. Summary sheet

20. Which of the following is NOT one of the general types of specifications used in construction contracts?

    A. Proprietary   B. Surety
    C. Descriptive   D. Performance

21. When negotiating a cost-plus contract, the owner and contractor must pay particular attention to each of the following considerations EXCEPT

    A. a list of job costs to be reimbursable to the contractor
    B. a common understanding regarding the accounting methods to be used
    C. the number of work units to be performed in executing the project
    D. a definite and mutually agreeable subcontract-letting procedure

22. According to construction contract law, what is the term for a promise by a party called the guarantor to make good the mistake, debt, or default of another party?

    A. Guaranty   B. Warranty   C. Guarantee   D. Surety

23. In a technical section that has been written according to the CSI standard format, which of the following descriptions would be sequenced FIRST?

    A. Warranty
    B. Summary
    C. Project/site conditions
    D. Maintenance

24. In a construction contract, addendum changes to _____ are typically sequenced first.

    A. drawings
    B. bid form
    C. prior addenda
    D. general conditions

25. Which of the following is typically added to a construction contract as a means of providing financial protection to a contractor?
    I. Value engineering clause
    II. Escalation clause
    III. Escape clause
    The CORRECT answer is:

    A. I only   B. I, II   C. I, III   D. II, III

KEY (CORRECT ANSWERS)

1. C		11. A	
2. C		12. A	
3. B		13. C	
4. D		14. D	
5. B		15. B	
6. C		16. D	
7. D		17. D	
8. B		18. C	
9. C		19. B	
10. A		20. B	

21. C
22. A
23. B
24. C
25. D

TEST 2

DIRECTIONS: Each question or incomplete statement is followed by several suggested answers or completions. Select the one that BEST answers the question or completes the statement. *PRINT THE LETTER OF THE CORRECT ANSWER IN THE SPACE AT THE RIGHT.*

1. Which type of specification is most commonly used for public work? 1.____

    A. Open
    C. Restricted
    B. Closed
    D. Bidder's choice

2. Changes in the general conditions of a contract are expressed in the form of 2.____

    A. contract modifications
    C. supplementary conditions
    B. change orders
    D. addenda

3. The listing of subcontractors is often troublesome for contractors when it comes to bidding on projects with 3.____

    A. unbalanced bids
    C. contract bonds
    B. alternates
    D. unit pricing

4. Of the following, it is NOT a typical right assigned to an owner under the terms of a construction contract to 4.____

    A. inspect the work as it proceeds
    B. terminate the contract for cause
    C. intervene in the direction and control of the work
    D. retain a specified portion of the contractor's periodic payments

5. In most states, oral purchase agreements are NOT enforceable when 5.____

    A. they are carried out without the knowledge or consent of the prime contractor
    B. the price of goods is $500 or more
    C. the seller has not been approved by the owner
    D. the seller is not required under the agreement to deliver the goods to the site

6. Which of the following elements of a project manual is NOT usually included under the Sample Forms heading? 6.____

    A. Bid bond
    B. Supplementary conditions
    C. Performance and payment bonds
    D. Agreement

7. As part of a construction contract, a retainage arrangement can substantially serve an owner in each of the following ways EXCEPT 7.____

    A. protection against a contractor's failure to remedy defective work
    B. collection of damages from the contractor for late completion
    C. protection against breach of contract
    D. protection against damages to others caused by the contractor's performance

8. In general, the submission of *qualified* bids by a contractor is not permissible in public bidding because it

    A. is considered to be an arbitrary and unfair practice.
    B. will make the bid subject to rejection
    C. avoids fixing a total cost for the project
    D. is an illegal practice

9. Which of the following bonds is given by a self-insured contractor to the state to guarantee payment of statutory benefits to injured employees?

    A. Union wage bond
    B. License bond
    C. Workman's compensation bond
    D. Fidelity bond

10. The Divisions of the CSI Masterformat of specifications are based on four major categories. Which of the following is NOT one of these categories?

    A. Trades
    C. Place relationships
    B. Levels of specialization
    D. Materials

11. In construction contract law, what is the term for the promise that certain facts are true as represented and that they will remain so?

    A. Guaranty   B. Guarantee   C. Surety   D. Warranty

12. An owner may occasionally want a contractor to start construction operations before the formalities associated with the signing of the contract can be completed. In this case, a(n) _____ should be conveyed to authorize the start of work.

    A. letter of intent
    C. proviso of estoppel
    B. escape clause
    D. writ of mediation

13. In performance specifying, the term *criterion* refers to a(n)

    A. set of physical measurements of the materials specified
    B. qualitative statement of the desired performance
    C. evaluative procedure to assure compliance with the standard
    D. quantitative statement of the desired performance

14. A construction contract may be terminated on the grounds of the doctrine of impossibility of performance. Which of the following would be most likely to be interpreted as constituting impossibility of performance?

    A. Prolonged infirmity of prime contractor
    B. Withdrawal of subbids that make the execution of construction too costly to be profitable
    C. Unexpected site conditions found that make the construction impracticable
    D. One party finds it an economic burden to continue

15. Which of the following contracts is NOT typically defined in a contractual liability insurance policy that is included in a construction contract?

    A. Hold-harmless agreements
    C. Easement agreements
    B. Lease of premises
    D. Sidetrack agreements

16. For a contractor, the main disadvantage associated with lump-sum contracts is that   16._____

    A. they increase the likelihood of impossibility of performance
    B. the total amount of payment will be unknown until project completion
    C. they make it more difficult to hold subcontractors to their subbids
    D. adverse changes in the contractor's project costs will not be compensated

17. When a bidder's list of substitutions is used in the specifications of a construction contract, each of the following is generally true EXCEPT   17._____

    A. the bid must include the net difference in cost if the substitutions are accepted
    B. each bidder is free to submit any substitution
    C. it is the best method for achieving pure competition
    D. each of the bidders is unaware of the substitution his competitor may offer

18. In a(n) _____ contract, it is especially important that the work must be of such a nature that it can be fairly well-defined and a reasonably good estimate of cost can be approximated at the time of negotiations.   18._____

    A. incentive   B. cost-plus-fixed-fee
    C. progress payment   D. cost-plus-percentage

19. In a typical surety bond arrangement written into a construction contract, the principal is the   19._____

    A. owner   B. surety company
    C. contractor   D. architect/engineer

20. When several prime contracts are desired in a construction project, the limits of each prime contract will usually be established in the   20._____

    A. specifications   B. general conditions
    C. agreement   D. bidding requirements

21. Under the terms of a *liquidated damages* bid bond, the surety agrees to pay the _____ as damages for a contractor's default on a bid.   21._____

    A. entire bond amount
    B. difference between the contractor's defaulted low bid and the price the owner must pay to the next lowest responsible bidder
    C. agreed-upon percentage, usually 5 to 10 percent, of the minimum bid price
    D. amount of the initial progress payment plus a penalty

22. Which of the following descriptions in a technical section would appear in Part 3, according to the CSI standard fornat?   22._____

    A. Manufacturers   B. Installation
    C. Definitions   D. Accessories

23. Before a contract award is made, the bids must be carefully studied and evaluated by the owner and architect-engineer, a process which is typically referred to as   23._____

    A. prepping   B. polling
    C. canvassing   D. bonding

24. On small projects, office functions are usually carried out in a contractor's main office and particular items of office overhead are difficult to establish. If the contractor is working such a project on a cost-plus basis, it is common practice to

    A. agree with the owner upon a disinterested third party who will estimate the total office overhead costs of the project, and incorporate this figure into the contract
    B. eliminate office overhead altogether as a reimbursed cost and increase the contractor's fee by a reasonable amount
    C. agree in advance with the owner upon an estimated percentage of total job costs that will be named as office overhead in the accounting of the contract
    D. agree in advance with the owner upon a fixed amount that will be named as office overhead in the accounting of the contract

25. In the absence of any clause in a construction contract that addresses the point of excusable delay by a contractor, the contractor may only expect relief from delays with specified causes. Which of the following is NOT one of these causes?

    A. The architect-engineer
    B. The law
    C. Subcontractors
    D. The owner

KEY (CORRECT ANSWERS)

1. A
2. C
3. B
4. C
5. B

6. B
7. C
8. B
9. C
10. B

11. D
12. A
13. D
14. C
15. A

16. D
17. C
18. B
19. C
20. A

21. A
22. B
23. C
24. B
25. C

DOCUMENTS AND FORMS
PREPARING WRITTEN MATERIALS
EXAMINATION SECTION
TEST 1

DIRECTIONS: Each question or incomplete statement is followed by several suggested answers or completions. Select the one that BEST answers the question or completes the statement. *PRINT THE LETTER OF THE CORRECT ANSWER IN THE SPACE AT THE RIGHT.*

1. Of the following types of documents, it is MOST important to retain and file
   A. working drafts of reports that have been submitted in final form
   B. copies of letters of good will which conveyed a message that could not be handled by phone
   C. interoffice orders for materials which have been received and verified
   D. interoffice memoranda regarding the routine of standard forms

   1.____

2. The MAXIMUM number of 2¾" x 4¼" size forms which may be obtained from one ream of 17" x 22" paper is
   A. 4,000   B. 8,000   C. 12,000   D. 16,000

   2.____

3. On a general organization chart, staff positions NORMALLY should be pictured
   A. directly above the line positions to which they report
   B. to the sides of the main flow lines
   C. within the box of the highest level subordinate positions pictured
   D. directly below the line positions which report to them

   3.____

4. When an administrator is diagramming an office layout, of the following, his PRIMARY job generally should be to indicate the
   A. lighting intensities that will be required by each operator
   B. noise level that will be produced by the various equipment employed in the office
   C. direction of the work flow and the distance involved in each transfer
   D. durability of major pieces of office equipment currently in use or to be utilized

   4.____

5. One common guideline or rule-of-thumb ratio for evaluating the efficiency of files is the number of records requested divided by the number of records filed. Generally, if this ratio is very low, it would point MOST directly to the need for
   A. improving the indexing and coding systems
   B. improving the charge-out procedures
   C. exploring the need for transferring records from active storage to the archives
   D. exploring the need to encourage employees to keep more records in their private files

   5.____

6. The GREATEST percentage of money spent on preparing and keeping the usual records in an office generally is expended for which one of the following?
   A. Renting space in which to place the record-keeping equipment
   B. Paying salaries of record-preparing and record-keeping personnel
   C. Depreciation of purchased record-preparation and record-keeping machines
   D. Paper and forms upon which to place the records

7. In a certain office, file folders are constantly being removed from the files for use by administrators. At the same time, new material is coming in to be filed in some of these folders.
   Of the following, the BEST way to avoid delays in filing of the new material and to keep track of the removed folders is to
   A. keep a sheet listing all folders removed from the file, who has them, and a follow-update to check on their return; attach to this list new material received for filing
   B. put an "out" slip in the place of any file folder removed, telling what folder is missing, date removed, and who has it; file new material received at front of files
   C. put a temporary "out" folder in place of the one removed, giving title or subject, date removed, and who has it; put into this temporary folder any new material received
   D. keep a list of all folders removed and who has them; forward any new material received for filing while a folder is out to the person who has it

8. Folders labeled "Miscellaneous" should be used in an alphabetic filing system MAINLY to
   A. provide quick access to recent material
   B. avoid setting up individual folders for infrequent correspondence
   C. provide temporary storage for less important documents
   D. temporarily hold papers which will not fit into already crowded individual folders

9. Out-of-date and seldom-used records should be removed periodically from the files because
   A. overall responsibility for records will be transferred to the person in charge of the central storage files
   B. duplicate copies of every record are not needed
   C. valuable filing space will be regained and the time needed to find a current record will be cut down
   D. worthwhile suggestions on improving the filing system will result whenever this is done

10. Of the following, the BEST reason for discarding certain material from office files would be that the
    A. files are crowded
    B. material in the files is old
    C. material duplicates information obtainable from other sources in the files
    D. material is referred to most often by employees in an adjoining office

11. Of the following, the MAIN factor contributing to the expense of maintaining an office procedure manual would be the
    A. infrequent use of the manual
    B. need to revise it regularly
    C. cost of loose-leaf binders
    D. high cost of printing

    11._____

12. The suggestion that memos or directives which circulate among subordinates be initialed by each employee is a
    A. *poor* one, because, with modern copying machines, it would be possible to supply every subordinate with a copy of each message for his personal use
    B. *good* one, because it relieves the supervisor of blame for the action of subordinates who have read and initialed the messages
    C. *poor* one, because initialing the memo or directive is no guarantee that the subordinate has read the material
    D. *good* one, because it can be used as a record by the supervisor to show that his subordinates have received the message and were responsible for reading it

    12._____

13. Of the following, the MOST important reason for microfilming office records is to
    A. save storage space needed to keep records
    B. make it easier to get records when needed
    C. speed up the classification of information
    D. shorten the time which records must be kept

    13._____

14. Your office filing cabinets have become so overcrowded that it is difficult to use the files.
    Of the following, the MOST desirable step for you to take FIRST to relieve this situation would be to
    A. assign your assistant to spend some time each day reviewing the material in the files and to give you his recommendations as to what material may be discarded
    B. discard all material which has been in the files more than a given number of years
    C. submit a request for additional filing cabinets in your next budget request
    D. transfer enough material to the central storage room of your agency to give you the amount of additional filing space needed

    14._____

15. In indexing names of business firms and other organizations, one of the rules to be followed is:
    A. The word "and" is considered an indexing unit
    B. When a firm name includes the full name of a person who is not well known, the person's first name is considered as the first indexing unit
    C. Usually, the units in a firm name are indexed in the order in which they are written
    D. When a firm's name is made up of single letters (such as ABC Corp.), the letters taken together are considered as more than one indexing unit

    15._____

16. Assume that your unit processes confidential forms which are submitted by persons seeking financial assistance. An individual comes to your office, gives you his name, and states that he would like to look over a form which he sent in about a week ago because he believes he omitted some important information. Of the following, the BEST thing for you to do FIRST is to
    A. locate the proper form
    B. call the individual's home telephone number to verify his identity
    C. ask the individual if he has proof of his identity
    D. call the security office

17. An employee has been assigned to open her division head's mail and place it on his desk. One day, the employee opens a letter which she then notices is marked "Personal."
    Of the following, the BEST action for her to take is to
    A. write "Personal" on the letter and staple the envelope to the back of the letter
    B. ignore the matter and treat the letter the same way as the others
    C. give it to another division head to hold until her own division head comes into the office
    D. leave the letter in the envelope and write "Sorry-opened by mistake" on the envelope, and initial it

18. The MOST important reason for having a filing system is to
    A. get papers out of the way
    B. have a record of everything that has happened
    C. retain information to justify your actions
    D. enable rapid retrieval of information

19. The system of filing which is used MOST frequently is called _____ filing.
    A. alphabetic   B. alphanumeric
    C. geographic   D. numeric

20. In judging the adequacy of a standard office form, which of the following is LEAST important?
    A. Date of the form   B. Legibility of the form
    C. Size of the form   D. Design of the form

21. Assume that the letters and reports which are dictated to you fall into a few distinct subject-matter areas.
    The practice of trying to familiarize yourself with the terminology in these areas is
    A. *good*, because you will have a basis for commenting on the dictated material
    B. *good*, because it will be easier to take the dictation at the rate at which it is given
    C. *poor*, because the functions and policies of an office are not of your concern
    D. *poor*, because it will take too much time away from your assigned work

22. A letter was dictated on June 9 and was ready to be typed on June 12. The
letter was typed on June 13, signed on June 14, and mailed on June 14.
The date that, ORDINARILY, should have appeared on the letter is June
    A. 9   B. 12   C. 13   D. 14

23. Of the following, the BEST reason for putting the "key point" at the beginning
of a letter is that it
    A. may save time for the reader
    B. is standard practice in writing letters
    C. will more likely to be typed correctly
    D. cannot logically be placed elsewhere

24. As a supervisor, you have been asked to attend committee meetings and take
the minutes.
The body of such minutes GENERALLY consists of
    A. the date and place of the meeting and the list of persons present
    B. an exact verbatim report of everything that was said by each person who
       spoke
    C. a clear description of each matter discussed and the action decided on
    D. the agenda of the meeting

25. When typing a rough draft from a recorded transcription, a stenographer under
your supervision reaches a spot on the recording that is virtually inaudible.
Of the following, the MOST advisable action that you should recommend to her
is to
    A. guess what the dictator intended to say based on what he said in the
       parts that are clear
    B. ask the dictator to listen to his unsatisfactory recording
    C. leave an appropriate amount of space for that portion that is inaudible
    D. stop typing the draft and send a note to the dictator identifying the item
       that could not be completed

KEY (CORRECT ANSWERS)

1.	D		11.	B
2.	D		12.	D
3.	B		13.	A
4.	C		14.	A
5.	C		15.	C
6.	B		16.	C
7.	C		17.	D
8.	B		18.	D
9.	C		19.	A
10.	C		20.	A

21.	B
22.	D
23.	A
24.	C
25.	C

TEST 2

DIRECTIONS: Each question or incomplete statement is followed by several suggested answers or completions. Select the one that BEST answers the question or completes the statement. *PRINT THE LETTER OF THE CORRECT ANSWER IN THE SPACE AT THE RIGHT.*

1. To tell a newly employed clerk to fill a top drawer of a four-drawer cabinet with heavy binders which will be often used and to keep lower drawers only partly filled is
    A. *good*, because a tall person would have to bend unnecessarily if he had to use a lower drawer
    B. *bad*, because the file cabinet may tip over when the top drawer is opened
    C. *good*, because it is the most easily reachable drawer for the average person
    D. *bad*, because a person bending down at another drawer may accidentally bang his head on the bottom of the drawer when he straightens up

2. If you have requisitioned a "ream" of paper in order to duplicate a single page office announcement, how many announcements can be printed from the one package of paper?
    A. 200   B. 500   C. 700   D. 1,000

3. In the operations of a government agency, a voucher is ORDINARILY used to
    A. refer someone to the agency for a position or assignment
    B. certify that an agency's records of financial transactions are accurate
    C. order payment from agency funds of a stated amount to an individual
    D. enter a statement of official opinion in the records of the agency

4. Of the following types of cards used in filing systems, the one which is generally MOST helpful in locating records which might be filed under more than one subject is the _____ card.
    A. out
    B. tickler
    C. cross-reference
    D. visible index

5. The type of filing system in which one does NOT need to refer to a card index in order to find the folder is called
    A. alphabetic   B. geographic   C. subject   D. locational

6. Of the following, records management is LEAST concerned with
    A. the development of the best method for retrieving important information
    B. deciding what records should be kept
    C. deciding the number of appointments a client will need
    D. determining the types of folders to be used

7. If records are continually removed from a set of files without "charging" them to the borrower, the filing system will soon become ineffective.
Of the following terms, the one which is NOT applied to a form used in the charge-out system is a
   A. requisition card
   B. out-folder
   C. record retrieval form
   D. substitution card

7._____

8. A new clerk has been told to put 500 cards in alphabetical order. Another clerk suggests that she divide the cards into four groups, such as A to F, G to L, M to R, and S to Z, and then alphabetize these four smaller groups.
The suggested method is
   A. *poor*, because the clerk will have to handle the sheets more than once and will waste time
   B. *good*, because it saves time, is more accurate, and is less tiring
   C. *good*, because she will not have to concentrate on it so much when it is in smaller groups
   D. *poor*, because this method is much more tiring than straight alphabetizing

8._____

9. In Microsoft Excel, data and records are entered into
   A. pages   B. forms   C. cells   D. contracts

9._____

10. Suppose a clerk has been given pads of pre-printed forms to use when taking phone messages for others in her office. The clerk is then observed using scraps of paper and not the forms for writing her messages.
It should be explained that the BEST reason for using the forms is that
   A. they act as a checklist to make sure that the important information is taken
   B. she is expected to do her work in the same way as others in the office
   C. they make sure that unassigned paper is not wasted on phone messages
   D. learning to use these forms will help train her to use more difficult forms

10._____

11. The high-speed printing process used for producing large quantities of superior quality copy and cost efficiency is called
   A. photocopying
   B. laser printing
   C. inkjet printing
   D. word processing

11._____

12. Of the following, the MAIN reason a stock clerk keeps a perpetual inventory of supplies in the storeroom is that such an inventory will
   A. eliminate the need for a physical inventory
   B. provide a continuous record of supplies on hand
   C. indicate whether a shipment of supplies is satisfactory
   D. dictate the terms of the purchase order

12._____

13. As a supervisor, you may be required to handle different types of correspondence.
Of the following types of letters, it would be MOST important to promptly seal which kind of letter?
    A. One marked "confidential"
    B. Those containing enclosures
    C. Any letter to be sent airmail
    D. Those in which copies will be sent along with the original

14. While opening incoming mail, you notice that one letter indicates that an enclosure was to be included but, even after careful inspection, you are not able to find the information to which this refers.
Of the following, the thing that you should do FIRST is
    A. replace the letter in its envelope and return it to the sender
    B. file the letter until the sender's office mails the missing information
    C. type out a letter to the sender informing him of his error
    D. make a notation in the margin of the letter that the enclosure was omitted

15. You have been given a checklist and assigned the responsibility of inspecting certain equipment in the various offices of your agency.
Which of the following is the GREATEST advantage of the checklist?
    A. It indicates which equipment is in greatest demand.
    B. Each piece of equipment on the checklist will be checked only once.
    C. It helps to insure that the equipment listed will not be overlooked.
    D. The equipment listed suggests other equipment you should look for.

16. The BEST way to evaluate the overall state of completion of a construction project is to check the progress estimate against the
    A. inspection worksheet   B. construction schedule
    C. inspector's checklist   D. equipment maintenance schedule

17. The usual contract for agency work includes a section entitled "Instructions to Bidders," which states that the
    A. contractor agrees that he has made his own examination and will make no claim for damages on account of errors or omissions
    B. contractor shall not make claims for damages of any discrepancy, error, or omission in any plans
    C. estimates of quantities and calculations are guaranteed by the agency to be correct and are deemed to be a representation of the conditions affecting the work
    D. plans, measurements, dimensions, and conditions under which the work is to be performed are guaranteed by the agency

18. In order to avoid disputes over payments for extra work in a contract for construction, the BEST procedure to follow would be to
    A. have contractor submit work progress reports daily
    B. insert a special clause in the contract specifications
    C. have a representative on the job at all times to verify conditions
    D. allocate a certain percentage of the cost of the job to cover such expenses

4 (#2)

19. Prior to the installation of equipment called for in the specifications, the contractor is USUALLY required to submit for approval
    A. sets of shop drawings
    B. a set of revised specifications
    C. a detailed description of the methods of work to be used
    D. a complete list of skilled and unskilled tradesmen he proposes to use

20. During the actual construction work, the CHIEF value of a construction schedule is to
    A. insure that the work will be done on time
    B. reveal whether production is falling behind
    C. show how much equipment and material is required for the project
    D. furnish data as to the methods and techniques of construction operations

KEY (CORRECT ANSWERS)

1.	B	11.	B
2.	B	12.	B
3.	C	13.	A
4.	C	14.	D
5.	A	15.	C
6.	C	16.	B
7.	C	17.	A
8.	B	18.	C
9.	C	19.	A
10.	A	20.	B

PREPARING WRITTEN MATERIAL
EXAMINATION SECTION
TEST 1

DIRECTIONS: Each of the sentences in this test may be classified under one of the following four categories:
- A. Faulty because of incorrect grammar or word usage
- B. Faulty because of incorrect punctuation
- C. Faulty because of incorrect capitalization or incorrect spelling
- D. Correct

Examine each sentence carefully to determine under which of the above four options it is best classified. Then, in the space to the right, print the capital letter preceding the option which is the BEST of the four suggested above. (Note that each faulty sentence contains but one type of error. Consider a sentence to be correct if it contains none of the types of errors mentioned, even though there may be other correct ways of expressing the same thought.)

1. He sent the notice to the clerk who you hired yesterday. 1.____

2. It must be admitted, however that you were not informed of this change. 2.____

3. Only the employee who have served in this grade for at least two years are eligible for promotion. 3.____

4. The work was divided equally between she and Mary. 4.____

5. He thought that you were not available at that time. 5.____

6. When the messenger returns; please give him this package. 6.____

7. The new secretary prepared, typed, addressed, and delivered, the notices. 7.____

8. Walking into the room, his desk can be seen at the rear. 8.____

9. Although John has worked here longer than She, he produces a smaller amount of work. 9.____

10. She said she could of typed this report yesterday. 10.____

11. Neither one of these procedures are adequate for the efficient performance of this task. 11.____

12. The typewriter is the tool of the typist; the cash register, the tool of the cashier. 12.____

2 (#1)

13. "The assignment must be completed as soon as possible" said the supervisor. 13._____

14. As you know, office handbooks are issued to all new Employees. 14._____

15. Writing a speech is sometimes easier than to deliver it before an audience. 15._____

16. Mr. Brown our accountant, will audit the accounts next week. 16._____

17. Give the assignment to whomever is able to do it most efficiently. 17._____

18. The supervisor expected either your or I to file these reports. 18._____

KEY (CORRECT ANSWERS)

1.	A	11.	A
2.	B	12.	C
3.	D	13.	B
4.	A	14.	C
5.	D	15.	A
6.	B	16.	B
7.	B	17.	A
8.	A	18.	A
9.	C		
10.	A		

TEST 2

DIRECTIONS: Each of the sentences in this test may be classified under one of the following four categories:
  A. Faulty because of incorrect grammar or word usage
  B. Faulty because of incorrect punctuation
  C. Faulty because of incorrect capitalization or incorrect spelling
  D. Correct

Examine each sentence carefully to determine under which of the above four options it is best classified. Then, in the space to the right, print the capital letter preceding the option which is the BEST of the four suggested above. (Note that each faulty sentence contains but one type of error. Consider a sentence to be correct if it contains none of the types of errors mentioned, even though there may be other correct ways of expressing the same thought.)

1. The fire apparently started in the storeroom, which is usually locked.   1.____

2. On approaching the victim, two bruises were noticed by this officer.   2.____

3. The officer, who was there examined the report with great care.   3.____

4. Each employee in the office had a seperate desk.   4.____

5. All employees including members of the clerical staff, were invited to the lecture.   5.____

6. The suggested Procedure is similar to the one now in use.   6.____

7. No one was more pleased with the new procedure than the chauffeur.   7.____

8. He tried to persaude her to change the procedure.   8.____

9. The total of the expenses charged to petty cash were high.   9.____

10. An understanding between him and I was finally reached.   10.____

KEY (CORRECT ANSWERS)

1.	D	6.	C
2.	A	7.	D
3.	B	8.	C
4.	C	9.	A
5.	B	10.	A

TEST 3

DIRECTIONS: Each of the sentences in this test may be classified under one of the following four categories:
- A. Faulty because of incorrect grammar or word usage
- B. Faulty because of incorrect punctuation
- C. Faulty because of incorrect capitalization or incorrect spelling
- D. Correct

Examine each sentence carefully to determine under which of the above four options it is best classified. Then, in the space to the right, print the capital letter preceding the option which is the BEST of the four suggested above. (Note that each faulty sentence contains but one type of error. Consider a sentence to be correct if it contains none of the types of errors mentioned, even though there may be other correct ways of expressing the same thought.)

1. They told both he and I that the prisoner had escaped.

2. Any superior officer, who, disregards the just complaint of his subordinates, is remiss in the performance of his duty.

3. Only those members of the national organization who resided in the Middle West attended the conference in Chicago.

4. We told him to give the national organization assignment to whoever was available.

5. Please do not disappoint and embarass us by not appearing in court.

6. Although the office's speech proved to be entertaining, the topic was not relevent to the main theme of the conference.

7. In February all new officers attended a training course in which they were learned in their principal duties and the fundamental operating procedure of the department.

8. I personally seen inmate Jones threaten inmates Smith and Green with bodily harm if they refused to participate in the plot.

9. To the layman, who on a chance visit to the prison observes everything functioning smoothly, the maintenance of prison discipline may seem to be a relatively easily realizable objective.

10. The prisoners in cell block fourty were forbidden to sit on the cell cots during the recreation hour.

KEY (CORRECT ANSWERS)

1. A
2. B
3. C
4. D
5. C
6. C
7. A
8. A
9. D
10. C

TEST 4

DIRECTIONS: Each of the sentences in this test may be classified under one of the following four categories:
- A. Faulty because of incorrect grammar or word usage
- B. Faulty because of incorrect punctuation
- C. Faulty because of incorrect capitalization or incorrect spelling
- D. Correct

Examine each sentence carefully to determine under which of the above four options it is best classified. Then, in the space to the right, print the capital letter preceding the option which is the BEST of the four suggested above. (Note that each faulty sentence contains but one type of error. Consider a sentence to be correct if it contains none of the types of errors mentioned, even though there may be other correct ways of expressing the same thought.)

1. I cannot encourage you any.   1._____
2. You always look well in those sort of clothes.   2._____
3. Shall we go to the park?   3._____
4. The man whome he introduced was Mr. Carey.   4._____
5. She saw the letter laying here this morning.   5._____
6. It should rain before the Afternoon is over.   6._____
7. They have already went home.   7._____
8. That Jackson will be elected is evident.   8._____
9. He does not hardly approve of us.   9._____
10. It was he, who won the prize.   10._____

KEY (CORRECT ANSWERS)

1.	A	6.	C
2.	A	7.	A
3.	D	8.	D
4.	C	9.	A
5.	A	10.	B

TEST 5

DIRECTIONS: Each of the sentences in this test may be classified under one of the following four categories:
  A. Faulty because of incorrect grammar or word usage
  B. Faulty because of incorrect punctuation
  C. Faulty because of incorrect capitalization or incorrect spelling
  D. Correct

Examine each sentence carefully to determine under which of the above four options it is best classified. Then, in the space to the right, print the capital letter preceding the option which is the BEST of the four suggested above. (Note that each faulty sentence contains but one type of error. Consider a sentence to be correct if it contains none of the types of errors mentioned, even though there may be other correct ways of expressing the same thought.)

1. Shall we go to the park.   1.____
2. They are, alike, in this particular way.   2.____
3. They gave the poor man sume food when he knocked on the door.   3.____
4. I regret the loss caused by the error.   4.____
5. The students' will have a new teacher.   5.____
6. They sweared to bring out all the facts.   6.____
7. He decided to open a branch store on 33rd street.   7.____
8. His speed is equal and more than that of a racehorse.   8.____
9. He felt very warm on that Summer day.   9.____
10. He was assisted by his friend, who lives in the next house.   10.____

KEY (CORRECT ANSWERS)

1.	B	6.	A
2.	B	7.	C
3.	C	8.	A
4.	D	9.	C
5.	B	10.	D

TEST 6

DIRECTIONS: Each of the sentences in this test may be classified under one of the following four categories:
- A. Faulty because of incorrect grammar or word usage
- B. Faulty because of incorrect punctuation
- C. Faulty because of incorrect capitalization or incorrect spelling
- D. Correct

Examine each sentence carefully to determine under which of the above four options it is best classified. Then, in the space to the right, print the capital letter preceding the option which is the BEST of the four suggested above. (Note that each faulty sentence contains but one type of error. Consider a sentence to be correct if it contains none of the types of errors mentioned, even though there may be other correct ways of expressing the same thought.)

1. The climate of New York is colder than California.   1.____
2. I shall wait for you on the corner.   2.____
3. Did we see the boy who, we think, is the leader.   3.____
4. Being a modest person, John seldom talks about his invention.   4.____
5. The gang is called the smith street bos.   5.____
6. He seen the man break into the store.   6.____
7. We expected to lay still there for quite a while.   7.____
8. He is considered to be the Leader of his organization.   8.____
9. Although I recieved an invitation, I won't go.   9.____
10. The letter must be here some place.   10.____

KEY (CORRECT ANSWERS)

1.	A	6.	A
2.	D	7.	A
3.	B	8.	C
4.	D	9.	C
5.	C	10.	A

TEST 7

DIRECTIONS: Each of the sentences in this test may be classified under one of the following four categories:
- A. Faulty because of incorrect grammar or word usage
- B. Faulty because of incorrect punctuation
- C. Faulty because of incorrect capitalization or incorrect spelling
- D. Correct

Examine each sentence carefully to determine under which of the above four options it is best classified. Then, in the space to the right, print the capital letter preceding the option which is the BEST of the four suggested above. (Note that each faulty sentence contains but one type of error. Consider a sentence to be correct if it contains none of the types of errors mentioned, even though there may be other correct ways of expressing the same thought.)

1. I though it to be he. 1.____
2. We expect to remain here for a long time. 2.____
3. The committee was agreed. 3.____
4. Two-thirds of the building are finished. 4.____
5. The water was froze. 5.____
6. Everyone of the salesmen must supply their own car. 6.____
7. Who is the author of Gone With the Wind? 7.____
8. He marched on and declaring that he would never surrender. 8.____
9. Who shall I say called? 9.____
10. Everyone has left but they. 10.____

KEY (CORRECT ANSWERS)

1.	A	6.	A
2.	D	7.	B
3.	D	8.	A
4.	A	9.	D
5.	A	10.	D

TEST 8

DIRECTIONS: Each of the sentences in this test may be classified under one of the following four categories:
  A. Faulty because of incorrect grammar or word usage
  B. Faulty because of incorrect punctuation
  C. Faulty because of incorrect capitalization or incorrect spelling
  D. Correct

Examine each sentence carefully to determine under which of the above four options it is best classified. Then, in the space to the right, print the capital letter preceding the option which is the BEST of the four suggested above. (Note that each faulty sentence contains but one type of error. Consider a sentence to be correct if it contains none of the types of errors mentioned, even though there may be other correct ways of expressing the same thought.)

1. Who did we give the order to?   1._____
2. Send your order in immediately.   2._____
3. I believe I paid the Bill.   3._____
4. I have not met but one person.   4._____
5. Why aren't Tom, and Fred, going to the dance?   5._____
6. What reason is there for him not going?   6._____
7. The seige of Malta was a tremendous event.   7._____
8. I was there yesterday I assure you   8._____
9. Your ukulele is better than mine.   9._____
10. No one was there only Mary.   10._____

KEY (CORRECT ANSWERS)

1.	A	6.	A
2.	D	7.	C
3.	C	8.	B
4.	A	9.	C
5.	B	10.	A

TEST 9

DIRECTIONS: In each of the following groups of sentences, one of the four sentences is faulty in grammar, punctuation, or capitalization. Select the INCORRECT sentence in each case.

1. A. If you had stood at home and done your homework, you would not have failed in arithmetic.
   B. Her affected manner annoyed every member of the audience.
   C. How will the new law affect our income taxes?
   D. The plants were not affected by the long, cold winter, but they succumbed to the drought of summer.

   1.____

2. A. He is one of the most able men who have been in the Senate.
   B. It is he who is to blame for the lamentable mistake.
   C. Haven't you a helpful suggestion to make at this time?
   D. The money was robbed from the blind man's cup.

   2.____

3. A. The amount of children in this school is steadily increasing.
   B. After taking an apple from the table, she went out to play.
   C. He borrowed a dollar from me.
   D. I had hoped my brother would arrive before me.

   3.____

4. A. Whom do you think I hear from every week?
   B. Who do you think is the right man for the job?
   C. Who do you think I found in the room?
   D. He is the man whom we considered a good candidate for the presidency.

   4.____

5. A. Quietly the puppy laid down before the fireplace.
   B. You have made your bed; now lie in it.
   C. I was badly sunburned because I had lain too long in the sun.
   D. I laid the doll on the bed and left the room.

   5.____

KEY (CORRECT ANSWERS)

1. A
2. D
3. A
4. C
5. A

PREPARING WRITTEN MATERIAL

PARAGRAPH REARRANGEMENT
COMMENTARY

The sentences that follow are in scrambled order. You are to rearrange them in proper order and indicate the letter choice containing the correct answer at the space at the right.

Each group of sentences in this section is actually a paragraph presented in scrambled order. Each sentence in the group has a place in that paragraph; no sentence is to be left out. You are to read each group of sentences and decide upon the best order in which to put the sentences so as to form a well-organized paragraph.

The questions in this section measure the ability to solve a problem when all the facts relevant to its solution are not given.

More specifically, certain positions of responsibility and authority require the employee to discover connection between events sometimes, apparently, unrelated. In order to do this, the employee will find it necessary to correctly infer that unspecified events have probably occurred or are likely to occur. This ability becomes especially important when action must be taken on incomplete information.

Accordingly, these questions require competitors to choose among several suggested alternatives, each of which presents a different sequential arrangement of the events. Competitors must choose the MOST logical of the suggested sequences.

In order to do so, they may be required to draw on general knowledge to infer missing concepts or events that are essential to sequencing the given events. Competitors should be careful to infer only what is essential to the sequence. The plausibility of the wrong alternatives will always require the inclusion of unlikely events or of additional chains of events which are NOT essential to sequencing the given events.

It's very important to remember that you are looking for the best of the four possible choices, and that the best choice of all may not even be one of the answers you're given to choose from.

There is no one right way to solve these problems. Many people have found it helpful to first write out the order of the sentences, as they would have arranged them, on their scrap paper before looking at the possible answers. If their optimum answer is there, this can save them some time. If it isn't, this method can still give insight into solving the problem. Others find it most helpful to just go through each of the possible choices, contrasting each as they go along. You should use whatever method feels comfortable and works for you.

While most of these types of questions are not that difficult, we've added a higher percentage of the difficult type, just to give you more practice. Usually there are only one or two questions on this section that contain such subtle distinctions that you're unable to answer confidently. And you then may find yourself stuck deciding between two possible choices, neither of which you're sure about.

EXAMINATION SECTION
TEST 1

DIRECTIONS: The sentences that follow are in scrambled order. You are to rearrange them in proper order and indicate the letter choice containing the correct answer. *PRINT THE LETTER OF THE CORRECT ANSWER IN THE SPACE AT THE RIGHT.*

1. Below are four statements labeled W, X, Y and Z.   1.____
    W. He was a strict and fanatic drillmaster.
    X. The word is always used in a derogatory sense and generally shows resentment and anger on the part of the user.
    Y. It is from the name of this Frenchman that we derive our English word, martinet.
    Z. Jean Martinet was the Inspector-General of Infantry during the reign of King Louis XIV.
    The PROPER order in which these sentences should be placed in a paragraph is:
    A. X, Z, W, Y   B. X, Z, Y, W   C. Z, W, Y, X   D. Z, Y, W, X

2. In the following paragraph, the sentences, which are numbered, have been jumbled.   2.____
    I. Since then it has undergone changes.
    II. It was incorporated in 1955 under the laws of the State of New York.
    III. Its primary purposes, a cleaner city, has, however, remained the same.
    IV. The Citizens Committee works in cooperation with the Mayor's Inter-departmental Committee for a Clean City.   3.____
    The order in which these sentences should be arranged to form a well-organized paragraph is:
    A. II, IV, I, III   B. III, IV, I, II   C. IV, II, I, III   D. IV, III, II, I

Questions 3-5.

DIRECTIONS: The sentences listed below are part of a meaningful paragraph but they are not given in their proper order. You are to decide what would be the BEST order in which to put the sentences so as to form a well-organized paragraph. Each sentence has a place in the paragraph; there are no extra sentences. You are then to answer Questions 3 through 5 inclusive on the basis of your rearrangements of these scrambled sentences into a properly organized paragraph.

In 1887 some insurance companies organized an Inspection Department to advise their clients on all phases of fire prevention and protection. Probably this has been due to the smaller annual fire losses in Great Britain than in the United States. It tests various fire prevention devices and appliances and determines manufacturing hazards and their safeguards. Fire research began earlier in the United States and is more advanced than in Great Britain. Later they established a laboratory specializing in electrical, mechanical, hydraulic, and chemical fields.

3. When the five sentences are arranged in proper order, the paragraph starts with the sentence which begins
   A. "In 1887…" B. "Probably this…" C. "It tests…"
   D. "Fire research…" E. "Later they…"

4. In the last sentence listed above, "they" refers to
   A. the insurance companies
   B. the United States and Great Britain
   C. the Inspection Department
   D. clients
   E. technicians

5. When the above paragraph is properly arranged, it ends with the words
   A. "…and protection."
   B. "…the United States."
   C. "…their safeguards."
   D. "…in Great Britain."
   E. "…chemical fields."

KEY (CORRECT ANSWERS)

1. C
2. C
3. D
4. A
5. C

TEST 2

DIRECTIONS: In each of the questions numbered I through V, several sentences are given. For each question, choose as your answer the group of number that represents the MOST logical order of these sentences if they were arranged in paragraph form. *PRINT THE LETTER OF THE CORRECT ANSWER IN THE SPACE AT THE RIGHT.*

1.
   I. It is established when one shows that the landlord has prevented the tenant's enjoyment of his interest in the property leased.
   II. Constructive eviction is the result of a breach of the covenant of quiet enjoyment implied in all leases.
   III. In some parts of the United States, it is not complete until the tenant vacates within a reasonable time.
   IV. Generally, the acts must be of such serious and permanent character as to deny the tenant the enjoyment of his possessing rights.
   V. In this event, upon abandonment of the premises, the tenant's liability for that ceases.
   The CORRECT answer is:
   A. II, I, IV, III, V
   B. V, II, III, I, IV
   C. IV, III, I, II, V
   D. I, III, V, IV, II

   1.____

2.
   I. The powerlessness before private and public authorities that is the typical experience of the slum tenant is reminiscent of the situation of blue-collar workers all through the nineteenth century.
   II. Similarly, in recent years, this chapter of history has been reopened by anti-poverty groups which have attempted to organize slum tenants to enable them to bargain collectively with their landlords about the conditions of their tenancies.
   III. It is familiar history that many of the worker remedied their condition by joining together and presenting their demands collectively.
   IV. Like the workers, tenants are forced by the conditions of modern life into substantial dependence on these who possess great political aid and economic power.
   V. What's more, the very fact of dependence coupled with an absence of education and self-confidence makes them hesitant and unable to stand up for what they need from those in power.
   The CORRECT answer is:
   A. V, IV, I, II, III
   B. II, III, I, V, IV
   C. III, I, V, IV, II
   D. I, IV, V, III, II

   2.____

3.
   I. A railroad, for example, when not acting as a common carrier may contract away responsibility for its own negligence.
   II. As to a landlord, however, no decision has been found relating to the legal effect of a clause shifting the statutory duty of repair to the tenant.
   III. The courts have not passed on the validity of clauses relieving the landlord of this duty and liability.
   IV. They have, however, upheld the validity of exculpatory clauses in other types of contracts.

   3.____

105

V. Housing regulations impose a duty upon the landlord to maintain leased premises in safe condition.
VI. As another example, a bailee may limit his liability except for gross negligence, willful acts, or fraud.

The CORRECT answer is:
A. II, I, VI, IV, III, V
B. I, III, IV, V, VI, II
C. III, V, I, IV, II, VI
D. V, III, IV, I, VI, II

4. I. Since there are only samples in the building, retail or consumer sales are generally eschewed by mart occupants, and in some instances, rigid controls are maintained to limit entrance to the mart only to those persons engaged in retailing.
II. Since World War I, in many larger cities, there has developed a new type of property, called the mart building.
III. It can, therefore, be used by wholesalers and jobbers for the display of sample merchandise.
IV. This type of building is most frequently a multi-storied, finished interior property which is a cross between a retail arcade and a loft building.
V. This limitation enables the mart occupants to ship the orders from another location after the retailer or dealer makes his selection from the samples.

The CORRECT answer is:
A. II, IV, III, I, V
B. IV, III, V, I, II
C. I, III, II, IV, V
D. I, IV, II, III, V

5. I. In general, staff-line friction reduces the distinctive contribution of staff personnel.
II. The conflicts, however, introduce an uncontrolled element into the managerial system.
III. On the other hand, the natural resistance of the line to staff innovations probably usefully restrains over-eager efforts to apply untested procedures on a large scale.
IV. Under such conditions, it is difficult to know when valuable ideas are being sacrificed.
V. The relatively weak position of staff, requiring accommodation to the line, tends to restrict their ability to engage in free, experimental innovation.

The CORRECT answer is:
A. IV, II, III, I, V
B. I, V, III, II, IV
C. V, III, I, II, IV
D. II, I, IV, V, III

KEY (CORRECT ANSWERS)

1. A
2. D
3. D
4. A
5. B

TEST 3

DIRECTIONS: Questions 1 through 4 consist of six sentences which can be arranged in a logical sequence. For each question, select the choice which places the numbered sentences in the MOST logical sequent. *PRINT THE LETTER OF THE CORRECT ANSWER IN THE SPACE AT THE RIGHT.*

1.
   I. The burden of proof as to each issue is determined before trial and remains upon the same party throughout the trial.
   II. The jury is at liberty to believe one witness' testimony as against a number of contradictory witnesses.
   III. In a civil case, the party bearing the burden of proof is required to prove his contention by a fair preponderance of the evidence.
   IV. However, it must be noted that a fair preponderance of evidence does not necessarily mean a greater number of witnesses.
   V. The burden of proof is the burden which rests upon one of the parties to an action to persuade the trier of the facts, generally the jury, that a proposition he asserts is true.
   VI. If the evidence is equally balanced, or if it leaves the jury in such doubt as to be unable to decide the controversy either way, judgment must be given against the party upon whom the burden of proof rests.

   The CORRECT answer is:
   A. III, II, V, IV, I, VI
   B. I, II, VI, V, III, IV
   C. III, IV, V, I, II, VI
   D. V, I, III, VI, IV, II

   1.____

2.
   I. If a parent is without assets and is unemployed, he cannot be convicted of the crime of non-support of a child.
   II. The term "sufficient ability" has been held to mean sufficient financial ability.
   III. It does not matter if his unemployment is by choice or unavoidable circumstances.
   IV. If he fails to take any steps at all, he may be liable to prosecution for endangering the welfare of a child.
   V. Under the penal law, a parent is responsible for the support of his minor child only if the parent is "of sufficient ability."
   VI. An indigent parent may meet his obligation by borrowing money or by seeking aid under the provisions of the Social Welfare Law.

   The CORRECT answer is:
   A. VI, I, V, III, II, IV
   B. I, III, V, II, IV, VI
   C. V, II, I, III, VI, IV
   D. I, VI, IV, V, II, III

   2.____

3.
   I. Consider, for example, the case of a rabble rouser who urges a group of twenty people to go out and break the windows of a nearby factory.
   II. Therefore, the law fills the indicated gap with the crime of inciting to riot.
   III. A person is considered guilty of inciting to riot when he urges ten or more persons to engage in tumultuous and violent conduct of a kind likely to create public alarm.
   IV. However, if he has not obtained the cooperation of at least four people, he cannot be charged with unlawful assembly.

   3.____

107

2 (#3)

V. The charge of inciting to riot was added to the law to cover types of conduct which cannot be classified as either the crime of "riot" or the crime of "unlawful assembly."
VI. If he acquires the acquiescence of at least four of them, he is guilty of unlawful assembly even if the project does not materialize.

The CORRECT answer is:
A. III, V, I, VI, IV, II
B. V, I, IV, VI, II, III
C. III, IV, I, V, II, VI
D. V, I, IV, VI, III, II

4. I. If, however, the rebuttal evidence presents an issue of credibility, it is for the jury to determine whether the presumption has, in fact, been destroyed.
    II. Once sufficient evidence to the contrary is introduced, the presumption disappears from the trial.
    III. The effect of a presumption is to place the burden upon the adversary to come forward with evidence to rebut the presumption.
    IV. When a presumption is overcome and ceases to exist in the case, the fact or facts which gave rise to the presumption still remain.
    V. Whether a presumption has been overcome is ordinarily a question for the court.
    VI. Such information may furnish a basis for a logical inference.

The CORRECT answer is:
A. IV, VI, II, V, I, III
B. III, II, V, I, IV, VI
C. V, III, VI, IV, II, I
D. V, IV, I, II, VI, III

KEY (CORRECT ANSWERS)

1. D
2. C
3. A
4. B

SUPERVISION STUDY GUIDE

Social science has developed information about groups and leadership in general and supervisor-employee relationships in particular. Since organizational effectiveness is closely linked to the ability of supervisors to direct the activities of employees, these findings are important to executives everywhere.

IS A SUPERVISOR A LEADER?

First-line supervisors are found in all large business and government organizations. They are the men at the base of an organizational hierarchy. Decisions made by the head of the organization reach them through a network of intermediate positions. They are frequently referred to as part of the management team, but their duties seldom seem to support this description.

A supervisor of clerks, tax collectors, meat inspectors, or securities analysts is not charged with budget preparation. He cannot hire or fire the employees in his own unit on his say-so. He does not administer programs which require great planning, coordinating, or decision making.

Then what is he? He is the man who is directly in charge of a group of employees doing productive work for a business or government agency. If the work requires the use of machines, the men he supervises operate them. If the work requires the writing of reports, the men he supervises write them. He is expected to maintain a productive flow of work without creating problems which higher levels of management must solve. But is he a leader?

To carry out a specific part of an agency's mission, management creates a unit, staffs it with a group of employees and designates a supervisor to take charge of them. Management directs what this unit shall do, from time to time changes directions, and often indicates what the group should not do. Management presumably creates status for the supervisor by giving him more pay, a title, and special privileges.

Management asks a supervisor to get his workers to attain organizational goals, including the desired quantity and quality of production. Supposedly, he has authority to enable him to achieve this objective. Management at least assumes that by establishing the status of the supervisor's position, it has created sufficient authority to enable him to achieve these goals— not his goals, nor necessarily the group's, but management's goals.

In addition, supervision includes writing reports, keeping records of membership in a higher-level administrative group, industrial engineering, safety engineering, editorial duties, housekeeping duties, etc. The supervisor as a member of an organizational network, must be responsible to the changing demands of the management above him. At the same time, he must be responsive to the demands of the work group of which he is a member. He is placed in the difficult position of communicating and implementing new decisions, changed programs and revised production quotas for his work group, although he may have had little part in developing them.

It follows, then, that supervision has a special characteristic: achievement of goals, previously set by management, through the efforts of others. It is in this feature of the supervisor's job that we find the role of a leader in the sense of the following definition: *A leader is that person who most effectively influences group activities toward goal setting and goal achievements.*

This definition is broad. It covers both leaders in groups that come together voluntarily and in those brought together through a work assignment in a factory, store, or government agency. In the natural group, the authority necessary to attain goals is determined by the group membership and is granted by them. In the working group, it is apparent that the establishment of a supervisory position creates a predisposition on the part of employees to accept the authority of the occupant of that position. We cannot, however, assume that mere occupation confers authority sufficient to assure the accomplishment of an organization's goals.

Supervision is different, then, from leadership. The supervisor is expected to fulfill the role of leader but without obtaining a grant of authority from the group he supervises. The supervisor is expected to influence the group in the achieving of goals but is often handicapped by having little influence on the organizational process by which goals are set. The supervisor, because he works in an organizational setting, has the burdens of additional organizational duties and restrictions and requirements arising out of the fact that his position is subordinate to a hierarchy of higher-level supervisors. These differences between leadership and supervision are reflected in our definition: *Supervision is basically a leadership role, in a formal organization, which has as its objective the effective influencing of other employees.*

Even though these differences between supervision and leadership exist, a significant finding of experimenters in this field is that supervisors must be leaders to be successful.

The problem is: How can a supervisor exercise leadership in an organizational setting? We might say that the supervisor is expected to be a natural leader in a situation which does not come about naturally. His situation becomes really difficult in an organization which is more eager to make its supervisors into followers rather than leaders.

LEADERSHIP: NATURAL AND ORGANIZATIONAL

Leadership, in its usual sense of *natural* leadership, and supervision are not the same. In some cases, leadership embraces broader powers and functions than supervision; in other cases, supervision embraces more than leadership. This is true both because of the organization and technical aspects of the supervisor's job and because of the relatively freer setting and inherent authority of the natural leader.

The natural leader usually has much more authority and influence than the supervisor. Group members not only follow his command but prefer it that way. The employee, however, can appeal the supervisor's commands to his union or to the supervisor's superior or to the personnel office. These intercessors represent restrictions on the supervisor's power to lead.

The natural leader can gain greater membership involvement in the group's objectives, and he can change the objectives of the group. The supervisor can attempt to gain employee support only for management's objectives; he cannot set other objectives. In these instances leadership is broader than supervision.

The natural leader must depend upon whatever skills are available when seeking to attain objectives. The supervisor is trained in the administrative skills necessary to achieve management's goals. If he does not possess the requisite skills, however, he can call upon management's technicians.

A natural leader can maintain his leadership, in certain groups, merely by satisfying members' need for group affiliation. The supervisor must maintain his leadership by directing and organizing his group to achieve specific organizational goals set for him and his group by management. He must have a technical competence and a kind of coordinating ability which is not needed by many natural leaders.

A natural leader is responsible only to his group which grants him authority. The supervisor is responsible to management, which employs him, and also to the work group of which he is a member. The supervisor has the exceedingly difficult job of reconciling the demands of two groups frequently in conflict. He is often placed in the untenable position of trying to play two antagonistic roles. In the above instance, supervision is broader than leadership.

ORGANIZATIONAL INFLUENCES ON LEADERSHIP

The supervisor is both a product and a prisoner of the organization wherein we find him. The organization which creates the supervisor's position also obstructs, restricts, and channelizes the exercise of his duties. These influences extend beyond prescribed functional relationships to specific supervisory behavior. For example, even in a face-to-face situation involving one of his subordinates, the supervisor's actions are controlled to a great extent by his organization. His behavior must conform to the organization policy on human relations, rules which dictate personnel procedures, specific prohibitions governing conduct, the attitudes of his own superior, etc. He is not a free agent operating within the limits of his work group. His freedom of action is much more circumscribed than is generally admitted. The organizational influences which limit his leadership actions can be classified as structure, prescriptions, and proscriptions.

The organizational structure places each supervisor's position in context with other designated positions. It determines the relationships between his position and specific positions which impinge on his. The structure of the organization designates a certain position to which he looks for orders and information about his work. It gives a particular status to his position within a pattern of statuses from which he perceives that (1) certain positions are on a par, organizationally, with his, (2) other positions are subordinate, and (3) still others are superior.

The organizational structure determines those positions to which he should look for advice and assistance, and those positions to which he should give advice and assistance.

For instance, the organizational structure has predetermined that the supervisor of a clerical processing unit shall report to a supervisory position in a higher echelon. He shall have certain relationships with the supervisors of the work units which transmit work to and receive work from his unit. He shall discuss changes and clarification of procedures with certain staff units, such as organization and methods, cost accounting, and personnel. He shall consult supervisors of units which provide or receive special work assignments.

The organizational structure, however, establishes patterns other than those of the relationships of positions. These are the patterns of responsibility, authority, and expectations.

The supervisor is responsible for certain activities or results; he is presumably invested with the authority to achieve these. His set of authority and responsibility is interwoven with other sets to the end that all goals and functions of the organization are parceled out in small, manageable lots. This, of course, establishes a series of expectations: a single supervisor can perform his particular set of duties only upon the assumption that preceding or contiguous sets of duties have been, or are being carried out. At the same time, he is aware of the expectations of others that he will fulfill his functional role.

The structure of an organization establishes relationships between specified positions and specific expectations for these positions. The fact that these relationships and expectations are established is one thing; whether or not they are met is another.

PRESCRIPTIONS AND PROSCRIPTIONS

But let us return to the organizational influences which act to restrict the supervisor's exercise of leadership. These are the prescriptions and proscriptions generally in effect in all organizations, and those peculiar to a single organization. In brief these are the *thou shalt's* and the *thou shalt not's*.

Organizations not only prescribe certain duties for individual supervisory positions, they also prescribe specific methods and means of carrying out these duties and maintaining management-employee relations. These include rules, regulations, policy, and tradition. It does no good for the supervisor to say, *This seems to be the best way to handle such-and-such,* if the organization has established a routine for dealing with problems. For good or bad, there are rules that state that firings shall be executed in such a manner, accompanied by a certain notification; that training shall be conducted, and in this manner. Proscriptions are merely negative prescriptions; you may not discriminate against any employee because of politics or race; you shall not suspend any employee without following certain procedures and obtaining certain approvals.

Most of these prohibitions and rules apply to the area of interpersonal relations, precisely the area which is now arousing most interest on the part of administrators and managers. We have become concerned about the contrast between formally prescribed relationships and interpersonal relationships, and this brings us to the often discussed informal organization.

FORMAL AND INFORMAL ORGANIZATIONS

As we well know, the functions and activities of any organization are broken down into individual units of work called positions. Administrators must establish a pattern which will link these positions to each other and relate them to a system of authority and responsibility. Man-to-man are spelled out as plainly as possible for all to understand. Managers, then, build an official structure which we call the formal organization.

In these same organizations, employees react individually and in groups to institutionally determined roles. John, a worker, rides in the same carpool as Joe, a foreman. An unplanned communication develops. Harry, a machinist knows more about high-speed machining than his foreman or anyone else in his shop. An unofficial tool boss comes into being. Mary, who fought with Jane, is promoted over her. Jane now gives Mary's directions. A planned relationship fails to develop. The employees have built a structure which we call the informal organization.

> *Formal organization is a system of management-prescribed relations between positions in an organization.*
>
> *Informal organization is a network of unofficial relations between people in an organization.*

These definitions might lead us to the absurd conclusion that positions carry out formal activities and that employe4es spend their time in unofficial activities. We must recognize that organizational activities are in all cases carried out by people. The formal structure provides a needed framework within which interpersonal relations occur. What we call informal organization is the complex of normal, natural relations among employees. These personal relationships may be negative or positive. That is, they may impede or aid the achievement of organizational goals. For example, friendship between two supervisors greatly increases the probability of good cooperation and coordination between their sections. On the other hand, *buck passing* nullifies the formal structure by failure to meet a prescribed and expected responsibility.

It is improbable that an ideal organization exists where all activities are carried out in strict conformity to a formally prescribed pattern of functional roles. Informal organization arises because of the incompleteness and ambiguities in the network of formally prescribed relationships, or in response to the needs or inadequacies of supervisors or managers who hold prescribed functional roles in an organization. Many of these relationships are not prescribed by the organizational pattern; many cannot be prescribed; many should not be prescribed.

Management faces the problem of keeping the informal organization in harmony with the mission of the agency. One way to do this is to make sure that all employees have a clear understanding of and are sympathetic with that mission. The issuance of organizational charts, procedural manuals, and functional descriptions of the work to be done by divisions and sections helps communicate management's plans and goals. Issuances alone, of course, cannot do the whole job. They should be accompanied by oral discussion and explanation. Management must ensure that there is mutual understanding and acceptance of charts and procedures. More important is that management acquaint itself with the attitudes, activities, and peculiar brands of logic which govern the informal organization. Only through this type of knowledge can they and supervisors keep informal goals consistent with the agency mission.

SUPERVISION STATUS AND FUNCTIONAL ROLE

A well-established supervisor is respected by the employees who work with him. They defer to his wishes. It is clear that a superior-subordinate relationship has been established. That is, status of the supervisor has been established in relation to other employees of the same work group. This same supervisor gains the respect of employees when he behaves in as certain manner. He will be expected, generally, to follow the customs of the group in such matters as dress, recreation, and manner of speaking. The group has a set of expectations as to his behavior. His position is a functional role which carries with it a collection of rights and obligations.

The position of supervisor usually has a status distinct from the individual who occupies it: it is much like a position description which exists whether or not there is an incumbent. The status of a supervisory position is valued higher than that of an employee position both because of the functional role of leadership which is assigned to it and because of the status symbols of titles, rights, and privileges which go with it.

Social ranking, or status, is not simple because it involves both the position and the man. An individual may be ranked higher than others because of his education, social background, perceived leadership ability, or conformity to group customs and ideals. If such a man is ranked higher by the members of a work group than their supervisor, the supervisor's effectiveness may be seriously undermined.

If the organization does not build and reinforce a supervisor's status, his position can be undermined in a different way. This will happen when managers go around rather than through the supervisor or designate him as a straw boss, acting boss, or otherwise not a real boss.

Let us clarify this last point. A role, and corresponding status, establishes a set of expectations. Employees expect their supervisor to do certain things and to act in certain ways. They are prepared to respond to that expected behavior. When the supervisor's behavior does not conform to their expectations, they are surprised, confused, and ill-at-ease. It becomes necessary for them to resolve their confusion, if they can. They might do this by turning to one of their own members for leadership. If the confusion continues, or their attempted solutions are not satisfactory, they will probably become a poorly motivated, non-cohesive group which cannot function very well.

COMMUNICATION AND THE SUPERVISOR

In a recent survey, railroad workers reported that they rarely look to their supervisor for information about the company. This is startling, at least to us, because we ordinarily think of the supervisor as the link between management and worker. We expect the supervisor to be the prime source of information about the company. Actually, the railroad workers listed the supervisor next to last in the o5rder of their sources of information. Most surprising of all, the supervisors, themselves, stated that rumor and unofficial contacts were their principal sources of information. Here we see one of the reasons why supervisors may not be as effective as management desires.

The supervisor is not only being bypassed by his work group, he is being ignored, and his position weakened, by the very organization which is holding him responsible for the activities of his workers. If he is management's representative to the employee, then management has an obligation to keep him informed of its activities. This is necessary if he is to carry out his functions efficiently and maintain his leadership in the work group. The supervisor is expected to be a source of information; when he is not, his status is not clear, and employees are dissatisfied because he has not lived up to expectations.

By providing information to the supervisor to pass along to employees, we can strengthen his position as leader of the group, and increase satisfaction and cohesion within the group. Because he has more information than the other members, receives information sooner, and passes it along at the proper times, members turn to him as a source and also provide him with information in the hope of receiving some in return. From this, we can see an increase in group cohesiveness because:

- Employees are bound closer to their supervisor because he is *in the know*.
- There is less need to go outside the group for answers
- Employees will more quickly turn to the supervisor for enlightenment

The fact that he has the answers will also enhance the supervisor's standing in the eyes of his men. This increased status will serve to bolster his authority and control of the group and will probably result in improved morale and productivity.

The foregoing, of course, does not mean that all management information should be given out. There are obviously certain policy determinations and discussions which need not or cannot be transmitted to all supervisors. However, the supervisor must be kept as fully informed as possible so that he can answer questions when asked and can allay needless fears and anxieties. Further, the supervisor has the responsibility of encouraging employee questions and submissions of information. He must be able to present information to employees so that it is clearly understood and accepted. His attitude and manner should make it clear that he believes in what he is saying, that the information is necessary or desirable to the group, and that he is prepared to act on the basis of the information.

SUPERVISION AND JOB PERFORMANCE

The productivity of work groups is a product; employees' efforts are multiplied by the supervision they receive. Many investigators have analyzed this relationship and have discovered elements of supervision which differentiate high and low production groups. These researchers have identified certain types of supervisory practices which they classify as *employee-centered* and other types which they classify as *production centered*.

The difference between these two kinds of supervision lies not in specific practices but in the approach or orientation to supervision. The employee-centered supervisor directs most of his efforts toward increasing employee motivation. He is concerned more with realizing the potential energy of persons than with administrative and technological methods of increasing efficiency and productivity. He is the man who finds ways of causing employees to want to work harder with the same tools. These supervisors emphasize the personal relations between their employees and themselves.

Now, obviously, these pictures are overdrawn. No one supervisor has all the virtues of the ideal type of employee-centered supervisor. And, fortunately, no one supervisor has all the bad traits found in many production-centered supervisors. We should remember that the various practices that researchers have fond which distinguish these two kinds of supervision represent the many practices and methods of supervisors of all gradations between these extremes. We should be careful, too, of the implications of the labels attached to the two types. For instance, being production-centered is not necessarily bad, since the principal responsibility of any supervisor is maintaining the production level that is expected of his work group. Being employee-centered may not necessarily be good, if the only result is a happy, chuckling crew of loafers. To return to the researchers' findings, employee-centered supervisors:

- Recommend promotions, transfers, pay increases
- Inform men about what is happening in the company
- Keep men posted on how well they are doing
- Hear complaints and grievances sympathetically
- Speak up for subordinates

Production-centered supervisors, on the other hand, don't do those things. They check on employees more frequently, give more detailed and frequent instructions, don't give reasons for changes, and are more punitive when mistakes are made. Employee-centered supervisors were reported to contribute to high morale and high production, whereas production-centered supervision was associated with lower morale and less production.

More recent findings, however, show that the relationship between supervision and productivity is not this simple. Investigators now report that high production is more frequently associated with supervisory practices which combine employee-centered behavior with concern for production. (This concern is not the same, however, as anxiety about production, which is the hallmark of our production-centered supervisor.) Let us examine these apparently contradictory findings and the premises from which they are derived.

SUPERVISION AND MORALE

Why do supervisory activities cause high or low production? As the name implies, the activities of the employee-centered supervisor tend to relate him more closely and satisfactorily to his workers. The production-centered supervisor's practices tend to separate him from his group and to foster antagonism. An analysis of this difference may answer our question.

Earlier, we pointed out that the supervisor is a type of leader and that leadership is intimately related to the group in which it occurs We discover, now, that an employee-centered supervisor's primary activities are concerned with both his leadership and his group membership. Such a supervisor is a member of a group and occupies a leadership role in that group.

These facts are sometimes obscured when we speak of the supervisor as management's representative, or as the organizational link between management and the employee, or as the end of the chain of command. If we really want to understand what it is we expect of the supervisor, we must remember that he is the designated leader of a group of employees to whom he is bound by interaction and interdependence.

Most of his actions are aimed, consciously or unconsciously, at strengthening membership ties in the group. This includes both making members more conscious that he is a member of their group) and causing members to identify themselves more closely with the group. These ends are accomplished by:

- making the group more attractive to the worker: they find satisfaction of their needs for recognition, friendship, enjoyable work, etc.;
- maintaining open communication: employees can express their views and obtain information about the organization
- giving assistance: members can seek advice on personal problems as well as their work; and
- acting as a buffer between the group and management: he speaks up for his men and explains the reasons for management's decisions.

Such actions both strengthen group cohesiveness and solidarity and affirm the supervisor's leadership position in the group.

DEFINING MORALE

This brings us back to a point mentioned earlier. We had said that employee-centered supervisors contribute to high morale as well as to high production. But how can we explain units which have low morale and high productivity, or vice versa? Usually production and morale are considered separately, partly because they are measured against different criteria and partly because, in some instances, they seem to be independent of each other.

Some of this difficulty may stem from confusion over definitions of morale. Morale has been defined as, or measured by, absences from work, satisfaction with job or company, dissension among members of work groups, productivity, apathy or lack of interest, readiness to help others, and a general aura of happiness as rated by observers. Some of these criteria of morale are not subject to the influence of the supervisor, and some of them are not clearly related to productivity. Definitions like these invite findings of low morale coupled with high production.

Both productivity and morale can be influenced by environmental factors not under the control of group members or supervisors. Such things as plant layout, organizational structure and goals, lighting, ventilation, communications, and management planning may have an adverse or desirable effect.

We might resolve the dilemma by defining morale on the basis of our understanding of the supervisor as leader of a group; morale is the degree of satisfaction of group members with their leadership. In this light, the supervisor's employee-centered activities bear a clear relation to morale. His efforts to increase employee identification with the group and to strengthen his leadership lead to greater satisfaction with that leadership. By increasing group cohesiveness and by demonstrating that his influence and power can aid the group, he is able to enhance his leadership status and afford satisfaction to the group.

SUPERVISION, PRODUCTION, AND MORALE

There are factors within the organization itself which determine whether increased production is possible:

- Are production goals expressed in terms understandable to employees and are they realistic?
- Do supervisors responsible for production respect the agency mission and production goals?
- If employees do not know how to do the job well, does management provide a trainer—often the supervisor—who can teach efficient work methods?

There are other factors within the work group which determine whether increased production will be attained:

- Is leadership present which can bring about the desired level of production?
- Are production goals accepted by employees as reasonable and attainable?
- If group effort is involved, are members able to coordinate their efforts?

Research findings confirm the view that an employee-centered supervisor can achieve higher morale than a production-centered supervisor. Managers may well ask what is the relationship between this and production.

Supervision is production-oriented to the extent that it focuses attention on achieving organizational goals, and plans and devises methods for attaining them; it is employee-centered to the extent that it focuses attention on employee attitudes toward those goals, and plans and works toward maintenance of employee satisfaction.

High productivity and low morale result when a supervisor plans and organizes work efficiently but cannot achieve high membership satisfaction. Low production and high morale result when a supervisor, though keeping members satisfied with his leadership, either has not gained acceptance of organizational goals or does not have the technical competence to achieve them.

The relationship between supervision, morale, and productivity is an interdependent one, with the supervisor playing an integral role due to his ability to influence productivity and morale independently of each other.

A supervisor who can plan his work well has good technical knowledge, and who can install better production methods can raise production without necessarily increasing group satisfaction. On the other hand, a supervisor who can motivate his employees and keep them satisfied with his leadership can gain high production in spite of technical difficulties and environmental obstacles.

CLIMATE AND SUPERVISION

Climate, the intangible environment of an organization made up of attitudes, beliefs, and traditions, plays a large part in morale, productivity, and supervision. Usually when we speak of climate and its relationship to morale and productivity, we talk about the merits of *democratic* versus *authoritarian* climate. Employees seem to produce more and have higher morale in a democratic climate, whereas in an authoritarian climate, the reverse seems to be true or so the researchers tell us. We would do well to determine what these terms mean to supervision.

Perhaps most of our difficulty in understanding and applying these concepts comes from our emotional reactions to the words themselves. For example, authoritarian climate is usually painted as the very blackest kind of dictatorship. This is not surprising, because we are usually expected to believe that it is invariably bad. Conversely, democratic climate is drawn to make the driven snow look impure by comparison.

Now these descriptions are most probably true when we talk about our political processes, or town meetings, or freedom of speech. However, the same labels have been used by social scientists in other contexts and have also been applied to government and business organizations, without it, it seems, any recognition that the meanings and their social values may have changed somewhat

For example, these labels were used in experiments conducted in an informal classroom setting using 11-year-old boys as subjects. The descriptive labels applied to the climate of the setting as well as the type of leadership practiced. When these labels were transferred to a management setting, it seems that many presumed that they principally meant the king of leadership rather than climate. We can see that there is a great difference between the experimental and management settings and that leadership practices for one might be inappropriate for the other.

It is doubtful that formal work organizations can be anything but authoritarian, in that goals are set by management and a hierarchy exists through which decisions and orders from the top are transmitted downward. Organizations are authoritarian by structure and need; direction and control are placed in the hands of a few in order to gain fast and efficient decision making. Now this does not mean to describe a dictatorship. It is merely the recognition of the fact that direction of organizational affairs comes from above. It should be noted that leadership in some natural groups is, in this sense, authoritarian.

Granting that formal organizations have this kind of authoritarian leadership, can there be a democratic climate? Certainly there can be, but we would want to define and delimit this term. A more realistic meaning of democratic climate in organizations is the use of permissive and participatory methods in management-employee relations. That is, a mutual exchange of information and explanation with the granting of individual freedom within certain restricted and defined limits. However, it is not our purpose to debate the merits of authoritarianism versus democracy. We recognize that within the small work group there is a need for freedom from constraint and an increase in participation in order to achieve organizational goals within the framework of the organizational movement.

Another aspect of climate is best expressed by this familiar, and true, saying: actions speak louder than words. Of particular concern to us is this effect of management climate on the behavior of supervisors, particularly in employee-centered activities.

There have been reports of disappointment with efforts to make supervisors ore employee-centered. Managers state that, since research has shown ways of improving human relations, supervisors should begin to practice these methods. Usually a training course in human relations is established; and supervisors are given this training. Managers then sit back and wait for the expected improvements, only to find that there are none.

If we wish to produce changes in the supervisor's behavior, the climate must be made appropriate and rewarding to the changed behavior. This means that top-level attitudes and behavior cannot deny or contradict the change we are attempting to effect. Basic changes in organizational behavior cannot be made with any permanence, unless we provide an environment that is receptive to the changes and rewards those persons who do change.

IMPROVING SUPERVISION

Anyone who has read this far might expect to find *A Dozen Rules for Dealing With Employees* or *29 Steps to Supervisory Success*. We will not provide such a list.

Simple rules suffer from their simplicity. They ignore the complexities of human behavior. Reliance upon rules may cause supervisors to concentrate on superficial aspects of their relations with employees. It may preclude genuine understanding.

The supervisor who relies on a list of rules tends to think of people in mechanistic terms. In a certain situation, he uses *Rule No. 3*. Employees are not treated as thinking and feeling persons, but rather as figures in a formula: Rule 3 applied to employee X = Production.

Employees usually recognize mechanical manipulation and become dissatisfied and resentful. They lose faith in, and respect for, their supervisor, and this may be reflected in lower morale and productivity.

We do not mean that supervisors must become social science experts if they wish to improve. Reports of current research indicate that there are two major parts of their job which can be strengthened through self-improvement: (1) Work planning, including technical skills, and (2) motivation of employees.

The most effective supervisors combine excellence in the administrative and technical aspects of their work with friendly and considerate personal relations with their employees.

CRITICAL PERSONAL RELATIONS

Later in this chapter we shall talk about administrative aspects of supervision, but first let us comment on *friendly and considerate personal relations.* We have discussed this subject throughout the preceding chapters, but we want to review some of the critical supervisory influences on personal relations.

Closeness of Supervision: The closeness of supervision has an important effect on productivity and morale. Mann and Dent found that supervisors of low-producing units supervise very closely, while high-producing supervisors exercise only general supervision. It was found that the low-producing supervisors:

- check on employees more frequently
- give more detailed and frequent instructions
- limit employee's freedom to do job in own way

Workers who felt less closely supervised reported that they were better satisfied with their jobs and the company. We should note that the manner or attitude of the supervisor has an important bearing on whether employees perceive supervision as being close or general.

These findings are another way of saying that supervision does not mean standing over the employee and telling him what to do and when and how to do it. The more effective supervisor tells his employees what is required, giving general instructions.

COMMUNICATION

Supervisors of high-production units consider communication as one of the most important aspects of their job. Effective communication is used by these supervisors to achieve better interpersonal relations and improved employee motivation. Low-production supervisors do not rate communications as highly important.

High-producing supervisors find that an important aid to more effective communication is listening. They are ready to listen to both personal problems or interests and questions about the work. This does not mean that they are *nosey* or meddle in their employees' personal lives, but rather that they show a willingness to listen, and do listen, if their employees wish to discuss problems.

These supervisors inform employees about forthcoming changes in work; they discuss agency policy with employees; and they make sure that each employee knows how well he is doing. What these supervisors do is use two-way communication effectively. Unless the supervisor freely imparts information, he will not receive information in return.

Attitudes and perception are frequently affected by communication or the lack of it. Research surveys reveal that many supervisors are not aware of their employees' attitudes, nor do they know what personal reactions their supervision arouses. Through frank discussion with employees, they have been surprised to discover employee beliefs about which they were ignorant. Discussion sometimes reveals that the supervisor and his employees have totally different impressions about the same event. The supervisor should be constantly on the alert for misconceptions about his words and deeds. He must remember that, although his actions are perfectly clear to himself, they may be, and frequently are, viewed differently by employees.

Failure to communicate information results in misconceptions and false assumptions. What you say and how you say it will strongly affect your employees' attitudes and perceptions. By giving them available information, you can prevent misconceptions; by discussion, you may be able to change attitudes; by questioning, you can discover what the perceptions and assumptions really are. And it need hardly be added that actions should conform very closely to words.

If we were to attempt to reduce the above discussion on communication to rules, we would have a long list which would be based on one cardinal principle: Don't make assumptions!

- Don't assume that your employees know; tell them.
- Don't assume that you know how they feel; find out.
- Don't assume that they understand; clarify.

20 SUPERVISORY HINTS

1. Avoid inconsistency.
2. Always give employees a chance to explain their action before taking disciplinary action. Don't allow too much time for a "cooling off" period before disciplining an employee.
3. Be specific in your criticisms.
4. Delegate responsibility wisely.
5. Do not argue or lose your temper, and avoid being impatient.
6. Promote mutual respect and be fair, impartial, and open-minded.
7. Keep in mind that asking for employees' advice and input can be helpful in decision making.
8. If you make promises, keep them.
9. Always keep the feelings, abilities, dignity and motives of your staff in mind.
10. Remain loyal to your employees' interests.
11. Never criticize employees in front of others, or treat employees like children.
12. Admit mistakes. Don't place blame on your employees, or make excuses.
13. Be reasonable in your expectations, give complete instructions, and establish well-planned goals.
14. Be knowledgeable about office details and procedures, but avoid becoming bogged down in details.
15. Avoid supervising too closely or too loosely. Employees should also view you as an approachable supervisor.
16. Remember that employees' personal problems may affect job performance, but become involved only when appropriate.
17. Work to develop workers, and to instill a feeling of cooperation while working toward mutual goals.
18. Do not overpraise or underpraise, be properly appreciative.
19. Never ask an employee to discipline someone for you.
20. A complaint, even if unjustified, should be taken seriously.

16

NOTES

ELECTRICAL ASPECTS OF A HOUSING INSPECTION

TABLE OF CONTENTS

		Page
I.	Definitions	1
II.	Flow of Electric Current	2
III.	Electric Service Entrance	4
IV.	Grounding	6
V.	Two- or Three-Way Electric Services	7
VI.	Residential Wiring Adequacy	8
VII.	Wire Size and Types	8
VIII.	Electric Service Panel	10
IX.	Overcurrent Devices	11
X.	Electric Circuits	13
XI.	Common Electrical Violations	16
XII.	Steps Involved in Actual Inspections	18
XIII.	Wattage Consumption of Electrical Appliances	20
XIV.	Motor Currents	20

ELECTRICAL ASPECTS OF A HOUSING INSPECTION

There are two basic codes concerned with residential wiring that are of importance to the housing inspector. The first is the local electrical code. The purpose of this code is to safeguard persons and buildings and their contents from hazards arising from the use of electricity for light, heat, and power. The electrical code contains basic minimum provisions considered necessary for safety. Compliance with this code and proper maintenance will result in an installation essentially free from hazard but not necessarily efficient, convenient, or adequate for good service or future expansion.

The majority of local electrical codes are modeled after the National Electrical Code, published by the National Fire Prevention Association.

Just because an electrical installation was safe and adequate under the provisions of the electrical code at the time of installation does not indicate that the system is safe and adequate for use today. Hazards often occur because of overloading of wiring systems by methods or usage not in conformity with the code. This occurs because initial wiring did not provide for increases in the use of electricity. For this reason it is recommended that the initial installation be adequate and that reasonable provisions for system changes be made as may be required for future increase in the use of electricity.

The other code that contains electrical provisions is the local housing code. It establishes minimum standards for artificial and natural lighting and ventilation, specifies the minimum number of electric outlets and lighting fixtures per room, and prohibits temporary wiring except under certain circumstances. In addition, the housing code usually requires that all components of the electrical system be installed and maintained in a safe condition so as to prevent fire or electric shock.

This chapter contains electrical terms and major features of a residential wiring system that should be familiar to the housing inspector. It also contains a review of the steps involved in the electrical inspection, as well as commonly found conditions.

I. Definitions

A **Electricity** - is energy that can be used to run household appliances; it can produce light and heat, shocks, and numerous other effects.

B **Current** - the flow of electricity through a circuit.

   1 **Alternating current** is an electrical current that reverses its direction of flow at regular intervals: For example, it would alternate 60 times every second in a 60-cycle system. This type of power is commonly found in homes.

   2 **Direct current** is an electric current flowing in one direction. This type of current is not commonly found in today's homes.

C **Ampere** - the unit used in measuring intensity of flow of electricity. Symbol for it is "I."

D **Volt** - the unit for measuring electrical pressure or force, which is known as electromotive force. Symbol for it is "E."

E **Watt** - is the unit of electric power. Volts X Amperes = Watts.

F **Circuit** - the flow of electricity through two or more wires from the supply source to one or more outlets and back to the source.

G **Circuit Breaker** - a safety device used to break the flow of electricity by opening the circuit automatically in the event of overloading or used to open or close it manually.

H **Short Circuit** - is a break in the flow of electricity through a circuit due to the load caused by improper connection between hot and neutral wires (have the electrical inspector check for its location).

I **Conductor** - any substance capable of conveying an electric current. In the home, copper wire is usually used.

    1 **Bare conductor** is one with no insulation or covering.

    2 **Covered conductor** is one covered with one or more layers of insulation.

J **Fuse** - a safety device that cuts off the flow of electricity when the current flowing through the fuse exceeds its rated capacity.

K **Ground** - to connect with the earth as to ground an electric wire directly to the earth or indirectly through a water pipe or some other conductor. Usually a green-colored wire is used for grounding the whole electrical system to the earth. A white wire is then usually used to ground individual electrical components of the whole system.

L **Conductor Gauge** - a numerical system used to label electric conductor sizes, given in American Wire Gauge (AWG). The larger the AWG number the smaller the wire size.

M **Hot Wires** - those that carry the electric current or power to the load; they are usually black or red.

N **Service** - the conductor and equipment for delivering energy from the electricity supply system to the wiring system of the premises.

O **Service Drop** - the overhead service connectors from the last pole or other aerial support to and including the splices, if any, connecting to the service entrance conductors at the building or other structure.

P **Insulator** - a material that will not permit the passage of electricity.

Q **Neutral Wire** - the third wire in a three-wire distribution circuit; it is usually white or light gray and is connected to the ground.

R **Service Panel** - main panel or cabinet through which electricity is brought to building and distributed. It contains the main disconnect switch and fuses or circuit breakers.

S **Voltage Drop** - a voltage loss when wires carry current. The longer the cord the greater the voltage drop.

II. Flow of Electric Current

Electricity is usually generated by a generator that converts mechanical energy into electrical energy. The electricity is then run through a transformer where voltage is increased to several hundred thousand volts and in some instances to a million or more volts. This high voltage is necessary in order to increase the efficiency of power transmission over long distances.

This high-transmission voltage is then stepped down (reduced) to normal 115/230-volt household current by a transformer located near the point of use (residence). The electricity is then transmitted to the house by a series of wires called a "service drop." In areas where the electric wiring is underground, the wires leading to the building are buried in the ground.

In order for electric current to flow, it must travel from a higher to a lower potential voltage. In an electrical system the hot wires (black or red) are at a higher potential than the neutral or ground wire (white or green). Therefore, current will flow between the hot wires and the neutral or ground wires.

The voltage is a measure of the force at which electricity is delivered. It is similar to pressure in a water supply system.

Current is measured in amperes and is the quantity of flow of electricity. It is similar to measuring water in gallons per second.

A watt is equal to volts times amperes. It is a measure of how much power is flowing. Electricity is sold in quantities of watt-hours.

The earth, by virtue of moisture contained within the soil, serves as a very effective conductor. Therefore, in power transmission, instead of having both the hot and neutral wires carried by the transmission poles, one lead of the generator is connected to the ground, which serves as a conductor (see Figure 1). Only hot wires are carried by the transmission towers. At the house, or point where the electricity is to be used, the circuit is completed by another connection to ground.

The electric power utility provides a ground somewhere in its local distribution system; therefore, there is a ground wire in addition to the hot wires within the service drop. In Figure 1 this ground can be seen at the power pole that contains the stepdown transformer.

In addition to the ground connection provided by the electric utility, every building is required to have an independent ground, called a "system ground."

The system ground provides for limiting the voltage upon the circuit, which might otherwise occur through exposure to lighting, or for limiting the maximum potential to ground due to normal voltage. Therefore, the system ground's main purpose is to protect the electric system itself and offer limited protection to the user.
The system ground serves the same purpose as the power company's ground, however, being closer to the building, it has a lower resistance.

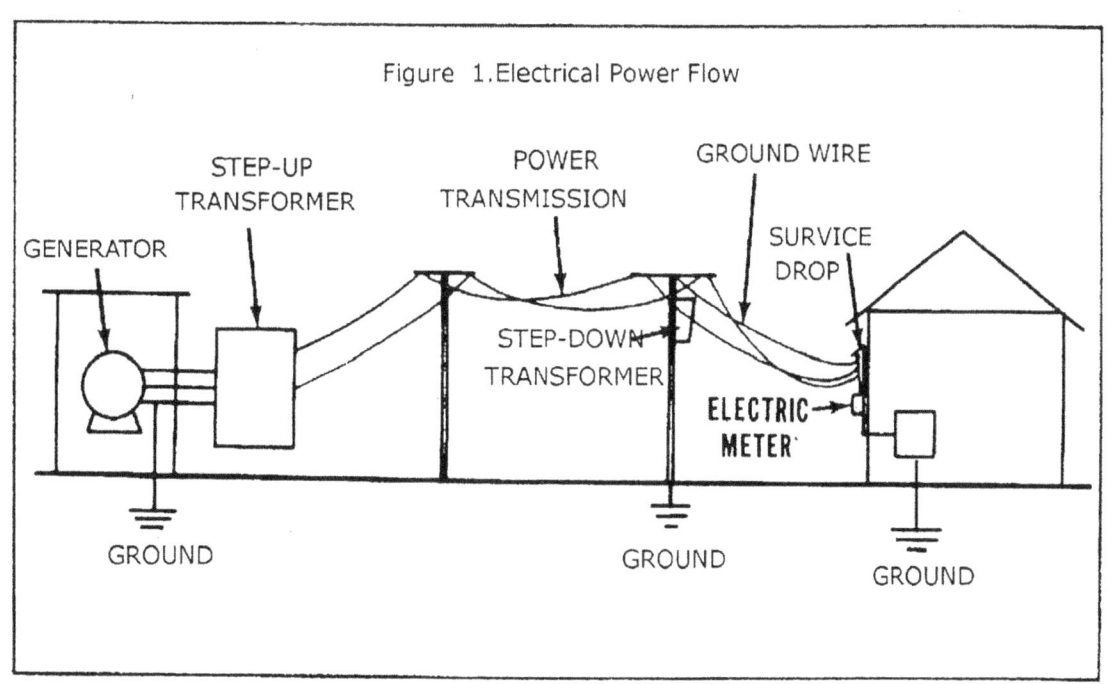

Figure 1. Electrical Power Flow

The "equipment ground," which we will discuss later in this chapter, protects man from potential harm during the use of certain electrical equipment.

The system ground should be a continuous wire of low resistance and of sufficient size to conduct current safely from lightning and overloads.

III. Electric Service Entrance

A Service Drop

The "Entrance Head" (see Figure 2) should be attached to the building at least 10 feet above ground, to prevent accidental contact by people. The conductor should clear all roofs by at least 8 feet and residential driveways by 12 feet. For public streets, alleys, roads, and driveways on other than residential property the clearance must be 18 feet.

The wires or conductor should be of sufficient size to carry the load and not smaller than No. 8 copper or equivalent.

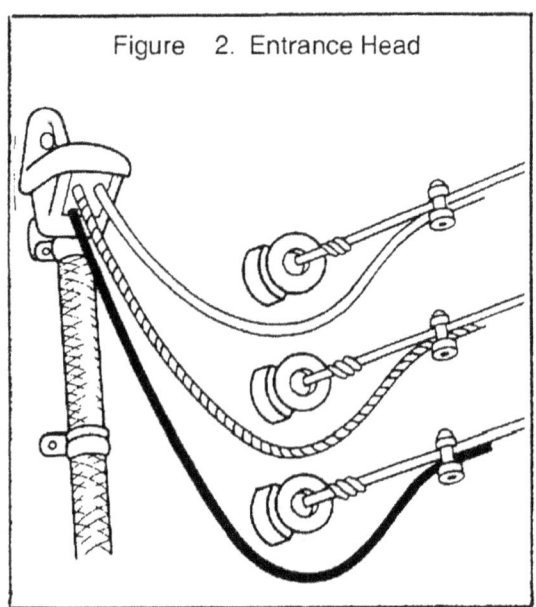

Figure 2. Entrance Head

For connecting wire from the entrance head to the service drop wires, the National Electrical Code requires that the service entrance conductors be installed either (1) below the level of the service head, or (2) below the termination of the service-entrance cable sheath. Drip loops must be formed on individual conductors. This will prevent water from entering the electric service system.

The wires that form "entrance cable" should extend 36 inches from the entrance head, to provide a sufficient length to connect service drop wires to the building with insulators (see Figure 2).

The entrance cable may be a special type of armored outdoor type of wire or it may be enclosed in a conduit. The electric power meter may be located either within or outside the building. In either instance, the meter must be located before the main power disconnect.

Figure 3 shows an armored cable service entrance. The armored cable is anchored to the building with metal straps spaced every 4 feet. The cable is run down the wall and through a hole drilled through the building. The cable is then connected to the service panel, which should be located within 1 foot of where the cable enters the building.

The ground wire need not be insulated. This ground wire may be either solid or stranded copper, or a material with an equivalent resistance.

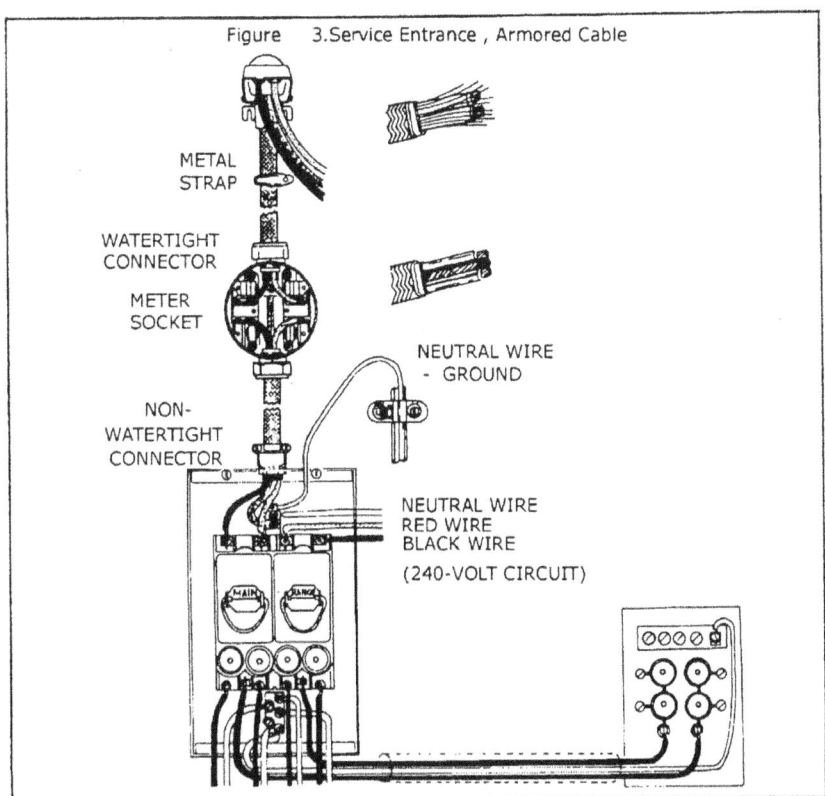

Figure 3. Service Entrance, Armored Cable

Figure 4 shows the use of thin-wall conduit in a service entrance.

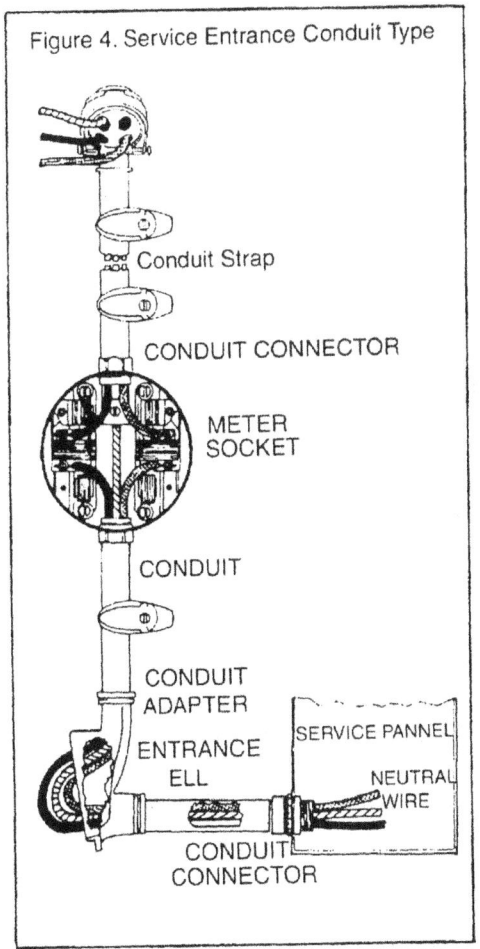

Figure 4. Service Entrance Conduit Type

B Underground Service

When wires are run underground they must be protected from moisture and physical damage. The opening in the building foundation where the underground service enters the building must be moisture proof. Local codes should be referred to, concerning allowable materials for this type of service entrance.

C Electric Meter

The electric meter may be located inside or outside the building, as shown in Figure 3 or 4. The meter itself is weatherproof and is plugged into a weatherproof socket (see Figure 5). The electric power company furnishes the meter, the socket may or may not be furnished by the power company.

IV. Grounding

The system ground consists of grounding the neutral incoming wire as well as the neutral wire of the branch circuits. The equipment ground consists of grounding the metal parts of the service entrance, such as the service switch, as well as the service entrance conduit, armor, or cable.

The usual ground connection is to a water pipe of the city water system. The connection should be made to the street side of the cold water meter as shown in Figure 6.

If the water meter is located near the street curb, then the ground connection should be made to the cold water pipe as close as possible to where it enters the building.

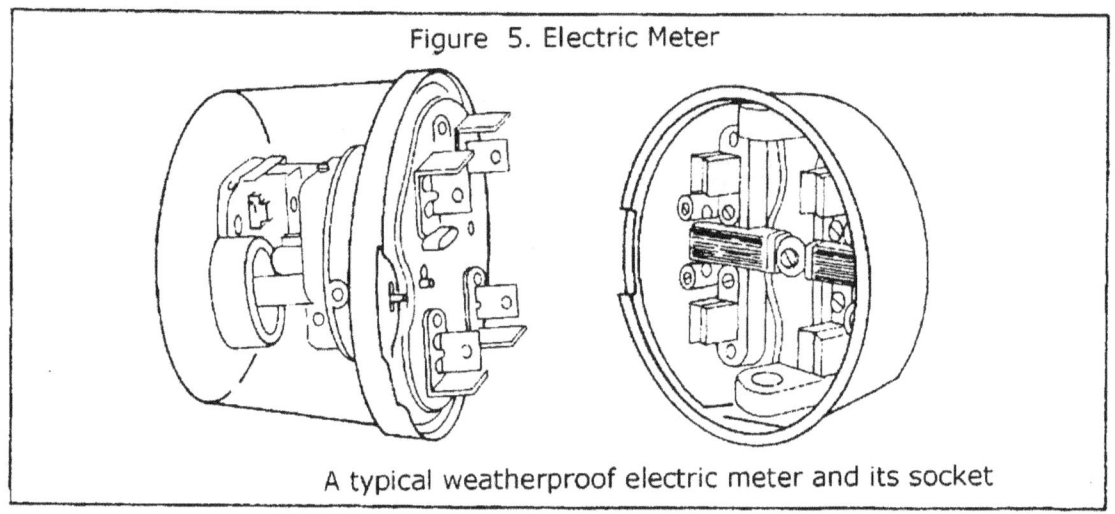

Figure 5. Electric Meter

A typical weatherproof electric meter and its socket

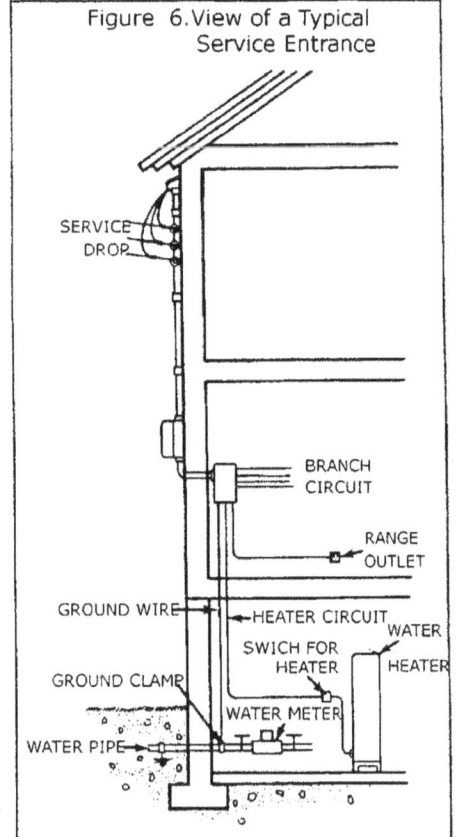

Figure 6. View of a Typical Service Entrance

It is not unusual for a water meter to be removed from a building for service. If the ground connection is made at a point in the water piping system on the building side of the water meter, the ground circuit will be broken upon removal of the meter. This broken ground circuit represents a shock hazard if both sides of the water meter connections should be touched simultaneously.

In some instances the connections between the water meter to pipes are electrically very poor. In this case, if the ground connection is made on the building side of the water meter, there may not be an effective ground.

In order to prevent the two aforementioned situations the code requires that an effective bonding shall be provided around any equipment that is likely to be disconnected for repairs or replacement. This is illustrated in Figure 7. The same jumper arrangement would be required for a water meter that is installed near the curb. In many installations the water meter mounting bracket is designed to serve as an electric jumper.

Often an amateur mechanic, in the process of doing a household repair, will disconnect the house ground. Therefore, the housing inspector should always check the house ground to see if it is properly connected.

Figure 8 shows a typical grounding scheme at the service box of a residence. In this figure, only the grounded neutral wires are shown. The neutral strap is an uninsulated metal strip that is riveted directly to the service box. The ground wires from the service entrance, branch circuits, and house ground are joined by this strip.

When a city water supply is not available for grounding, a substitute must be made. The most common ground is a pipe or rod that is driven into the ground a distance of at least 8 feet. If the pipe is made of steel or iron, it must be 3/4 inch in diameter and galvanized. A copper ground pipe of 1/2 inch diameter is sufficient.

The code requires that a ground rod be entirely independent of and kept at least 6 feet from any other ground of the type used for radio, telephone, or lightning rods.

V. Two- or Three-Wire Electric Services

One of the wires in every installation is grounded. This neutral wire is always white. The hot wires are usually black or red or some other color, but never white.

The potential difference or voltage between the hot wires and the ground or neutral of a normal residential electrical system is 115

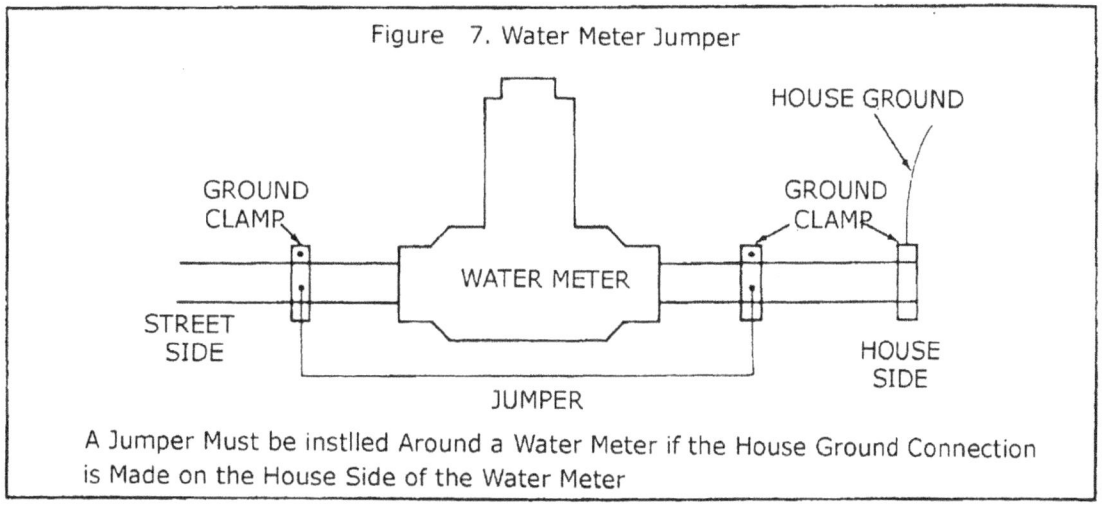

Figure 7. Water Meter Jumper

A Jumper Must be instlled Around a Water Meter if the House Ground Connection is Made on the House Side of the Water Meter

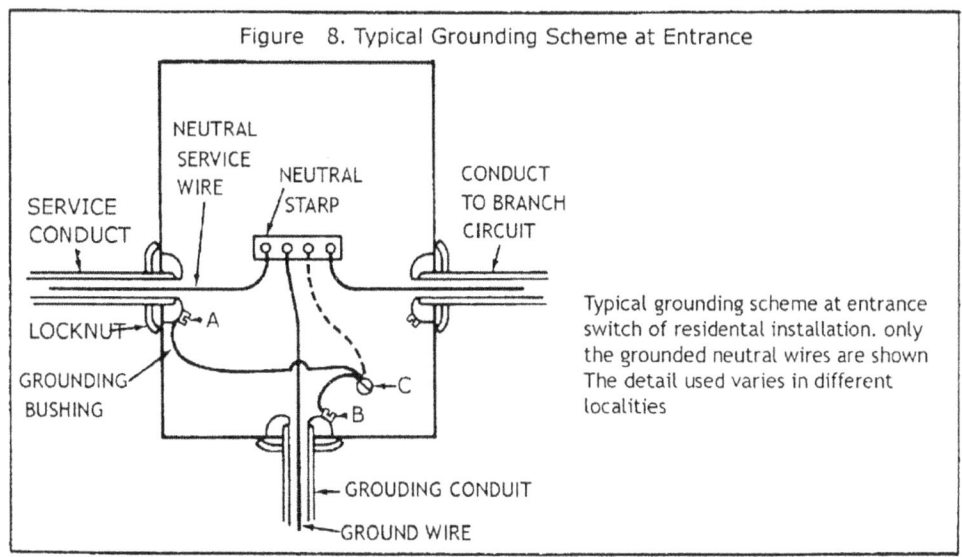

Figure 8. Typical Grounding Scheme at Entrance

Typical grounding scheme at entrance switch of residental installation. only the grounded neutral wires are shown The detail used varies in different localities

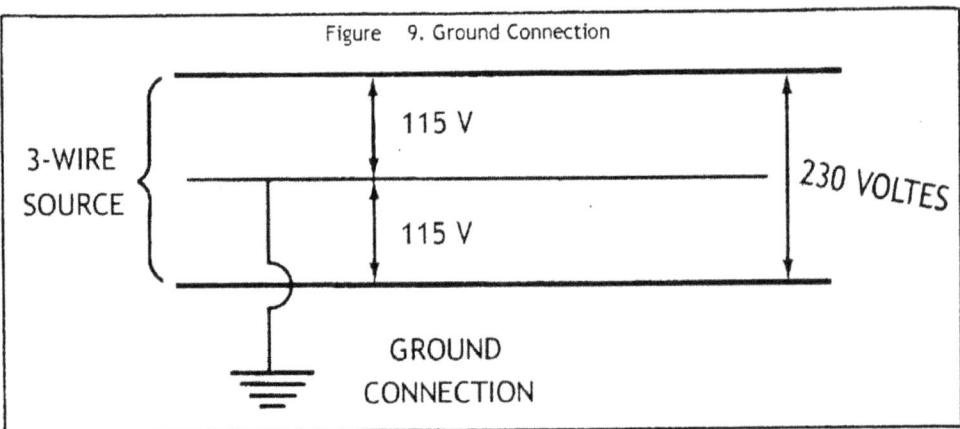

Figure 9. Ground Connection

volts. Thus, where we have a two-wire installation (one hot and one neutral) only 115-volt power is available (see Figure 9).

When three wires are installed (two hot and one neutral) either 115- or 230-volt power is available. In a three-wire system the voltage between the neutral and either of the hot wires is 115; between the two hot wires it is 230 volts.

The major advantage of a three-wire system is that it permits the operation of heavy electrical equipment such as laundry dryers, cooking ranges, and air conditioners, the majority of which require 230-volt circuits. In addition, the three-wire system is split at the service panel into two 115-volt systems to supply power for small appliances and electric lights. The result is a doubling of the number of circuits, and possibly a corresponding increase in the number of branch circuits, with a reduction of the probability of fire caused by overloading electrical circuits.

VI. Residential Wiring Adequacy

The use of electricity in the home has risen sharply since the 1930's. Many home owners have failed to repair or improve their wiring to keep it safe and up to date. The National Electrical Code recommends that individual residences be provided with a minimum of 100-ampere three-wire service. This type service is sufficient in a one-family house or dwelling unit to provide safe and adequate electric supply for the lighting, refrigerator, iron, and an 8,000-watt cooking range, plus other appliances requiring a total of up to 10,000 watts altogether.

Some homes have a 60-ampere, three-wire service. It is recommended that these homes be rewired for at least the minimum of 100 amperes recommended in the National Code since they are safely capable of supplying current only for lighting and portable appliances such as a cooking range and regular dryer (4,500 watts), or an electric hot-water heater (2,500 watts) and cannot handle additional major appliances.

Other homes today have only a 30-ampere, 115-volt, two-wire service. This system can safely handle only a limited amount of lighting, a few minor appliances, and no major appliances. Therefore, this size service is substandard in terms of modern household needs for electricity. Furthermore, it constitutes a fire hazard and a threat to the safety of the home and the occupants.

VII. Wire Size and Types

A Wire Size

Electric power flows over wire. It flows with relative ease (little resistance) in some materials such as copper and with a substantial amount of resistance in iron. If iron wire were used it would have to be 10 times as large as copper wire.

Copper wire sizes are indicated by a number. No. 14 is most commonly used in residential branch circuits. No. 14 is the smallest permitted by the Code for use in a branch circuit with a 15-ampere capacity. No. 16, 18, and 20 are progressively smaller than No. 14 and are usually used for extension wires. As the number of the wire becomes smaller the size and current capacity of the wire increases. No. 1 is the heaviest wire usually used in ordinary household wiring.

Wire of correct size must be used for two reasons: current capacity and voltage drop.

1. When current flows through a wire it creates heat. The greater the amount of flow, the greater the amount of heat generated. (Doubling the amperes without changing the wire size increases the amount of heat by four times.) The heat is electric energy that has been converted into heat energy by the resistance of the wire; the heat created by the coils in a toaster is an example. This heat developed in an electrical conductor is wasted, and thus the electric energy used to generate it is wasted. If the amount of heat generated by the flow of current through the wire becomes excessive, a fire may result. Therefore, the code sets the maximum permissible current that may flow through a certain type and size wire.
The following are examples of current capacities for copper wire of various sizes.

Size wire (AWG)	#14	#12	#10	#8
Max. capacity, amperes	15	20	30	40

2. In addition to heat generation there will be a reduction in voltage as a result of attempting to force more current through a wire than it is capable of carrying. Certain appliances, such as induction-type electric motors, may be damaged if operated at too low a voltage.

B Wire Types

1. **Wire markings** - All wires must be marked to indicate the maximum working voltage, the proper type letter or letters for the type wire specified in the code, the manufacturer's name or trademark, and the AWG size or circular-mil area.

2. **Insulations used** There are a variety of wire types which can be used for a wide range of temperature and moisture conditions. The 1975 National Electrical Code should be consulted to determine the proper wire for specific conditions.

C Types of Cable

1. **Nonmetallic Sheathed Cable** - This type of cable consists of wires wrapped in a paper layer, followed by another spiral layer of paper, and enclosed in a fabric braid, which is treated with moisture-resistant and fire-resistant compounds. Figure 10 shows this type of cable, which often is marketed under the "Romex" name. This type of cable can be used only indoors and in permanently dry locations.

2. **Armored Cable** - This type of cable is commonly known by the BX or Flex-steel trade names. Wires are wrapped in a tough paper and covered with a strong spiral flexible steel armor. This type of cable is shown in Figure 11 and may be used only in permanently dry indoor locations. Armored cable must be supported by a strap or staple every 6 feet and within 24 inches of every switch or junction box, except for concealed runs in old work where it is impossible to mount straps.

3. **Other Cable** Cables are also available with other outer coatings of metals such as copper, bronze, and aluminum for use in a variety of conditions.

D Flexible Cords

Flexible cords are used to connect lamps, appliances, and other devices to outlets. Each wire consists of many strands of fine wire for flexibility. Extension cords in AWG sizes 16 to 18 are usually fine for lamps and smaller appliances, if the cord is not too long. A commonly accepted standard limits their length to 8 feet of unspliced cord. This keeps the cords short enough to prevent the excessive voltage drops, minimizes the possibility of fire caused by overheating of the wire due to overload, and also minimizes the danger of someone's tripping over them.

E Open Wiring

Open wiring is a wiring method using knobs, nonmetallic tubes, cleats, and flexible tubing for the protection and support of insulated conductors in or on buildings and not concealed by the structure. The term "open wiring" does not mean exposed, bare wiring. In dry locations when not exposed to severe

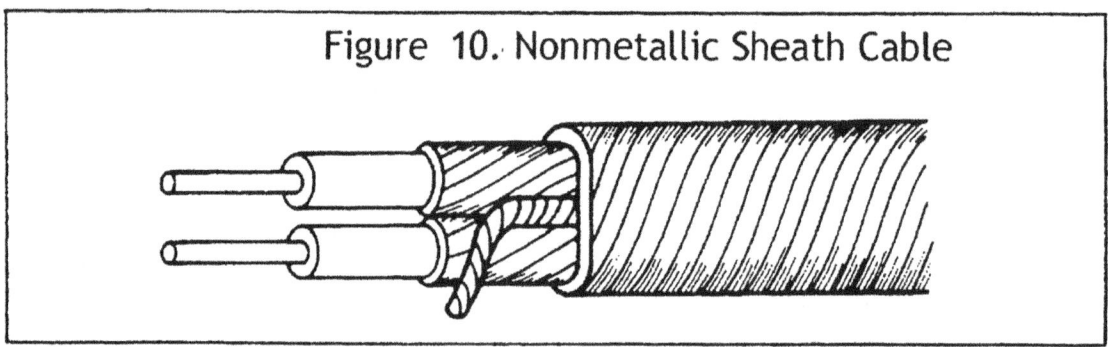

Figure 10. Nonmetallic Sheath Cable

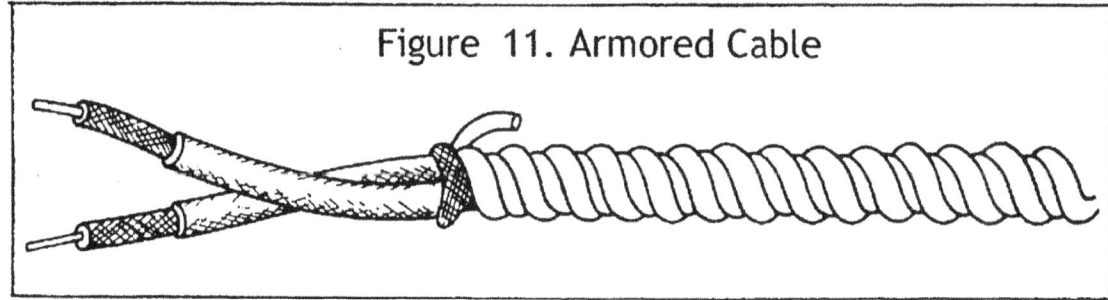

Figure 11. Armored Cable

physical damage, conductors may be separately encased in flexible tubing. Tubing should be in continuous lengths not exceeding 15 feet and secured to the surface by straps not more than 4 1/2 feet apart. They should be separated from other conductors by at least 2 1/2 inches and should have a permanently maintained airspace between them and any and all pipes they cross.

F Concealed Knob and Tube Wiring

Concealed knob and tube wiring is a wiring method using knobs, tubes, and flexible nonmetallic tubing for the protection and support of insulated wires concealed in hollow spaces of walls and ceilings of buildings. This wiring method is similar to open wiring, and like open wiring, is usually found only in older buildings.

VIII. Electric Service Panel

Service Switch

This is a main switch that will disconnect the entire electrical system at one time. The main fuses or circuit breakers are usually located within the "Service Switch" box. The branch circuit fuse or circuit breaker may also be located within this box.

According to the code, the switch must be "externally operable." This condition is fulfilled if the switch can be operated without the operator's being exposed to electrically active parts. Older switches use external handles as shown in Figure 12.

Most of today's service switches do not have hinged switch blades. Instead, the main fuse is mounted on a small insulated block that can be pulled out of the switch. When this block is removed, the circuit is broken just as if the blades had been operated with a handle.

The neutral terminal or wire of a grounded circuit must never be interrupted by a fuse or circuit breaker. In some installations the service switch is a "solid neutral" switch. This means that the neutral wire in the switch is not broken by the switch or a fuse.

When circuit breakers instead of fuses are used in homes, the use of main circuit breakers may or may not be required. If it takes not more than six movements of the hand to open all the branch-circuit breakers, no main breaker or switch or fuse will be required ahead of the branch-circuit breakers. Thus, a house with seven or more branch circuits requires a separate disconnect means or a main circuit breaker ahead of the branch-circuit breakers (see Figure 13).

IX. Overcurrent Devices

The amperage (current flow) in any wire is limited to the maximum permitted by using an overcurrent device of a

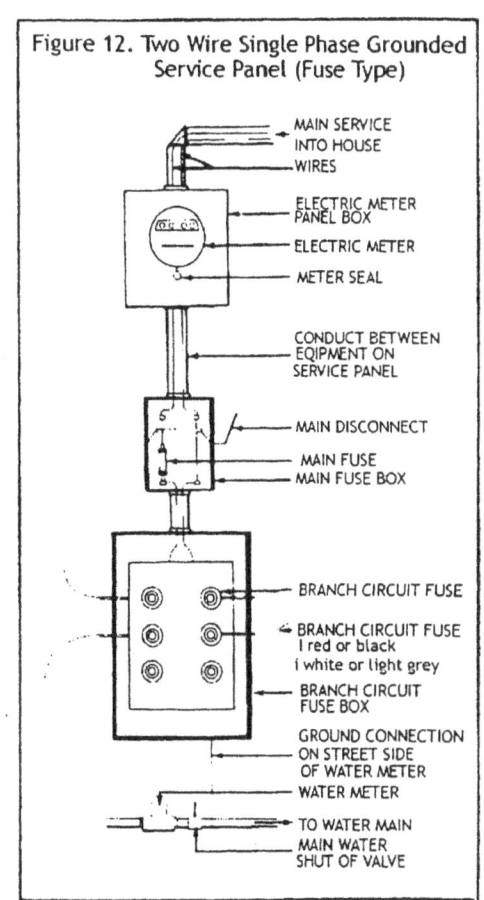

Figure 12. Two Wire Single Phase Grounded Service Panel (Fuse Type)

specific size as specified by the code. Two types of overcurrent devices are in common use: circuit breakers and fuses; both are rated in amperes. The overcurrent device must be rated at equal or lower capacity than the wire of the circuit it protects.

A Circuit Breakers (Fuseless) Service Panels

A circuit breaker (see Figure 14) looks something like an ordinary electric light switch. There is a handle that may be used to turn power on or off. Inside is a simple mechanism that, in case of a circuit overload, trips the switch and breaks the circuit. The circuit breaker may be reset by simply flipping the switch. A circuit breaker is capable of taking harmless short-period overloads (such as the heavy initial current required in the starting of a washing machine or air conditioner) without tripping but protects against prolonged overloads. After the cause of trouble

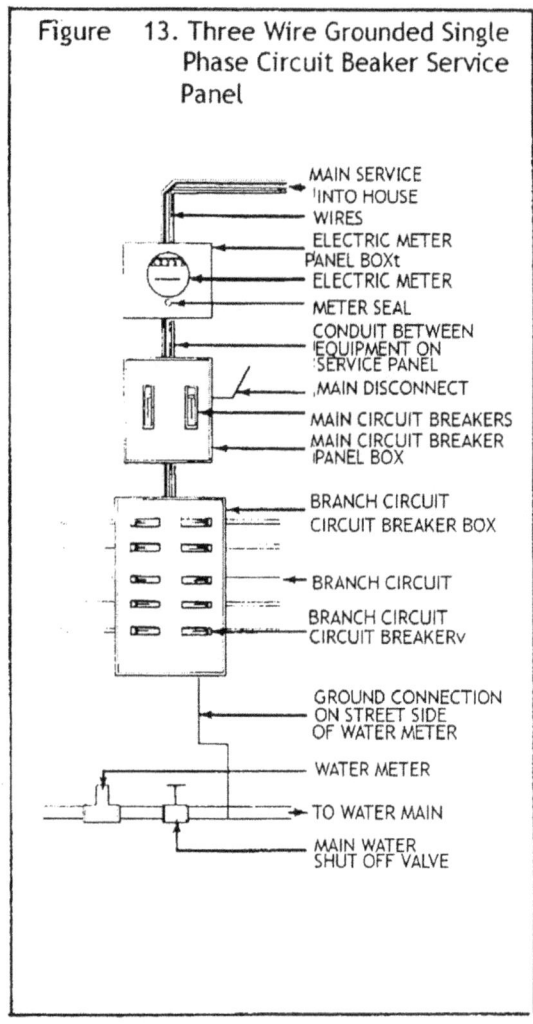

Figure 13. Three Wire Grounded Single Phase Circuit Beaker Service Panel

has been located and corrected, the power is easily restored by flipping the circuit breaker switch (circuit breakers are modern substitutes for fuses). Fuseless service panels are usually broken up into the following circuits.

1. A 100-ampere or larger main circuit breaker that shuts off all power.
2. A 40-ampere circuit for an appliance such as an electric cooking range. against the dangers of overloading
3. A 30-ampere circuit for clothes dryer, hot water heater, or central air conditioning.
4. A 20-ampere circuit for kitchen, small appliances, and power tools.
5. A 15-ampere circuit for general purpose lighting, TV, and vacuum cleaner.
6. Space for circuits to be added if needed for future use.

B Fused Ampere Service Panel or Fuse Box

Fuse-type panel boxes are generally found in older homes. They are equally as safe and adequate as a circuit breaker of equivalent capacity, provided fuses of the proper size are used.

A fuse (see Figure 15), like a circuit breaker, is designed to protect a circuit and short circuits and does this in two manners.

a. When a fuse is blown by a short circuit the metal strip is instantly heated to an extremely high temperature, and this heat causes it to vaporize. A fuse blown by a short circuit may be easily recognized because the window of the fuse usually becomes discolored.

b. In a fuse blown by overload the metal strip is melted at its weakest point, and this breaks the flow of current to the load. In this case the window of the fuse remains clear; therefore, a blown fuse caused by an overload may also be easily recognized.

Sometimes, although a fuse has not been blown, the bottom of the fuse may be severely discolored and pitted. This indicates a loose connection due to the fuse's not being screwed in properly.

Generally, all fused panel boxes are wired similarly for two- and three-wire systems. In a two-wire-circuit panel box the black or red hot wire is connected to a terminal of the main disconnect, and the white or light gray neutral wire is connected to the neutral strip, which is then grounded to the pipe on the street side of the water meter.

In a three-wire system the black and red hot wires are connected to separate terminals of the main disconnect, and the neutral wire is grounded the same as for a two-wire system (see Figure 12). Below each fuse is a terminal to which a black or red wire is connected. The white or light gray neutral wires are then connected to the neutral strip. Each fuse indicates a separate circuit.

1. **Non-tamperable Fuses** - All ordinary plug fuses, shown in Figure 15, have the same diameter and physical appearance regardless of their current capacity. Thus, if a circuit designed for a 15-ampere fuse is overloaded so that the 15-ampere fuse blows out, nothing will prevent a person from replacing the 15-ampere fuse with a 20- or 30-ampere fuse, which may not blow out. If a circuit wired with No. 14 wire (current capacity 15 amperes) is fused with a 20- or 30-ampere fuse and an overload develops, more current than the No. 14 wire is safely capable of carrying could pass through the circuit. The result would be a heating of the wire and a potential fire.

Type S fuses, shown in Figure 15, have different lengths and diameter threads for each different amperage capacity. An adapter is first inserted into the ordinary fuse holder, which adapts the fuse holder for only one capacity fuse. Once the adapter is inserted, it cannot be removed.

2. **Cartridge Fuses**

Figure 15 shows two different types of cartridge fuses. A cartridge fuse protects an electric circuit in the same manner as an ordinary plug fuse already described protects it. Cartridge fuses are often used as main fuses.

X. Electric Circuits

An electric circuit in good repair carries electricity through two or three wires from the source of supply to an outlet and back to the source.

A Branch Circuit

A branch circuit is an electric circuit that supplies electric current to a limited number of electric outlets and fixtures. A residence generally has many branch circuits. Each is protected against short circuits and overloads by a 15- or 20-ampere fuse or circuit breaker.

The number of outlets per branch circuit varies from building to building. The code requires enough light circuits so that 3 watts of power will be available for each square foot of floor area

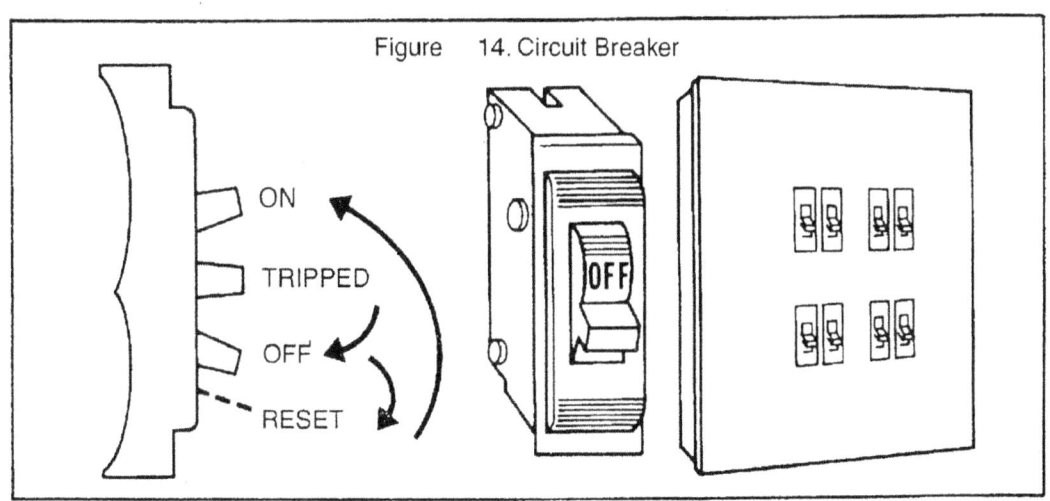
Figure 14. Circuit Breaker

Figure 15. Types of Fuses

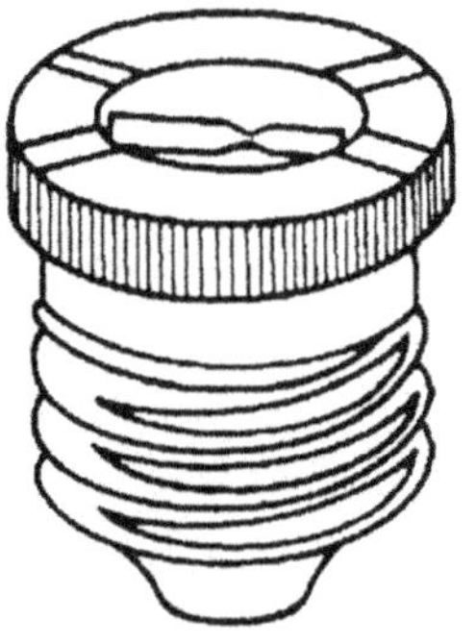

Plug fuses are not made in ratings over 30 amp.

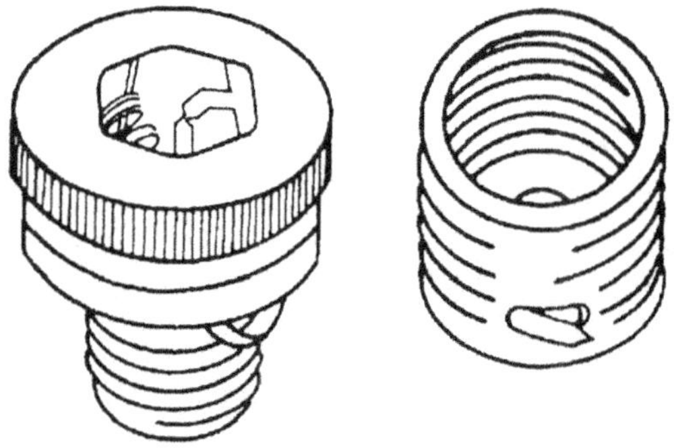

A typical Type-S non-tamperable fuse, and its adapter. Once an adapter has been screwed into a fuse-holder, it cannot be removed. This prevents use of fuses larger than originally intended.

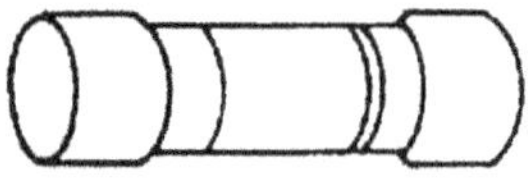

Cartridge fuses rated 60 amps, or less are of the ferrule type shown.

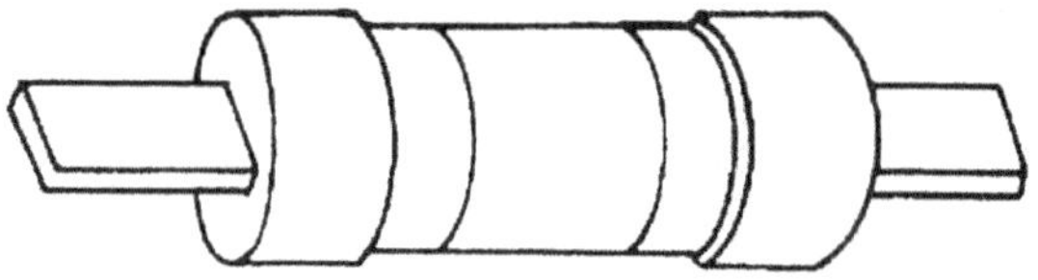

Cartridge fuses rated more than 60 amp. have knife-blade terminals shown.

in a house. A circuit wired with No. 14 wire and protected by a 15-ampere overcurrent protection device provides 15 X 115 or 1,725 watts; each circuit is obviously enough for 1,725/3 or 575 square feet.

Note that 575 is a minimum figure; if future use is considered, 500 or even 400 square feet per branch circuit should be used.

B   Special Appliance Circuits

The branch circuit will provide electric power for lighting, radio, television, and small portable appliances. However, the larger electric appliances usually found in the kitchen consume more power and must have their own special circuit.

Section 220-3b of the code requires two special circuits to serve only appliance outlets in kitchen, laundry, pantry, family-room, dining room, and breakfast room. Both circuits must be extended to the kitchen; the other rooms may be served by either one or both of these circuits. No lighting outlets may be connected to these circuits, and they must be wired with No. 12 wire and protected by a 20-ampere overcurrent device. Each circuit will have a capacity of 20 X 115 or 2,300 watts, which is not too much when one considers that toasters often require over 1,600 watts.

C   Individual Appliance Circuits

It is customary to provide a circuit for each of the following appliances:

1. Range
2. Water heater
3. Automatic laundry
4. Clothes dryer

5   Garbage disposer
6   Dishwasher
7   Furnace
8   Water pump

Note that these circuits may be either 115 volts or 230 volts, depending on the particular appliance or motor installed.

D Outlet Switch and Junction Boxes

The code requires that every switch, outlet, and joint in wire or cable be housed in a box. Every fixture must be mounted on a box. Most boxes are made of metal with a galvanized finish. Figure 16 shows a typical outlet box.

When a cable of any style is used for wiring, the code requires that it be securely anchored with a connector to each box it enters.

E Grounding Outlets

An electrical appliance may appear to be in good repair, and yet it might be a danger to the user. Consider a portable electric drill. It consists of an electric motor inside a metal casing. When the switch is depressed, the current flows to the motor, and the drill rotates. As a result of wear, however, the insulation on the wire inside the drill may deteriorate and allow the hot side of the power cord to come in contact with the metal casing. This will not affect the operation of the drill.

A person fully clothed using the drill in the living room, which has a dry floor, will not receive a shock, even though he is in contact with the electrified drill case. His body is not grounded, because of the dry floor. If, however, the operator should be standing on a wet basement floor, his body might be grounded, and when he touches the electrified drill case, current will pass through his body.

In order to protect man, the drill case is usually connected to the system ground by means of a wire called an "appliance ground." In this instance, as the drill is plugged in, current will flow between the shorted hot wire and the drill case and cause the overcurrent device to break the circuit. Thus the appliance ground has protected man. The appliance ground is the third wire found on many appliances.

The appliance ground on the appliance will be of no use unless the outlet into which the appliance is plugged is grounded. The outlet is grounded by being in physical contact with a ground outlet box. The outlet box is grounded by having a third ground wire, or a grounded conduit, as part of the circuit wiring.

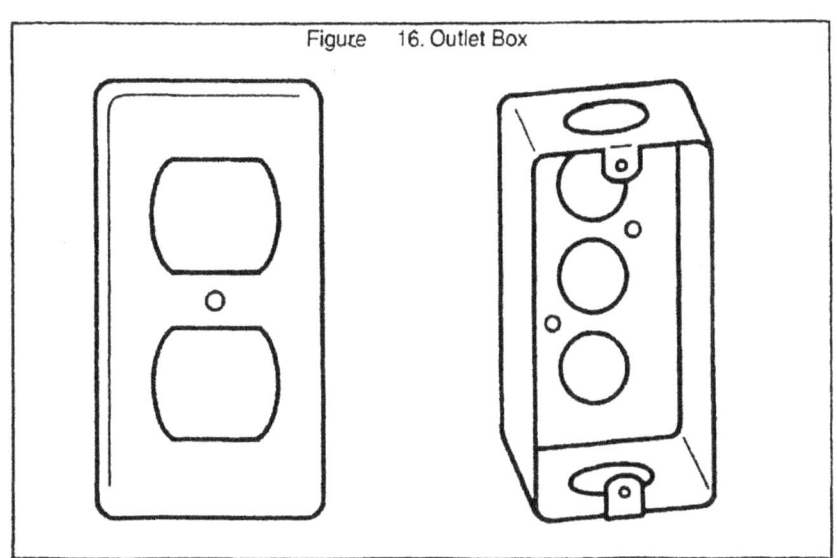
Figure 16. Outlet Box

All new buildings are required to have grounded outlets (as shown in Figure 17). The outlet may be tested by using a circuit tester. The circuit tester should light when both of its leads are plugged into the two elongated parallel openings of the outlet. In addition, the tester should light when one lead is plugged into the round third opening and the other is plugged into the hot side of the outlet.

If the conventional two-opening outlet is used, it still may be grounded. In this instance the screw that holds the outlet cover plate is the third-wire ground. The tester should light when one lead is in contact with a clean paint-free metal outlet cover plate screw and the hot side of the outlet. If the tester fails to light then the outlet is not grounded. If the outlet is not grounded then the tester will not function.

If a two-opening outlet is grounded, it may be adapted for use by a three-wire appliance by using an adapter. The loose-wire portion of the adapter should be secured behind the metal screw of the outlet plate cover.

Many appliances such as electric shavers and some new hand tools are double insulated and are safe without having a third ground wire.

XI. Common Electrical Violations

A The most apparent requirements that a housing inspector must check are the existence of the power supply; the types, locations, and conditions of the wiring in use; and the existence of the number of wall outlets or ceiling fixtures required by his local code and their condition. In making his investigations, these considerations will serve as useful guides:

1 **Power Supply** - Where is it located, is it grounded properly, and is it at least of minimum capacity required to supply current safely for lighting and the major and minor appliances in the dwelling?

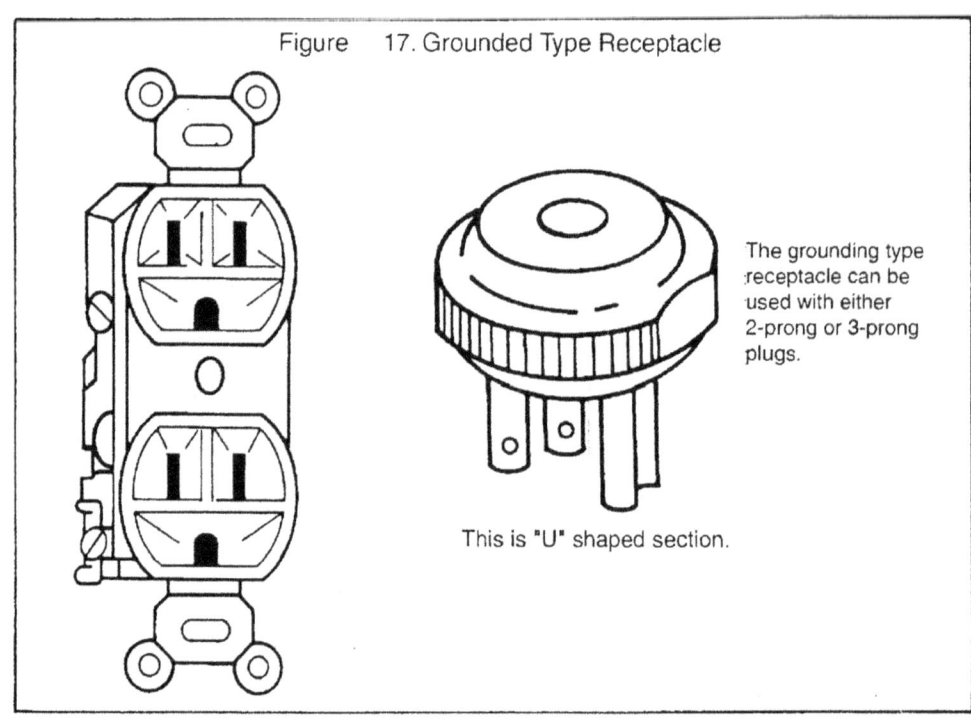

Figure 17. Grounded Type Receptacle

The grounding type receptacle can be used with either 2-prong or 3-prong plugs.

This is "U" shaped section.

2. **Panel Box Covers or Doors** - These should be accessible only from the front and should be sealed in such a way that they can be operated safely without the danger of contact with live or exposed parts of the wiring system.

3. **Switch, Outlets, and Junction Boxes** - These also must be covered to protect against danger of electric shock.

4. **Frayed or Bare Wires** - These are usually the result of long use and a drying out and cracking of the insulation, which leave the wires exposed, or else a result of constant friction and rough handling of the wire, which cause it to fray or become bare. Wiring in this condition constitutes a safety hazard, and correction of such defects should be ordered immediately.

5. **Electric Cords Under Rugs or Other Floor Coverings** - Putting electric cords in locations such as these is prohibited because of the potential fire hazard caused by continuing contact over a period of time between these heat-bearing cords and the flammable floor coverings. Direct the occupant to shift the cords to a safe location, explain why, and make sure it is done before you leave.

6. **Bathroom Lighting** - It should include at least one permanently installed ceiling or wall light fixture with a wall switch and plate so located and maintained that there is no danger of short circuiting from use of other bathroom facilities or splashing of water. Fixture or cover plates should be insulated or grounded.

7. **Lighting of Public Hallways, Stairways, Landings, and Foyers** A common standard here is sufficient lighting to provide illumination of 10 foot-candles on every part of these areas at all times. Sufficient lighting means that a person can clearly see his feet on all parts of the stairways and halls. Every public hall and stairway in a structure containing *less than three* dwelling units may be supplied with conveniently located light switches controlling an adequate lighting system that may be turned on when needed, instead of full-time lighting.

8. **Habitable Room Lighting** - The standard here may be two floor convenience outlets although floor outlets are dangerous unless protected by proper dust and water covers or one convenience outlet and one wall or ceiling electric light fixture. This number constitutes an absolute and often inadequate minimum given the contemporary widespread use of electricity in the home. The minimum should be that number required to provide adequate lighting and power to accommodate lighting and appliances normally used in each room.

9. **Octopus Outlets or Wiring** - This term is applied to outlets into which plugs have been inserted and are being used to permit more than two lights or portable appliances, such as a TV, lamp, or radio, to be connected to the electrical system. The condition occurs where the number of outlets is insufficient to accommodate the normal use of the room. This practice overloads the circuit and is a potential source of fire, which may be caused by overloading the circuit.

10. **Outlet Covers** - Every outlet and receptacle must be covered by a protective plate to prevent contact of its wiring or terminals with the body, combustible object or splashing water.

The following items are conditions that cause needless dangers and must also be corrected:

a. **Excessive or faulty fusing** - The wire's capacity must not be exceeded by the fuse or circuit breaker capacity or be left unprotected by faulty fusing or circuit breakers. Fuses and circuit breakers are safety devices designed to "blow" as a means of protection against overloadings of the electrical system or one or more of its circuits. Pennies under fuses are put there to bypass the fuse. These are illegal and must be removed. Overfusing is done for the same reason. The latter can be prevented by the installation of modern fuse stats, which prevent use of any fuse of a higher amperage than can be handled by the circuit it serves.

b **Cords run through walls or doorways and hanging cords or wires** - This is a makeshift-type installation and most often is installed by an unqualified handyman or do-it-yourself occupant. The inspector should check with his local electrical section to determine the policy regarding this type of insulation and govern his action in accordance with the electrical section's policies.

c **Temporary wiring** - This type of installation should not be allowed, with the exception of extension cords that go directly from portable lights and electric fixtures to convenience outlets.

d **Excessively long extension cords** - This requirement does not apply to specially designed extension cords for operating portable tools and trouble lights. Cities operating under modern code standards limit the length of loose cords or extension lines to a maximum of 8 feet. This is necessary because those that are too long will overheat if overloaded or if a short circuit develops and thus create a fire hazard. Even shorter lengths are feasible in housing with new or updated wiring systems that include one convenience outlet every 12 feet around the perimeter of the room.

e **Dead or dummy outlets** - These are sometimes installed to deceive the inspection agency. This is why all outlets must be tested or the occupants questioned to see if these are alive and functioning properly. A dead outlet cannot be counted to determine compliance with the code.

XII. Steps Involved in Actual Inspection

A **Testing Tools**
The basic tools required by an inspector of housing for making an electrical inspection are a fuse and circuit tester and a flashlight.

B **Danger of Techniques**

The first thing is to remember you are in a strange house and the layout is unfamiliar to you. The second thing to remember is that you are dealing with electricity *take no chances*. Go to the water meter and check the ground. It should connect to the water line on the street side of the water meter or else be equipped with a jumper wire. Do not touch any box or wire until you are sure of the ground. Go to the main fuse box and check all fuses in all boxes. Note the condition of the wiring and of the box itself and check whether it is overfused or not. Examine all wiring in the cellar. Make sure you are standing in a dry spot before touching any electrical device. Do not disassemble the fuse box or other devices. Decisions must be made on what you see. If in doubt, consult your supervisor.

Make note whether any fuse boxes or junction boxes are uncovered. Examine all wiring for frayed or bare spots, improper splicing, or rotted, worn, or inadequate insulation. Avoid all careless touching. When in doubt DON'T! If you see bare wire, have the owner call an electrician. Look for wires or cords in use in the cellar. Many work benches are lighted by an old lamp that was once in the parlor and now has a spliced or badly frayed cord or both. Be certain all switch boxes and outlets are in a tight, sound condition.

Make sure that the emergency switch for the oil burner is at the top of the cellar stairs, not on top of the unit.

If you find an electric clothes washer-clothes dryer combination in a dwelling, it should have a 240-volt circuit 30-ampere service connected to a separate fuse or circuit breaker. Washer-dryer combinations and other portable appliances in the entire house should be served by sufficiently heavy service. If either of these special lines is not available under the above-stated conditions, consult your supervisor.

An electric range needs a 50-ampere circuit, 240 volts. A dishwasher needs a 20-ampere, 120-volt circuit. A separate three-wire circuit must be installed for an electric water heater. Continue your inspection this way through the house. In the bathroom look for the usual items, but also check for dangerous items such as radios or plug-in portable electric heaters. Have them removed immediately. Such items have killed thousands of people either has a spliced or badly frayed cord or both. Be certain all switch boxes and outlets are in a tight, sound condition. Make sure that the emergency switch for the oil burner is at the top of the cellar stairs, not on top of the unit.

If you find an electric clothes washer-clothes dryer combination in a dwelling, it should have a 240-volt circuit 30-ampere service connected to a separate fuse or circuit breaker. Washer-dryer combinations and other portable appliances in the entire house should be served by sufficiently heavy service. If either of these special lines is not available under the above-stated conditions, consult your supervisor.

An electric range needs a 50-ampere circuit, 240 volts. A dishwasher needs a 20-ampere, 120-volt circuit. A separate three-wire circuit must be installed for an electric water heater. Continue your inspection this way through the because they touched them after getting out of the bathtub or shower while still wet or because the appliance fell into the water. Look for brass pull chains in bathroom lighting fixtures. If one exists, have owner attach a string to the end of it as a temporary precaution, then order it replaced with a wall switch as required by the electrical code.

To sum up, in broad terms, the housing inspector's investigation of specified electrical elements in a house is made to detect any obvious evidence of an insufficient power supply, to ensure the availability of adequate and safe lighting and electrical facilities, and to discover and correct any obvious hazard. Because electricity is a technical, complicated field, the housing inspector, when in doubt, should consult his supervisor. He cannot, however, close the case until appropriate corrective action has been taken on all such referrals.

XIII. Wattage Consumption of Electrical Appliances

(100 watts = approximately 1 ampere)

Appliance	Watts
Air conditioner (central)	5,000
Air conditioner (window)	see name plate
Blanket	150
Blender	250
Chaffing Dish	600
Clock	3
Coffee Maker	600
Deep fryer	1,320
Dishwasher	1,800
Egg boiler	250
Electric shaver	10
Fan	75
Food mixer	200
Furnace (fuel fixed)	800
Frying pan	600
Garbage disposer	900
Griddle	1,300
Grill	600
Heater (radiant)	1,600
Heating pad	50
Hot-plate (2 burners)	1,650
Humidifier	500
Immersion heater	300
Iron	1,000
Ironer	1,650
Lighting	
Bed lamp	40
Ceiling light	100
Decorative lights	80
Dining light	150
Dresser lamps	60
Drop light	60
Floor lamp	400
Fluorescent	80
Sun lamp	275
Table lamp	100

Appliance	Watts
Radio	100
Range	8,000 to 16,000
Refrigerator	250
Roaster (large)	1,380
Rotisserie	1,400
Sewing machine	75
Soldering iron	200
Stereo hi-fi	300
Sump pump	300
Television	300
Toaster	1,100
Vacuum cleaner	400
Waffle iron	660
Washing machine	5,200
Water heater	2,500-4,500
Water pump	300

XIV. Motor Currents

Horsepower	Full load amperes			
	115 v	230 1-phase	230 2-phase	230 3-phase
1/4	5.8	2.9		
1/2	9.8	4.9	2.0	2.0
3/4	13.8	6.9	2.4	2.8
1	16.0	8.0	3.2	3.6

PLUMBING ELEMENTS OF A HOUSING INSPECTION

CONTENTS

	PAGE
I. Background Factors	1
II. Definitions	1
III. Main Features of an Indoor Plumbing System	3
IV. Elements of a Plumbing System	3

PLUMBING ELEMENTS OF A HOUSING INSPECTION

Plumbing may be defined as practice, materials, and fixtures used in the installation, maintenance, and alteration of all piping, fixtures, appliances, and appurtenances in connection with sanitary or storm drainage facilities, the venting system, and the public or private water supply systems. **Plumbing** does not include the trade of drilling water wells, installing water softening equipment, or the business of manufacturing or selling plumbing fixtures, appliances, equipment, or hardware. A plumbing system consists of three separate parts: an adequate potable water supply system; a safe, adequate drainage system; and ample fixtures and equipment.

I. Background Factors

The generalized inspector of housing is concerned with a safe water supply system, an adequate drainage system, and ample and proper fixtures and equipment. This chapter covers the major features of a residential plumbing system and the basic plumbing terms the inspector must know and understand to identify properly housing code violations involving plumbing and the more complicated defects that he will refer to the appropriate agencies.

II. Definitions

1 **Air Chambers** — Air Chambers are pressure absorbing devices that eliminate water hammer. They should be installed as close as possible to the valves or faucet and at the end of long runs of pipe.

2 **Air Gap (Drainage System)** — The unobstructed vertical distance through the free atmosphere between the outlet of a water pipe and the flood level rim of the receptacle into which it is discharging.

3 **Air Gap (Water Distribution System)** — The unobstructed vertical distance through the free atmosphere between the lowest opening from any pipe or faucet supplying water to a tank, plumbing fixture, or other device and the flood level rim of the receptacle.

4 **Air Lock** — An air lock is a bubble of air which restricts the flow of water in a pipe.

5 **Backflow** — Backflow is the flow of water or other liquids, mixtures, or substances into the distributing pipes of a potable water supply from any source or sources other than the intended source. Back siphonage is one type of backflow.

6 **Back Siphonage** — Back siphonage is the flowing back of used, contaminated, or polluted water from a plumbing fixture or vessel into a potable water supply due to a negative pressure in the pipe.

7 **Branch** — A branch is any part of the piping system other than the main, riser, or stack.

8 **Branch Vent** — A vent connecting one or more individual vents with a vent stack.

9 **Building Drain** — The building (house) drain is the part of the lowest piping of a drainage system that receives the discharge from soil, waste, or other drainage pipes inside the walls of the building (house) and conveys it to the building sewer beginning 3 feet outside the building wall.

10 **Cross Connection** — Any physical connection or arrangement between two otherwise separate piping systems, one of which contains potable water and the other either water of unknown or questionable safety or steam, gas, or chemical whereby there may be a flow from one system to the other, the direction of flow depending on the pressure differential between the two systems. (See Backflow and Back siphonage.)

11 **Disposal Field** — An area containing a series of one or more trenches lined with coarse aggregate and conveying the effluent from the septic tank through vitrified clay pipe or

perforated, non-metallic pipe, laid in such a manner that the flow will be distributed with reasonable uniformity into natural soil.

12 **Drain** — A drain is any pipe that carries waste water or water-borne waste in a building (house) drainage system.

13 **Flood Level Rim** — The top edge of a receptacle from which water overflows.

14 **Flushometer Valve** — A device that discharges a predetermined quantity of water to fixtures for flushing purposes and is closed by direct water pressures.

15 **Flush Valve** — A device located at the bottom of the tank for flushing water closets and similar fixtures.

16 **Grease Trap** — See Interceptor

17 **Hot Water** — Hot water means potable water that is heated to at least 120°F and used for cooking, cleaning, washing dishes, and bathing.

18 **Insanitary** — Contrary to sanitary principles — injurious to health.

19 **Interceptor** — A device designed and installed so as to separate and retain deleterious, hazardous, or undesirable matter from normal wastes and permit normal sewage or liquid wastes to discharge into the drainage system by gravity.

20 **Leader** — An exterior drainage pipe for conveying storm water from roof or gutter drains to the building storm drain, combined building sewer, or other means of disposal.

21 **Main Vent** — The principal artery of the venting system, to which vent branches may be connected.

22 **Main Sewer** — See Public Sewer.

23 **Pneumatic** — The word pertains to devices making use of compressed air as in pressure tanks boosted by pumps.

24 **Potable Water** — Water having no impurities present in amounts sufficient to cause disease or harmful physiological effects and conforming in its bacteriological and chemical quality to the requirements of the Public Health Service drinking water standards or meeting the regulations of the public health authority having jurisdiction.

25 **P & T (Pressure and Temperature) Relief Valve** — A safety valve installed on a hot water storage tank to limit temperature and pressure of the water.

26 **P Trap** — A trap with a vertical inlet and a horizontal outlet.

27 **Public Sewer** — A common sewer directly controlled by public authority.

28 **Relief Vent** — An auxiliary vent that permits additional circulation of air in or between drainage and vent systems.

29 **Septic Tank** — A watertight receptacle that receives the discharge of a building's sanitary drain system or part thereof and is designed and constructed so as to separate solid from the liquid, digest organic matter through a period of detention, and allow the liquids to discharge into the soil outside of the tank through a system of open-joint or perforated piping, or through a seepage pit.

30 **Sewerage System** — A sewerage system comprises all piping, appurtenances, and treatment facilities used for the collection and disposal of sewage, except plumbing inside and in connection with buildings served, and the building drain.

31 **Soil Pipe** — The pipe that directs the sewage of a house to the receiving sewer, building drain, or building sewer.

32 **Soil Stack** — The vertical piping that terminates in a roof vent and carries off the vapors of a plumbing system.

33 **Stack Vent** — An extension of a solid or waste stack above the highest horizontal drain connected to the stack. Sometimes called a waste vent or a soil vent.

34 **Storm Sewer** — A sewer used for conveying rain water, surface water, condensate, cooling water, or similar liquid waste.

35 **Trap** — A trap is a fitting or device that provides a liquid seal to prevent the emission of sewer gases without materially affecting the flow of sewage or waste water through it.

36 **Vacuum Breaker** — A device to prevent backflow (back siphonage) by means of an opening through which air may be drawn to relieve negative pressure (vacuum).

37 **Vent Stack** — The vertical vent pipe installed to provide air circulation to and from the drainage system and that extends through one or more stories.

38 **Water Hammer** — The loud thump of water in a pipe when a valve or faucet is suddenly closed.

39 **Water Service Pipe** — The pipe from the water main or other sources of potable water supply to the water-distributing system of the building served.

40 **Water Supply System** — The water supply system consists of the water service pipe, the water-distributing pipes, the necessary connecting pipes, fittings, control valves, and all appurtenances in or adjacent to the building or premises.

41 **Wet Vent** — A vent that receives the discharge of waste other than from water closets.

42 **Yoke Vent** — A pipe connecting upward from a soil or waste stack to a vent stack for the purpose of preventing pressure changes in the stacks.

III. Main Features of an Indoor Plumbing System

The primary functions of the plumbing system within the house are as follows:

1 To bring an adequate and potable supply of hot and cold water to the users of the dwelling.

2 To drain all waste water and sewage discharged from these fixtures into the public sewer, or private disposal system.

It is, therefore, very important that the housing inspector familiarize himself fully with all elements of these systems so that he may recognize inadequacies of the structure's plumbing as well as other code violations. In order to aid the inspector in understanding the plumbing system, a series of drawings and diagrams has been included at the end of this chapter.

IV. Elements of a Plumbing System

A Supply System

1 Water Service: The piping of a house service line should be as short as possible. Elbows and bends should be kept to a minimum since these reduce the pressure and therefore the supply of water to fixtures in the house.

The house service line should also be protected from freezing. The burying of the line under 4 feet of soil is a commonly accepted depth to prevent freezing. This depth varies, however, across the country from north to south. The local or state plumbing code should be consulted for the recommended depth in your area of the country.

A typical house service installation is pictured in Figure 1.

The materials used for a house service may be copper, cast iron, steel or wrought iron. The connections used should be compatible with the type of pipe used.

a **Corporation stop** — The corporation stop is connected to the water main. This connection is usually made of brass and can be connected to the main by use of a special tool without shutting off the municipal supply. The valve incorporated in the corporation stop permits the pressure to be maintained in the main while the service to the building is completed.

b **Curb stop** — The curb stop is a similar valve used to isolate the building from the main for repairs, nonpayment of water bills, or flooded basements.

Since the corporation stop is usually under the street and would necessitate breaking the pavement to reach the valve, the curb stop is used as the isolation valve.

c **Curb stop box** — The curb stop box is an access box to the curb stop for opening and closing the valve. A long-handled wrench is used to reach the valve.

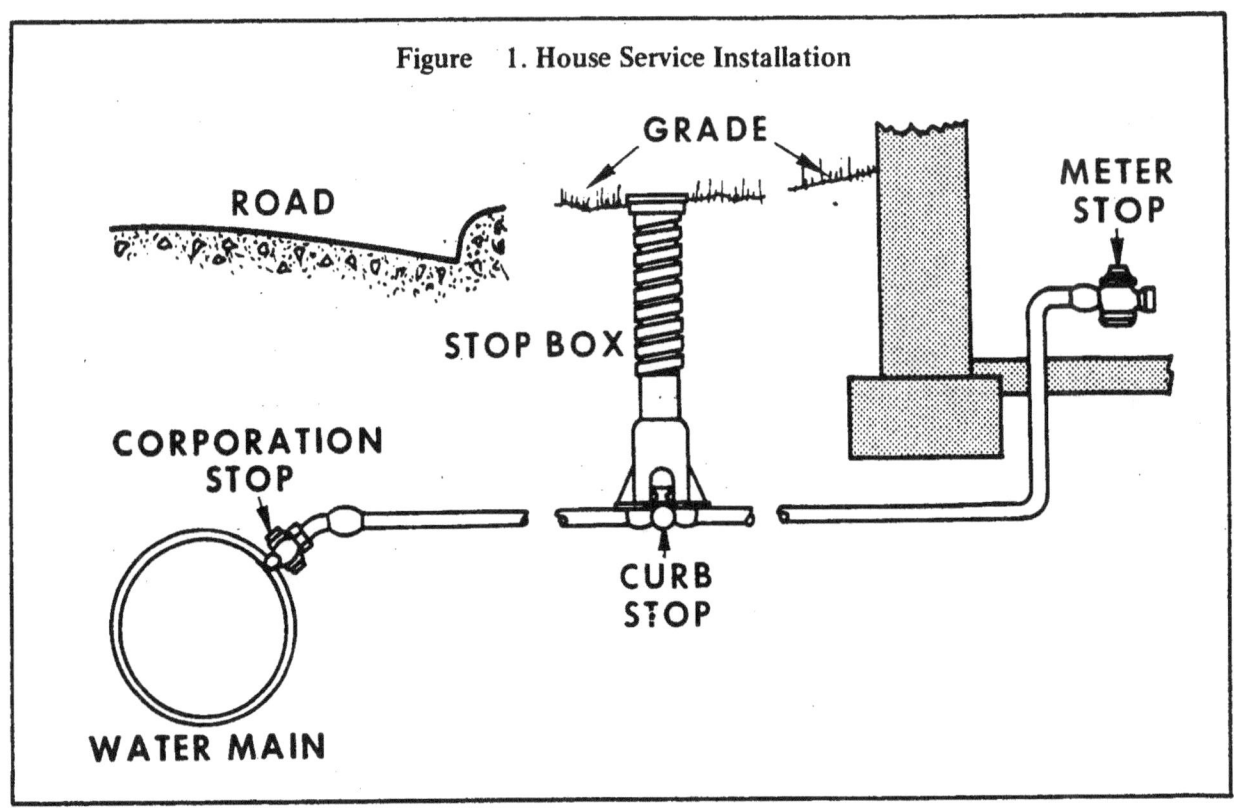

Figure 1. House Service Installation

- d **Meter stop** — The meter stop is a valve placed on the street side of the water meter to isolate the meter for installation or maintenance. Many codes require a gate valve on the house side of the meter to shut off water for house plumbing repairs. The curb and meter stops are not to be used frequently and can be ruined in a short time if used very frequently.

- e **Water meter** — The water meter is a device used to measure the amount of water used in the house. It is usually the property of the city and is a very delicate instrument that should not be abused.

  Since the electric system is usually grounded to the water line, a grounding loop-device should be installed around the meter. Many meters come with a yoke that maintains electrical continuity even though the meter is removed.

2 **Hot and Cold Water Main Lines:** The hot and cold water main lines are usually hung from the basement ceiling and are attached to the water meter and hot-water tank on one side and the fixture supply risers on the other.

These pipes should be installed in a neat manner and should be supported by pipe hangers or straps of sufficient strength and number to prevent sagging.

Hot and cold water lines should be approximately 6 inches apart unless the hot water line is insulated. This is to insure that the cold water line does not pick up heat from the hot water line.

The supply mains should have a drain valve or stop and waste valve in order to remove water from the system for repairs. These valves should be on the low end of the line or on the end of each fixture riser.

- a **The fixture risers** start at the basement main and rise vertically to the fixtures on the upper floors. In a one-family dwelling, riser branches will usually proceed from the main riser to each fixture grouping. In any event the fixture risers should not depend on the branch risers for support but should be supported with a pipe bracket.

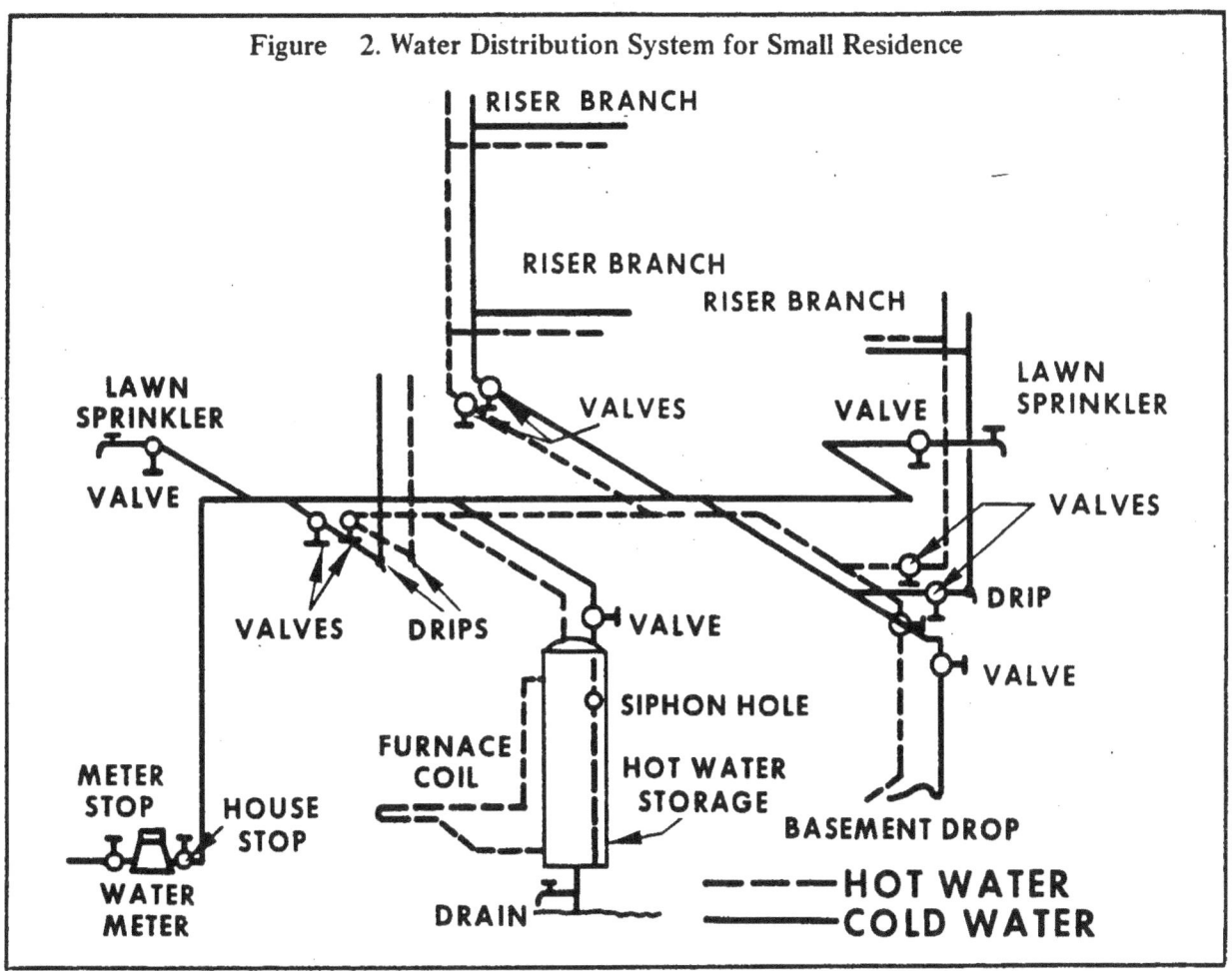

Figure 2. Water Distribution System for Small Residence

b Each fixture is then connected to the branch riser by a separate line. The last fixture on a line is usually connected directly to the branch riser. Figure 2 is a diagram of a typical single-family-residence water supply system.

3 Hot Water Heaters: Hot water heaters are usually powered by electricity, fuel oil, gas, or in rare cases, coal or wood. They consist of a space for heating the water and a storage tank for providing hot water over a limited period of time.

All hot water heaters should be fitted with a temperature-pressure relief valve no matter what fuel is used.

This valve will operate when either the temperature or the pressure becomes too high due to an interruption of the water supply or a faulty thermostat.

Figure 3 shows the correct installation of a hot water heater.

4 Pipe Sizes: The size of basement mains and risers depends on the number of fixtures supplied. However, a ¾ inch pipe is usually the minimum size used. This allows for deposits on the pipe due to hardness in the water and will usually give satisfactory volume and pressure.

B Drainage System

The water supply brought into the house and used is discharged through the drainage system. This system is either a sanitary drainage system carrying just interior waste water or a combined system carrying interior waste and roof runoff. The sanitary system will be discussed first.

1 Sanitary Drainage System: The proper sizing of the sanitary drain or house drain depends on the number of fixtures it serves. The usual

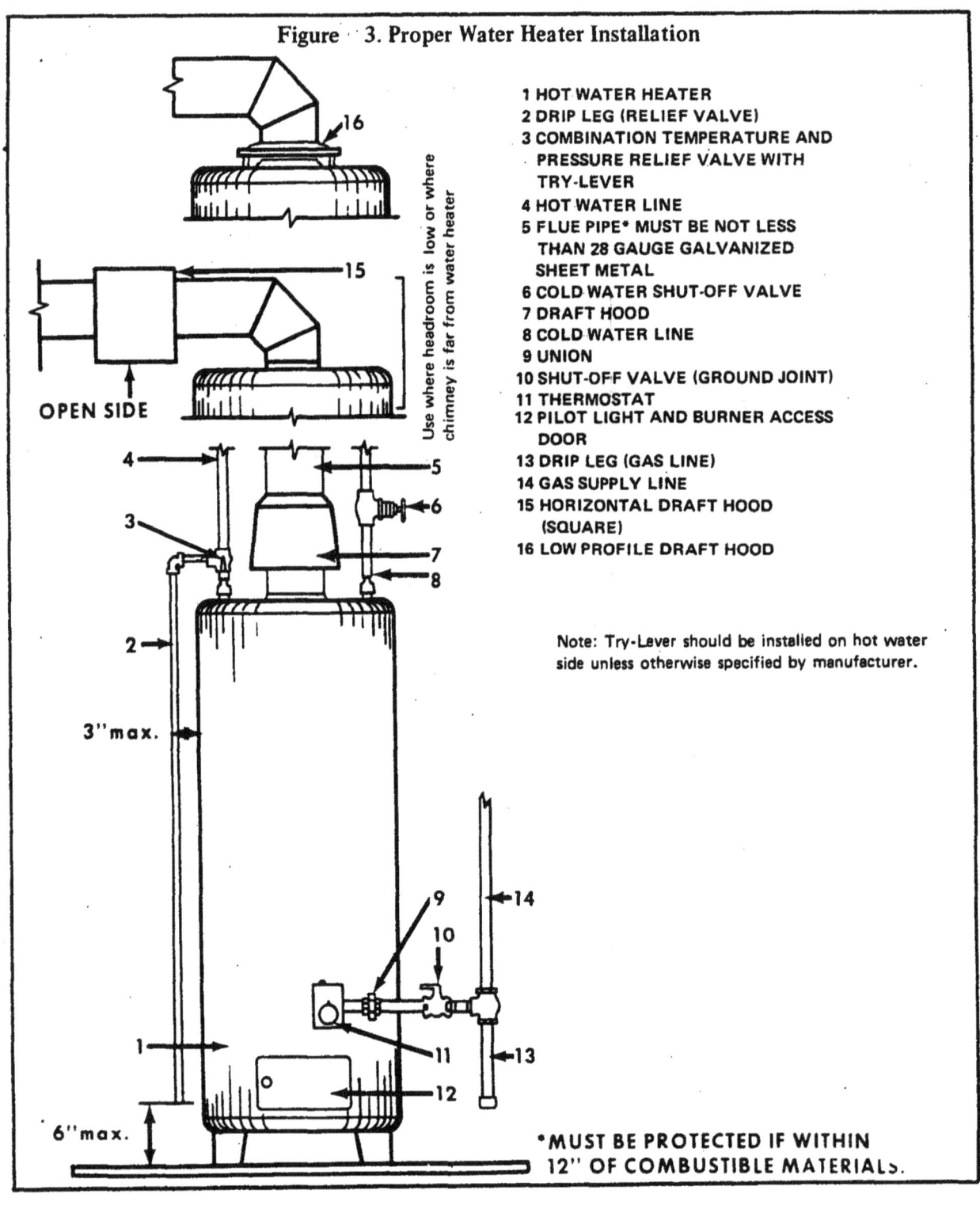

Figure 3. Proper Water Heater Installation

minimum size is 6 inches in diameter. The materials used are usually cast iron, vitrified clay, plastic, and in rare cases, lead. For proper flow in the drain the pipe should be sized so that it flows approximately one-half full. This ensures proper scouring action so that the solids contained in the waste will not be deposited in the pipe.

a   **Sizing of house drain** — The Uniform Plumbing Code Committee has developed a method of sizing of house drains in terms of "fixture units." One "fixture unit" equals approximately 7½ gallons of water per minute. This is the surge flow-rate of water discharged from a wash basin in 1 minute. All other fixtures have been related to this unit.

A table fixture unit values is shown in Table 1.

The maximum number of fixture units attached to a sanitary drain is shown in Table 2.

b   **Grade of house drain** — A house drain or building sewer should be sloped toward the sewer to ensure scouring of the drain. Figure 4 shows the results of proper and improper pitch of a house drain.

The usual pitch of a house or building sewer is ¼ inch fall in 1 foot of length.

Table 1. FIXTURE UNIT VALUES

Fixture	Units
Lavatory/wash basin	1
Kitchen sink	2
Bathtub	2
Laundry tub	2
Combination fixture	3
Urinal	5
Shower bath	2
Floor drain	1
Slop sinks	3
Water closet	6
One bathroom group (water closet, lavatory, bathtub, and shower; or water closet, lavatory, and shower)	8
180 square feet of roof drained	1

c   **House drain installation** — A typical house drain installation is shown in Figure 5. Typical branch connections to the main are shown in Figure 6.

d   **Fixture and branch drains** — A branch drain is a waste pipe that collects the waste from two or more fixtures and conveys it to the building or house sewer. It is sized in the same way as the house sewer, taking into account that all water closets must have a minimum 3-inch diameter drain, and

Table 2. SANITARY DRAIN SIZES

Maximum number of fixture units

Diameter of pipe, in.	Slope 1/8"/Ft.	Slope 1/4"/Ft.	Slope 1/2"/Ft.
1¼	1	1	1
1½	2	2	3
2	5	6	8
3	15	18	21
4	84	96	114
6	300	450	600
8	990	1,392	2,220
12	3,084	4,320	6,912

*A water closet must enter a 3 inch diameter drain and no more than 2 water closets may enter a 3 inch horizontal branch.

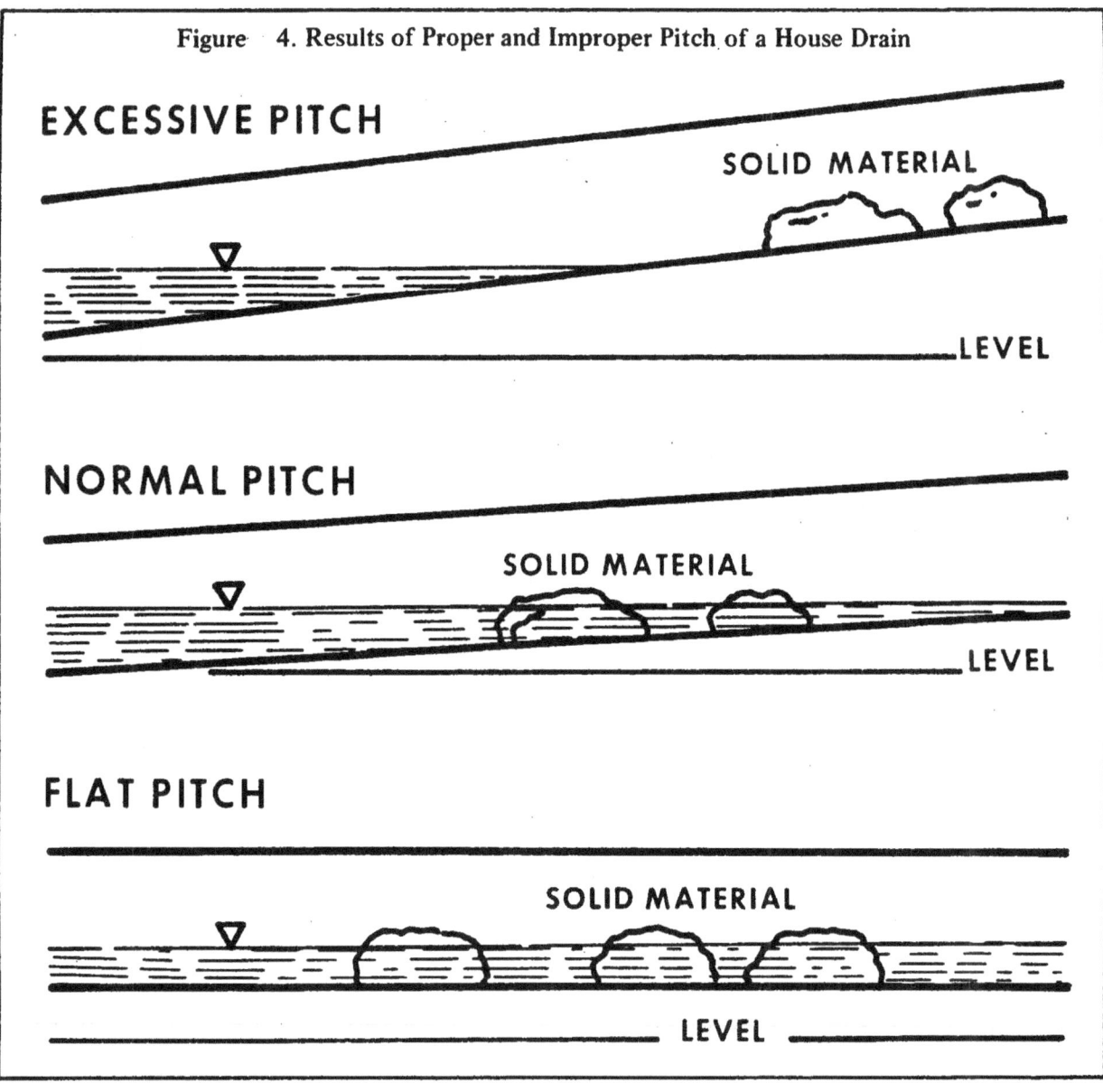

Figure 4. Results of Proper and Improper Pitch of a House Drain

only two water closets may connect into one 3-inch drain.

All branch drains must join the house drain with a "Y"-type fitting as shown in Figure 6. The same is true for fixture drains joining branch drains.

The "Y" fitting is used to eliminate, as much as possible, the deposit of solids in or near the connection. A build-up of these solids will cause a blockage in the drain.

The recommended minimum size of fixture drain is shown in Table 3.

e Traps – A plumbing trap is a device used in a waste system to prevent the passage of sewer gas into the structure and yet not hinder the fixture's discharge to any great extent. All fixtures connected to a household plumbing system should have a trap installed in the line.

Table 3. MINIMUM FIXTURE SERVICE

Fixture	Supply line, in.	Vent line, in.	Drain line, in.
Bathtub	½	1½	1½-2
Kitchen sink	½	1½	1½
Lavatory	3/8	1¼	1¼
Laundry sink	½	1½	1½
Shower	½	2	2
Water closet (tank)	3/8	3	3

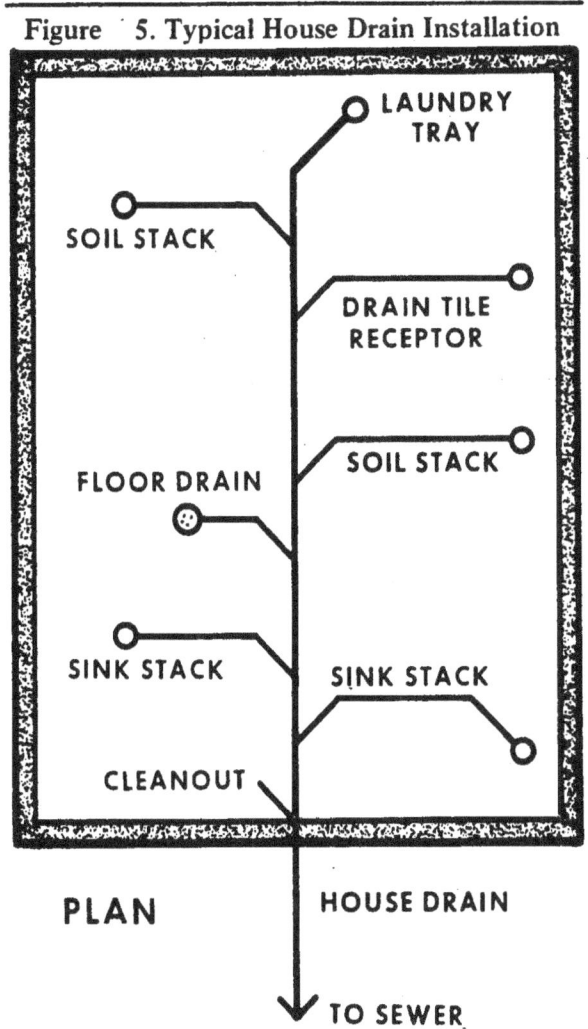

Figure 5. Typical House Drain Installation

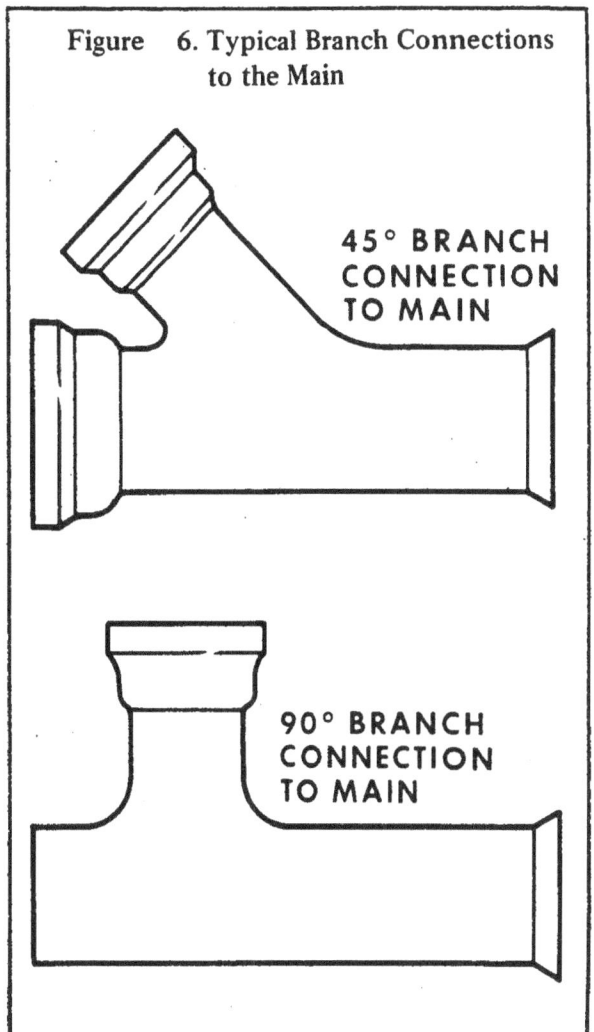

Figure 6. Typical Branch Connections to the Main

The effect of sewer gases on the human body are known; many are extremely harmful. Additionally, certain sewer gases are explosive. A trap will prevent these gases from passing into the structure.

1) "P" trap — The most common trap found today is the "P" trap. Figure 6-7 is a drawing of a "P" trap.

The depth of the seal in a trap is usually 2 inches. A deep seal trap has a 4-inch seal.

As was mentioned earlier, the purpose of a trap is to seal out sewer gases from the structure. Since a plumbing system is subject to wide variations in flow, and this flow originates in many different sections of the system, there is a wide variation in pressures in the waste lines. These pressure differences tend to destroy the water seal in the trap.

To counteract this problem mechanical traps were introduced. It has been found, however, that the corrosive liquids flowing in the system corrode or jam these mechanical traps. It is for this reason that most plumbing codes prohibit mechanical traps.

There are many manufacturers of traps, and all have varied the design somewhat. Figures 8 and 9 show various types of "P" traps. The "P" trap is usually found in lavatories, sinks, urinals, drinking fountains, showers, and other installations that do not discharge a great deal of water.

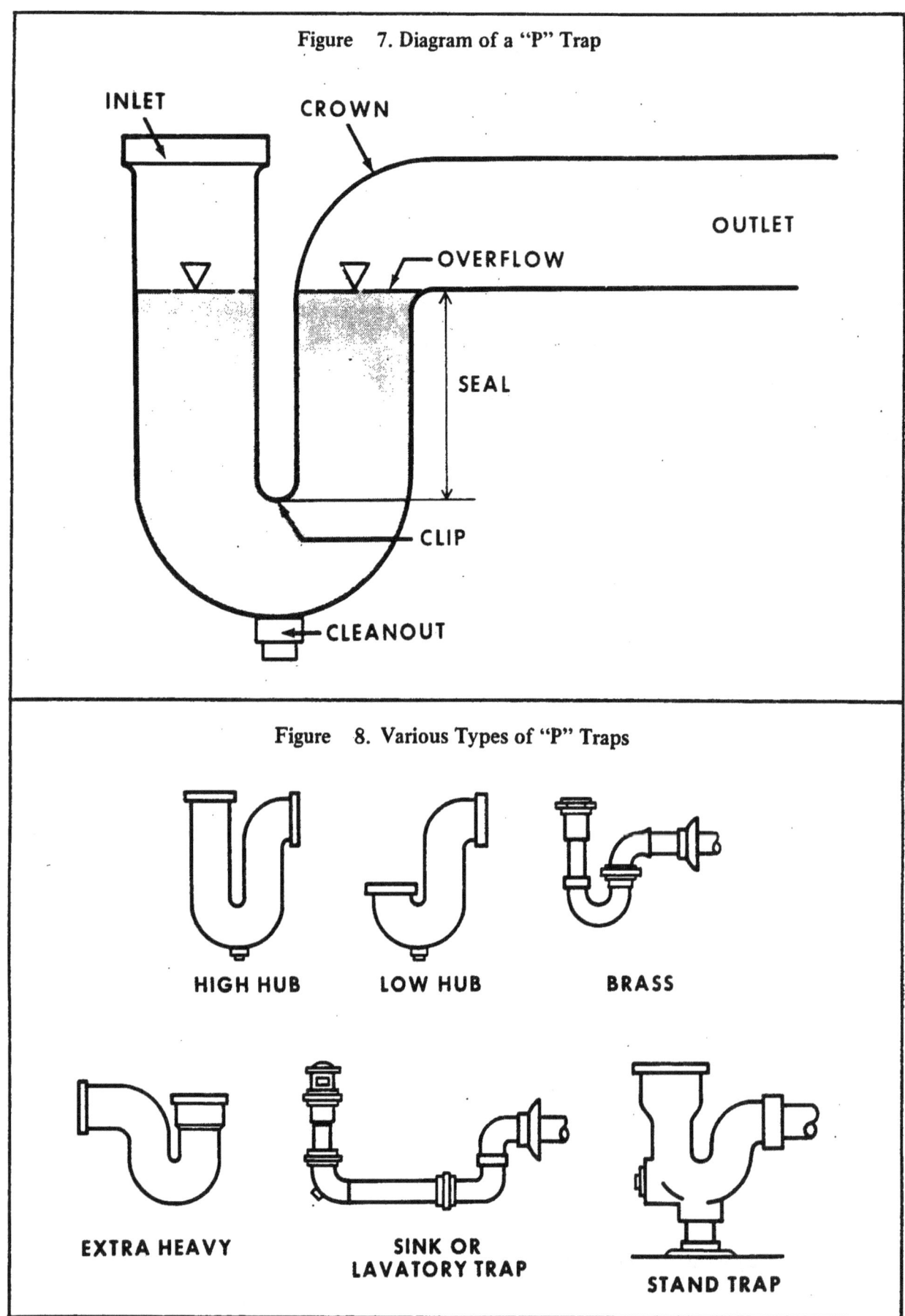

Figure 7. Diagram of a "P" Trap

Figure 8. Various Types of "P" Traps

2) Drum trap — The drum trap is another water seal-type trap. They are usually used in the 4- x 5-inch or 4- x 8-inch sizes. These traps have a greater sealing capacity than the "P" trap and pass large amounts of water quickly. Figure 10 shows a drum trap.

Drum traps are commonly connected to bathtubs, foot baths, sitz baths, and modified shower baths. Figure 11 shows a drum trap connected to a bathtub and shower.

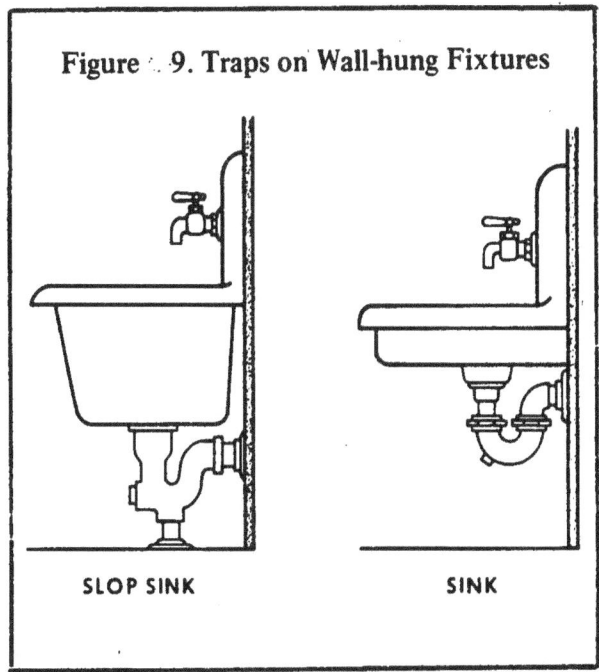

Figure 9. Traps on Wall-hung Fixtures

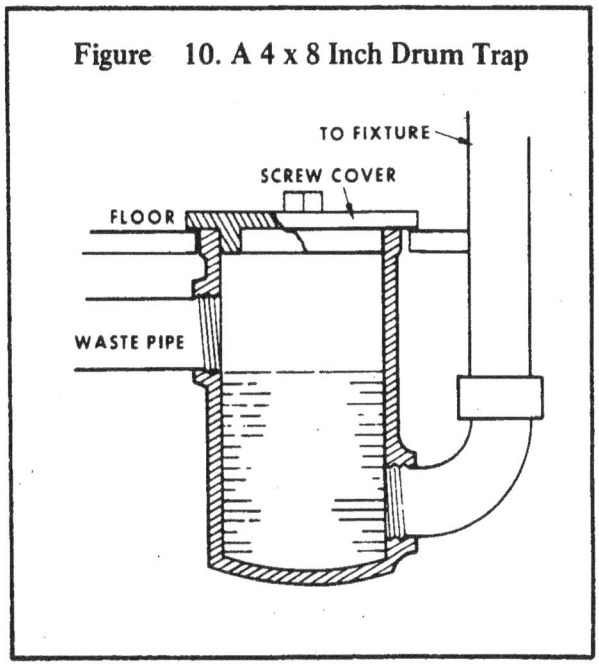

Figure 10. A 4 x 8 Inch Drum Trap

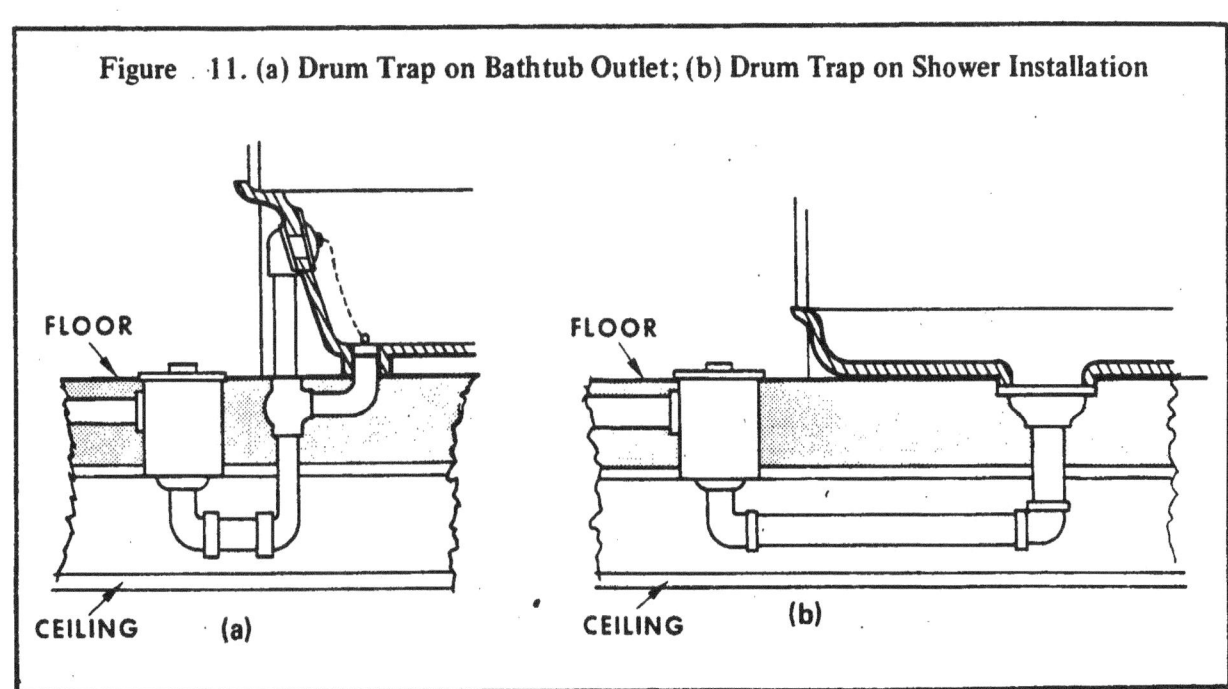

Figure 11. (a) Drum Trap on Bathtub Outlet; (b) Drum Trap on Shower Installation

3) Objectionable traps — The "S" trap and the ¾ "S" trap should not be used in plumbing installations. They are almost impossible to ventilate properly, and the ¾ "S" trap forms a perfect siphon.

The bag trap, an extreme form of "S" trap, is seldom found. Figure 12 shows these types of "S" traps.

Figure 13 shows one type of mechanically sealed trap. Any trap that depends on a moving part for its effectiveness is usually inadequate and has been prohibited by the local plumbing codes.

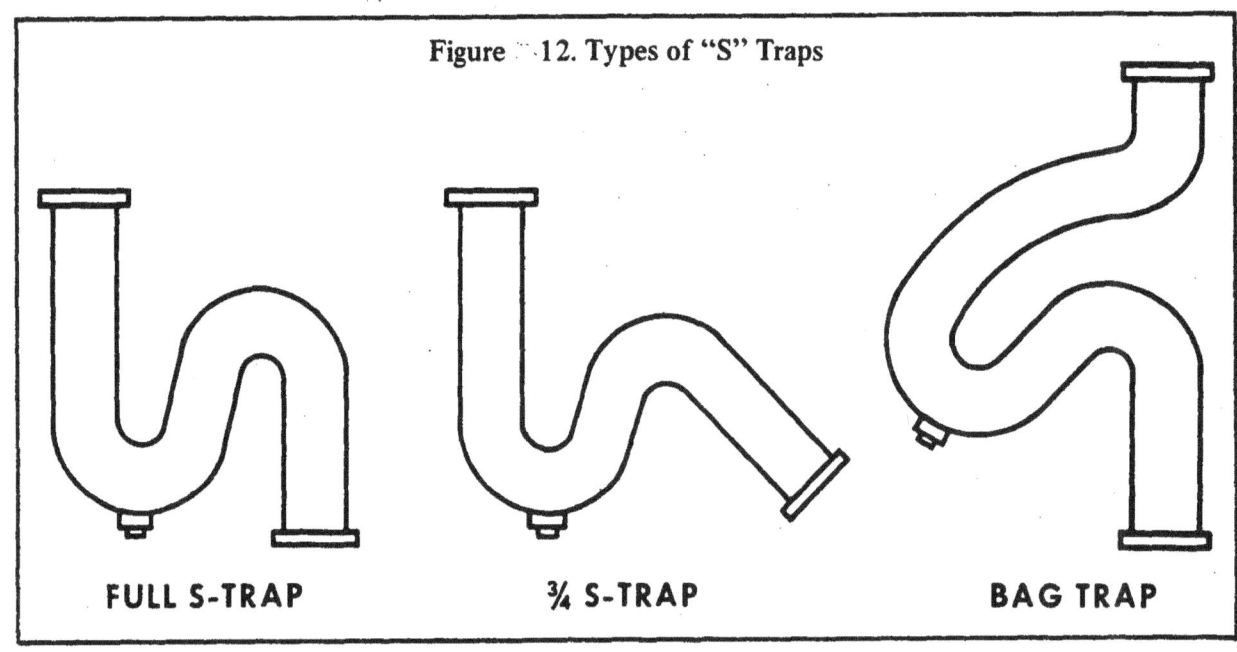

Figure 12. Types of "S" Traps

FULL S-TRAP   ¾ S-TRAP   BAG TRAP

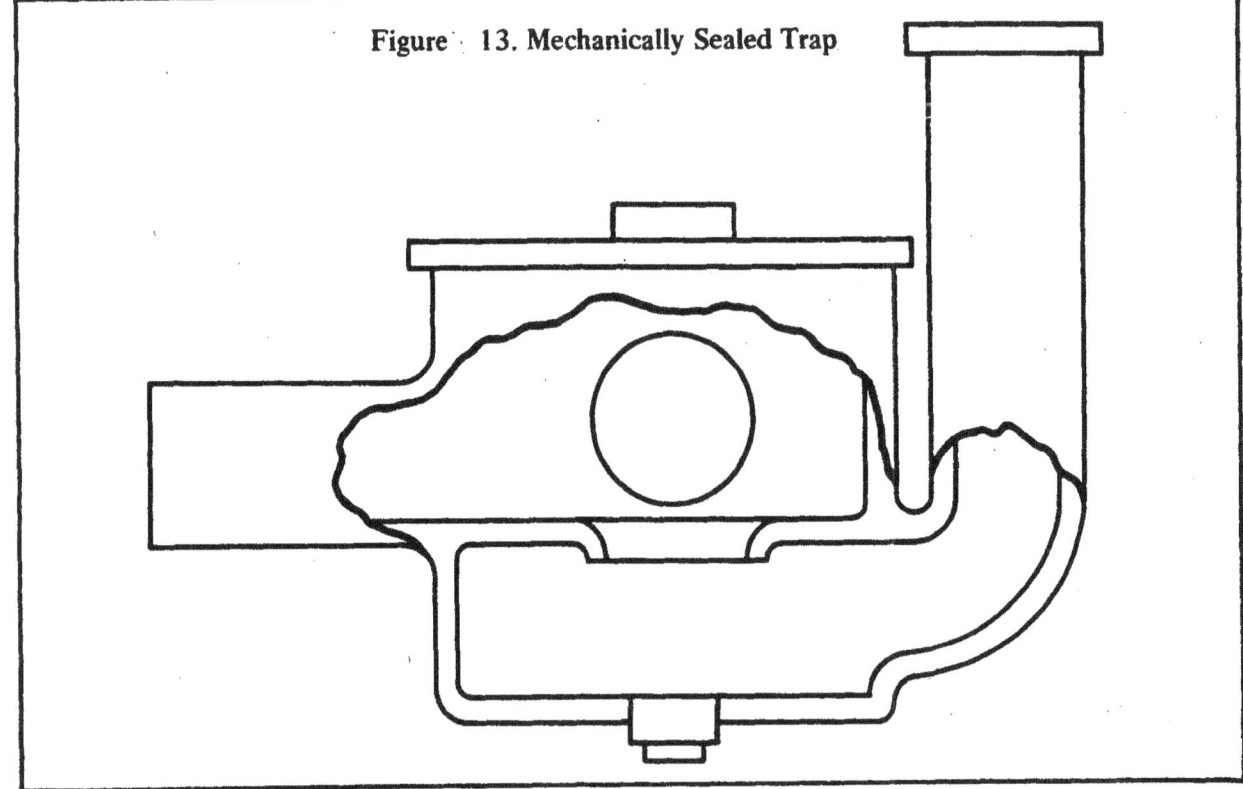

Figure 13. Mechanically Sealed Trap

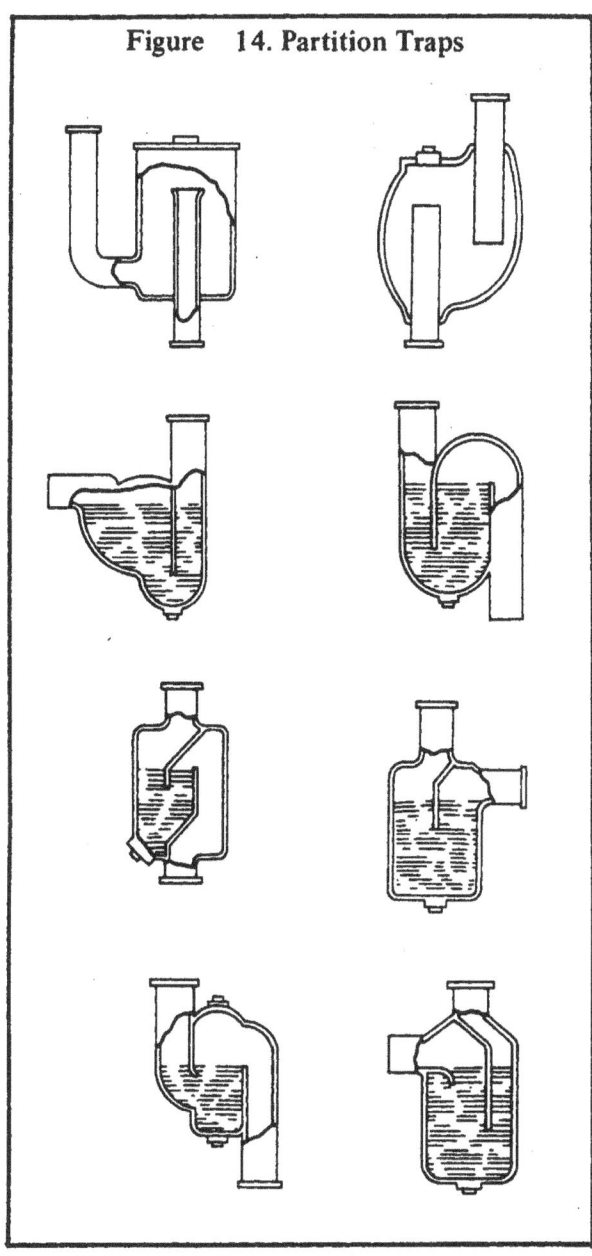

Figure 14. Partition Traps

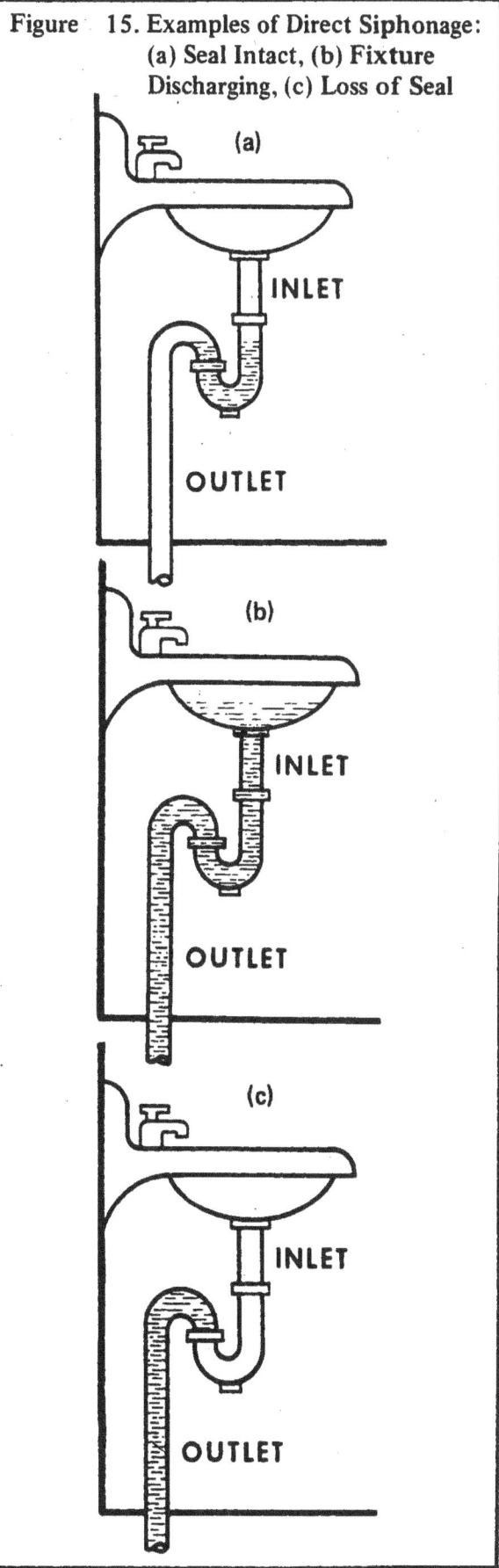

Figure 15. Examples of Direct Siphonage: (a) Seal Intact, (b) Fixture Discharging, (c) Loss of Seal

Figure 14 shows various types of internal partition traps. These traps work, but their design usually results in their being higher priced than the "P" or drum traps.

It should be remembered that traps are used only to prevent the escape of sewer gas into the structure. They do not compensate for pressure variations. Only proper venting will eliminate pressure problems.

f **Ventilation** — A plumbing system is ventilated to prevent trap seal loss, material deterioration, and flow retardation.

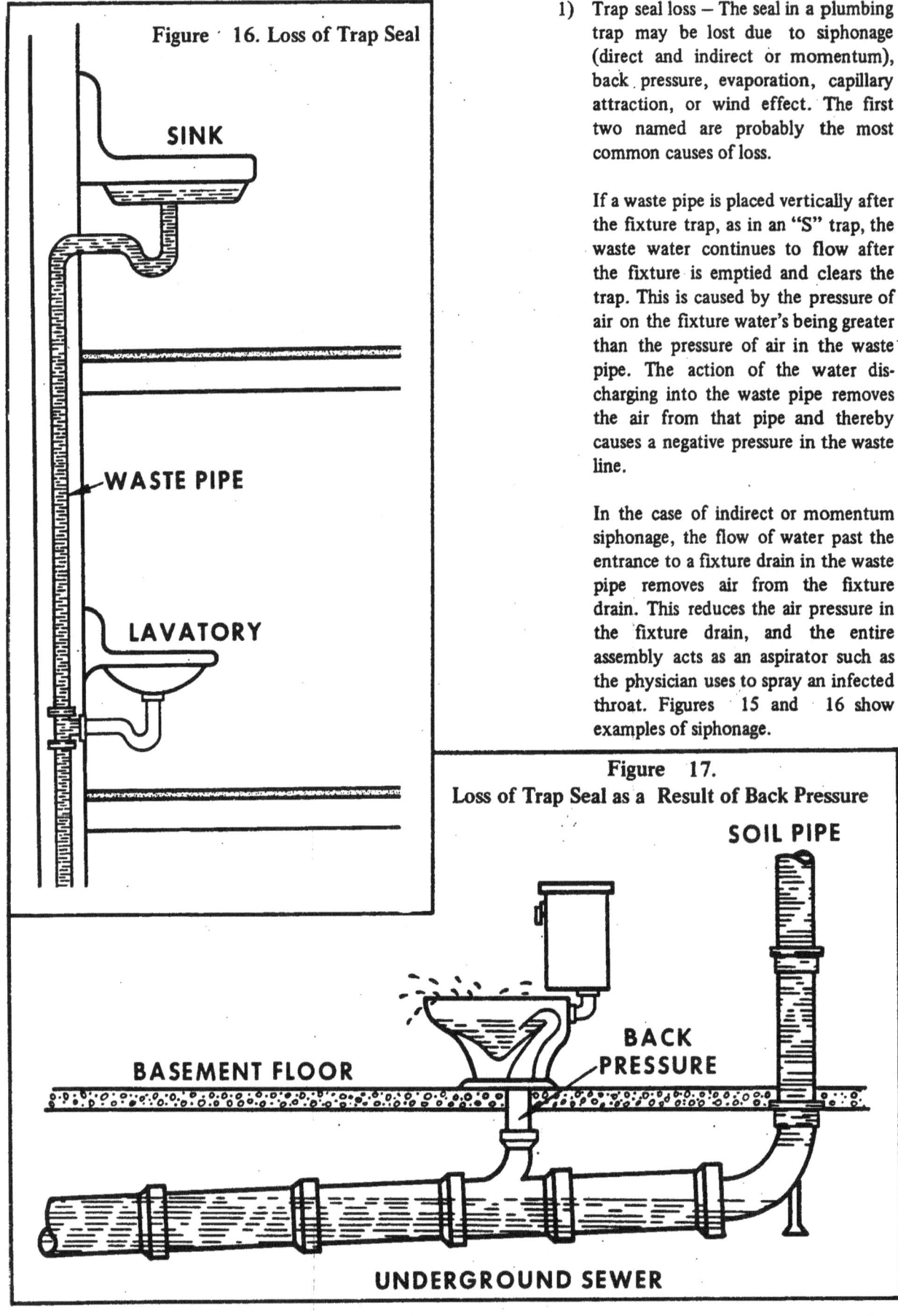

Figure 16. Loss of Trap Seal

Figure 17. Loss of Trap Seal as a Result of Back Pressure

1) Trap seal loss — The seal in a plumbing trap may be lost due to siphonage (direct and indirect or momentum), back pressure, evaporation, capillary attraction, or wind effect. The first two named are probably the most common causes of loss.

If a waste pipe is placed vertically after the fixture trap, as in an "S" trap, the waste water continues to flow after the fixture is emptied and clears the trap. This is caused by the pressure of air on the fixture water's being greater than the pressure of air in the waste pipe. The action of the water discharging into the waste pipe removes the air from that pipe and thereby causes a negative pressure in the waste line.

In the case of indirect or momentum siphonage, the flow of water past the entrance to a fixture drain in the waste pipe removes air from the fixture drain. This reduces the air pressure in the fixture drain, and the entire assembly acts as an aspirator such as the physician uses to spray an infected throat. Figures 15 and 16 show examples of siphonage.

2) Back pressure — The flow of water in a soil pipe varies according to the fixtures being used. A lavatory gives a small flow and a water closet a large flow. Small flows tend to cling to the sides of the pipe, but large ones form a slug of waste as they drop. As this slug of water falls down the pipe the air in front of it becomes pressurized. As the pressure builds it seeks an escape point. This point is either a vent or a fixture outlet. If the vent is plugged or there is no vent, the only escape for this air is the fixture outlet. The air pressure forces the trap seal up the pipe into the fixture. If the pressure is great enough the seal is blown out of the fixture entirely. Figures 17 and 18 illustrate this type of problem.

3) Vent sizing — Vent pipe installation is similar to that of soil and waste pipe. The same fixture unit criteria are used. Table 3 shows minimum vent pipe sizes.

Vent pipes of less than 1¼ inches in diameter should not be used. Vents smaller than this diameter tend to clog and do not perform their function.

4) Individual fixture ventilation — Figure 19 shows a typical installation of a wall-hung plumbing unit. This type of ventilation is generally used for sinks, lavatories, drinking fountains, and so forth.

Figure 20 shows a typical installation of a bathtub or shower ventilation system.

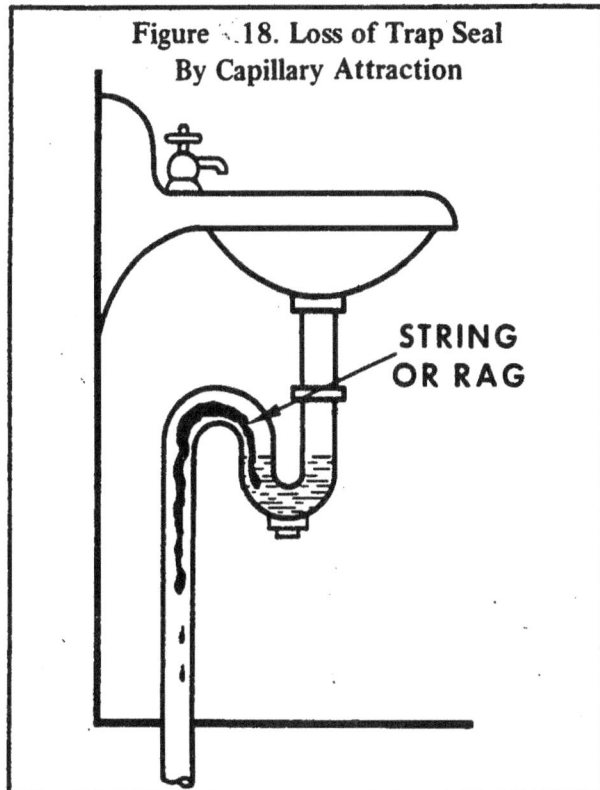

Figure 18. Loss of Trap Seal By Capillary Attraction

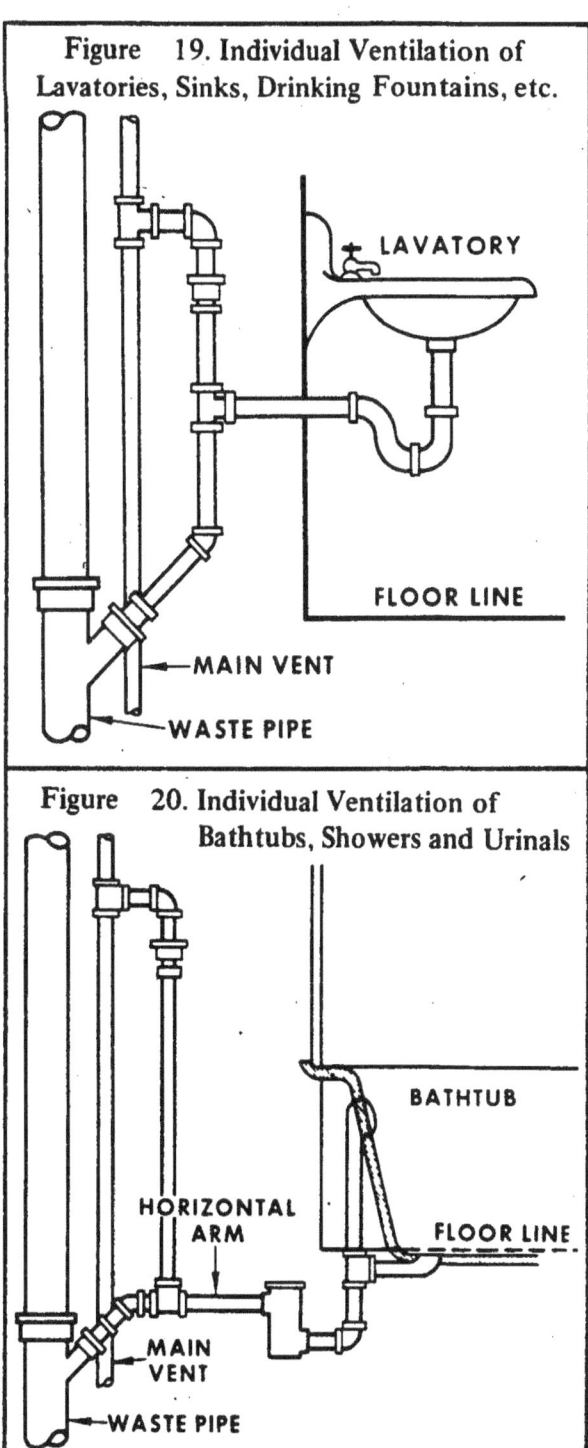

Figure 19. Individual Ventilation of Lavatories, Sinks, Drinking Fountains, etc.

Figure 20. Individual Ventilation of Bathtubs, Showers and Urinals

Figure 21 shows the proper vent connection for a water closet or slop sink. The water closet can be either a tank type or a flushometer valve type.

5) Unit venting — Figures 22 to 24 picture a back-to-back ventilation system for various common plumbing fixtures. The unit venting system is commonly used in apartment buildings. This type of system saves a great deal of money and space when fixtures are placed back to back in separate apartments.

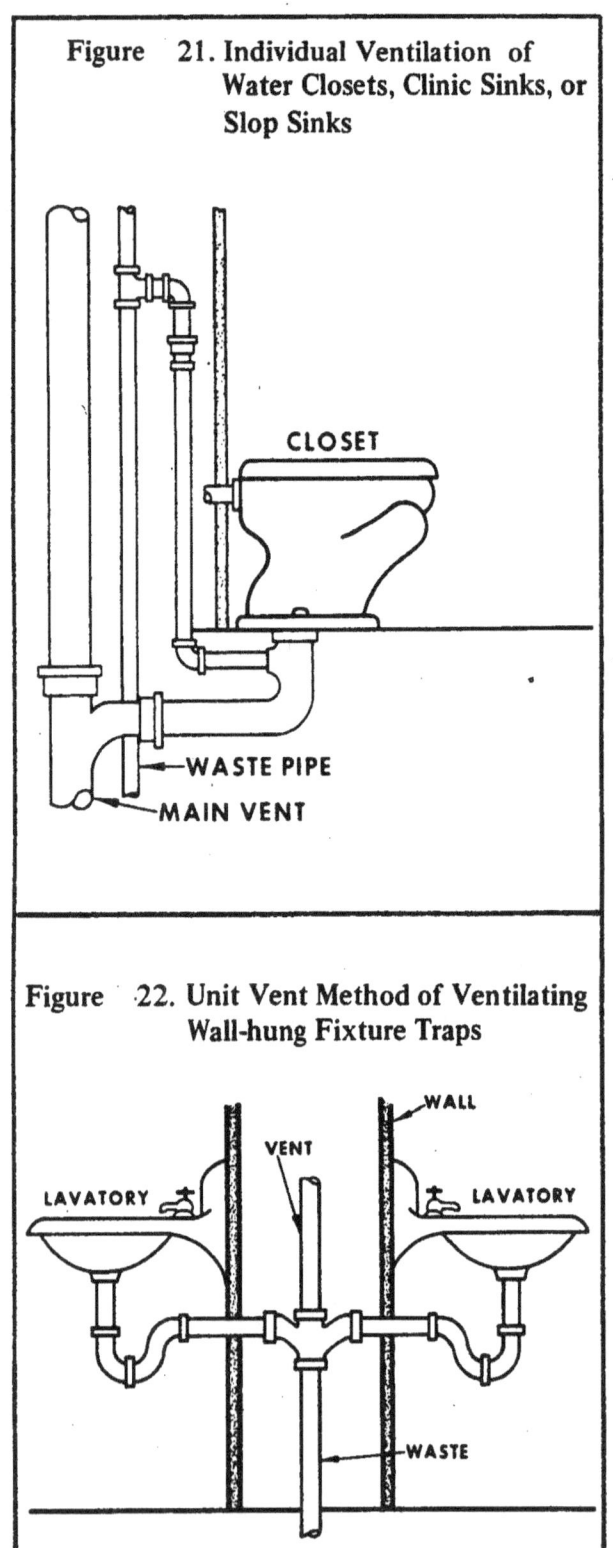

Figure 21. Individual Ventilation of Water Closets, Clinic Sinks, or Slop Sinks

Figure 22. Unit Vent Method of Ventilating Wall-hung Fixture Traps

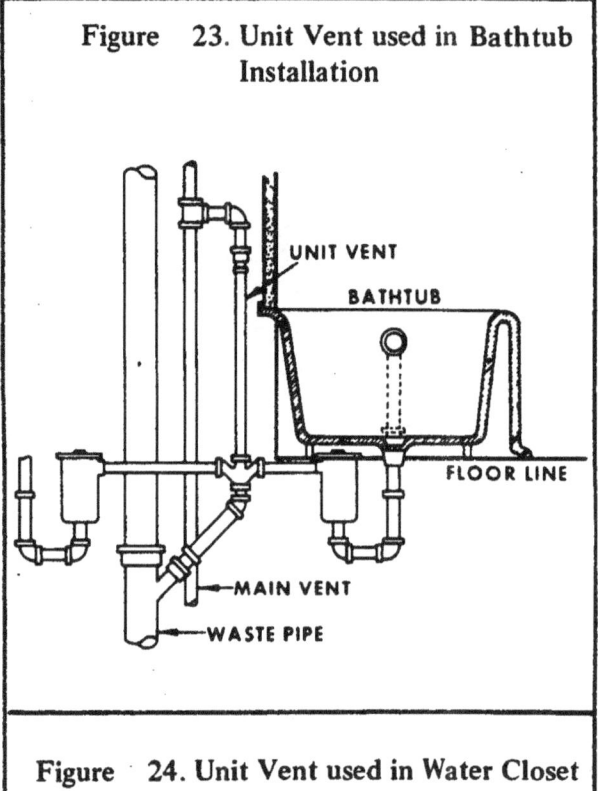

Figure 23. Unit Vent used in Bathtub Installation

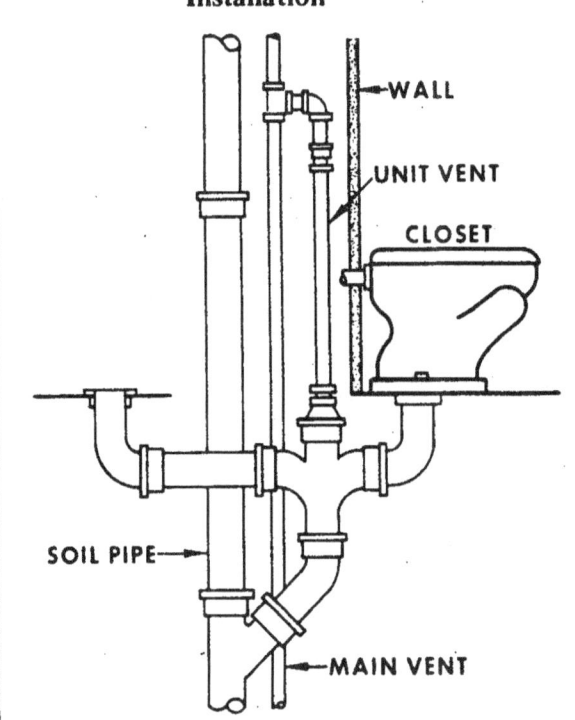

Figure 24. Unit Vent used in Water Closet Installation

Figure 25 shows a double combination "Y" used for joining the fixtures to the common soil pipe. The deflectors are to prevent waste from one fixture flowing back up into the waste in the attached fixture on the other side of the wall.

6) Wet venting — Wet venting of a plumbing system is common in household bathroom fixture grouping. It is exactly what the name implies: the vent pipe is used as a waste line. Figure 26 shows a typical wet-vent installation in a home.

7) Total drainage system — Up to now we have talked about the drain, soil waste, and vent systems of a plumbing system separately. For a working system, however, they must all be connected. Figures 27 through 32 show some typical drainage systems that are found in homes and small apartment buildings.

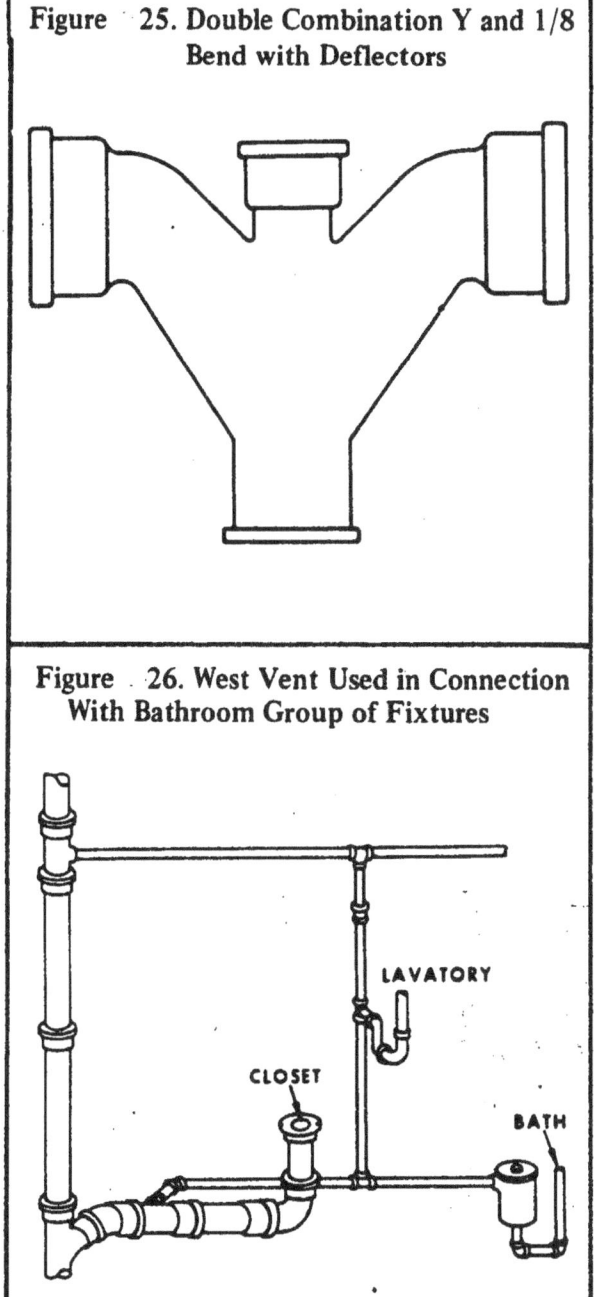

Figure 25. Double Combination Y and 1/8 Bend with Deflectors

Figure 26. West Vent Used in Connection With Bathroom Group of Fixtures

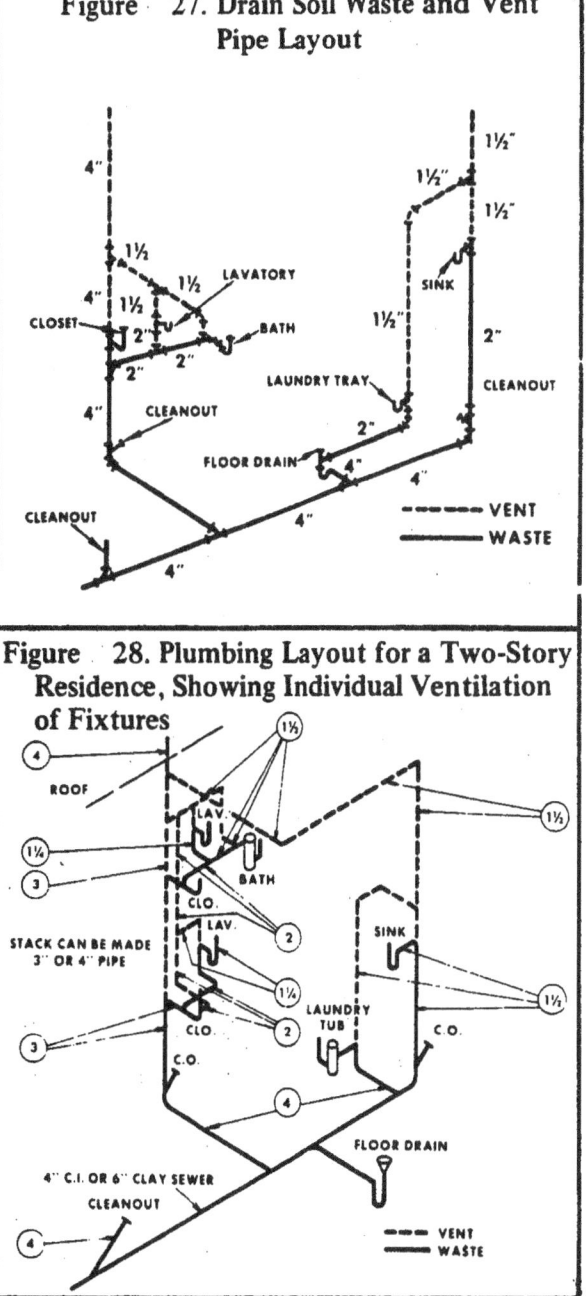

Figure 27. Drain Soil Waste and Vent Pipe Layout

Figure 28. Plumbing Layout for a Two-Story Residence, Showing Individual Ventilation of Fixtures

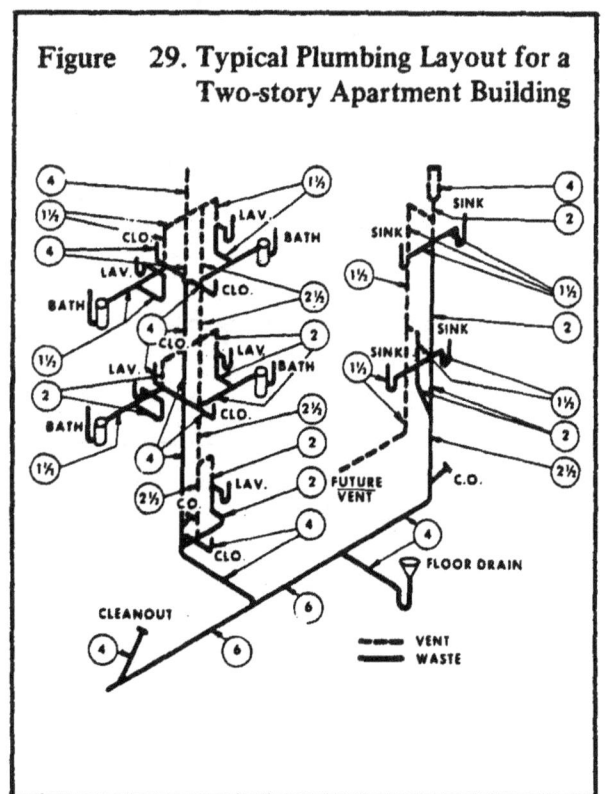

Figure 29. Typical Plumbing Layout for a Two-story Apartment Building

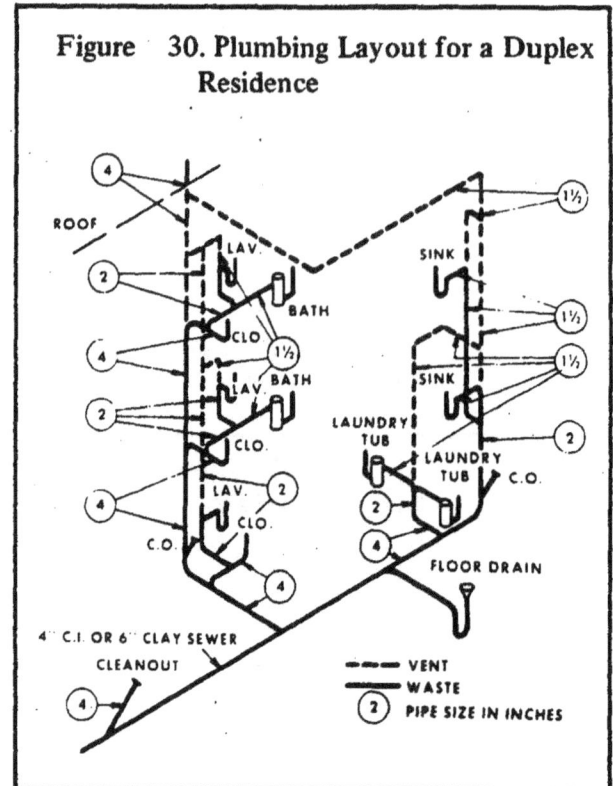

Figure 30. Plumbing Layout for a Duplex Residence

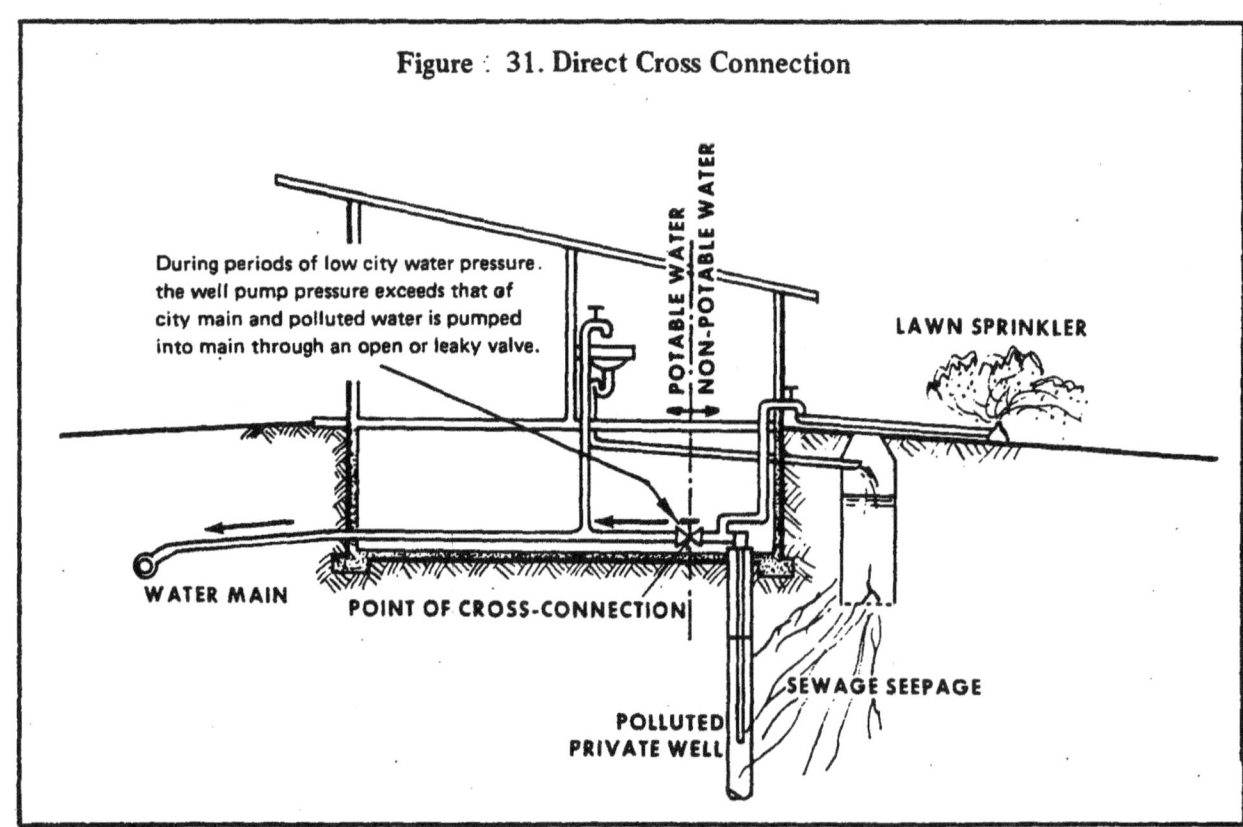

Figure 31. Direct Cross Connection

Figure 32. Cross Connection

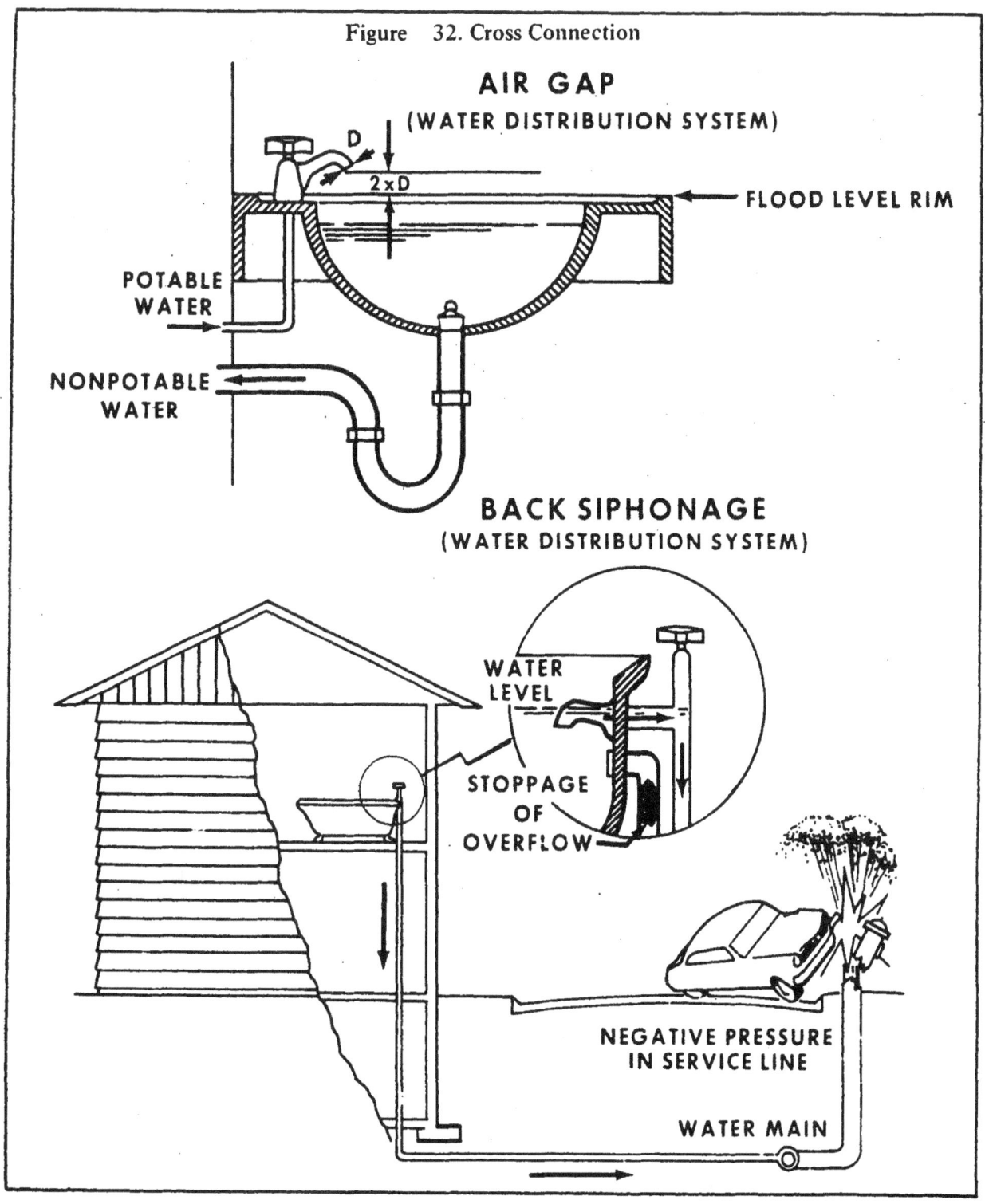

BASIC FUNDAMENTALS OF DRAWINGS AND SPECIFICATIONS

A building project may be broadly divided into two major phases: (1) the DESIGN phase, and (2) the CONSTRUCTION phase. In accordance with a number of considerations, of which the function and desired appearance of the building are perhaps the most important, the architect first conceives the building in his mind's eye, as it were, and then sets his concept down on paper in the form of PRESENTATION drawings. Presentation drawings are usually done in PERSPECTIVE, by employing the PICTORIAL drawing techniques.

Next the architect and the engineer, working together, decide upon the materials to be used in the structure and the construction methods which are to be followed. The engineer determines the loads which supporting members will carry and the strength qualities the members must have to bear the loads. He also designs the mechanical systems of the structure, such as the lighting, heating, and plumbing systems. The end-result of all this is the preparation of architectural and engineering DESIGN SKETCHES. The purpose of these sketches is to guide draftsmen in the preparation of CONSTRUCTION DRAWINGS.

The construction drawings, plus the SPECIFICATIONS to be described later, are the chief sources of information for the supervisors and craftsman responsible for the actual work of construction. Construction drawings consist mostly of ORTHOGRAPHIC views, prepared by draftsmen who employ the standard technical drawing techniques, and who use the symbols and other designations

You should make a thorough study of symbols before proceeding further with this chapter. Figure 1 illustrates the conventional symbols for the more common types of material used on structures. Figure 2 shows the more common symbols used for doors and windows.

Before you can interpret construction drawings correctly, you must also have some knowledge of the structure and of the terminology for common structural members.

I. STRUCTURES

The main parts of a structure are the LOAD-BEARING STRUCTURAL MEMBERS, which support and transfer the loads on the structure while remaining in equilibrium with each other. The places where members are connected to other members are called JOINTS. The sum total of the load supported by the structural members at a particular instant is equal to the total DEAD LOAD plus the total LIVE LOAD.

The total dead load is the total weight of the structure, which gradually increases, of course, as the structure rises, and remains constant once it is completed. The total live load is the total weight of movable objects (such as people, furniture, bridge traffic or the like) which the structure happens to be supporting at a particular instant.

The live loads in a structure are transmitted through the various load-bearing structural members to the ultimate support of the earth as follows. Immediate or direct support for the live loads is provided by HORIZTONAL members; these are in turn supported by VERTICAL members; which in turn are supported by FOUNDATIONS and/or FOOTINGS; and these are, finally, supported by the earth.

The ability of the earth to support a load is called the SOIL BEARING CAPACITY; it is determined by test and measured in pounds per square foot. Soil bearing capacity varies considerably with different types of soil, and a soil of given bearing capacity will bear a heavier load on a wide foundation or footing than it will on a narrow one.

VERTICAL STRUCTURAL MEMBERS

Vertical structural members are high-strength columns; they are sometimes called PILLARS in buildings. Outside wall columns and inside bottom-floor columns, usually rest directly on footings. Outside-wall columns usually extend from the footing or foundation to the roof line. Inside bottom-floor columns extend upward from footings or foundations to horizontal members which in turn support the

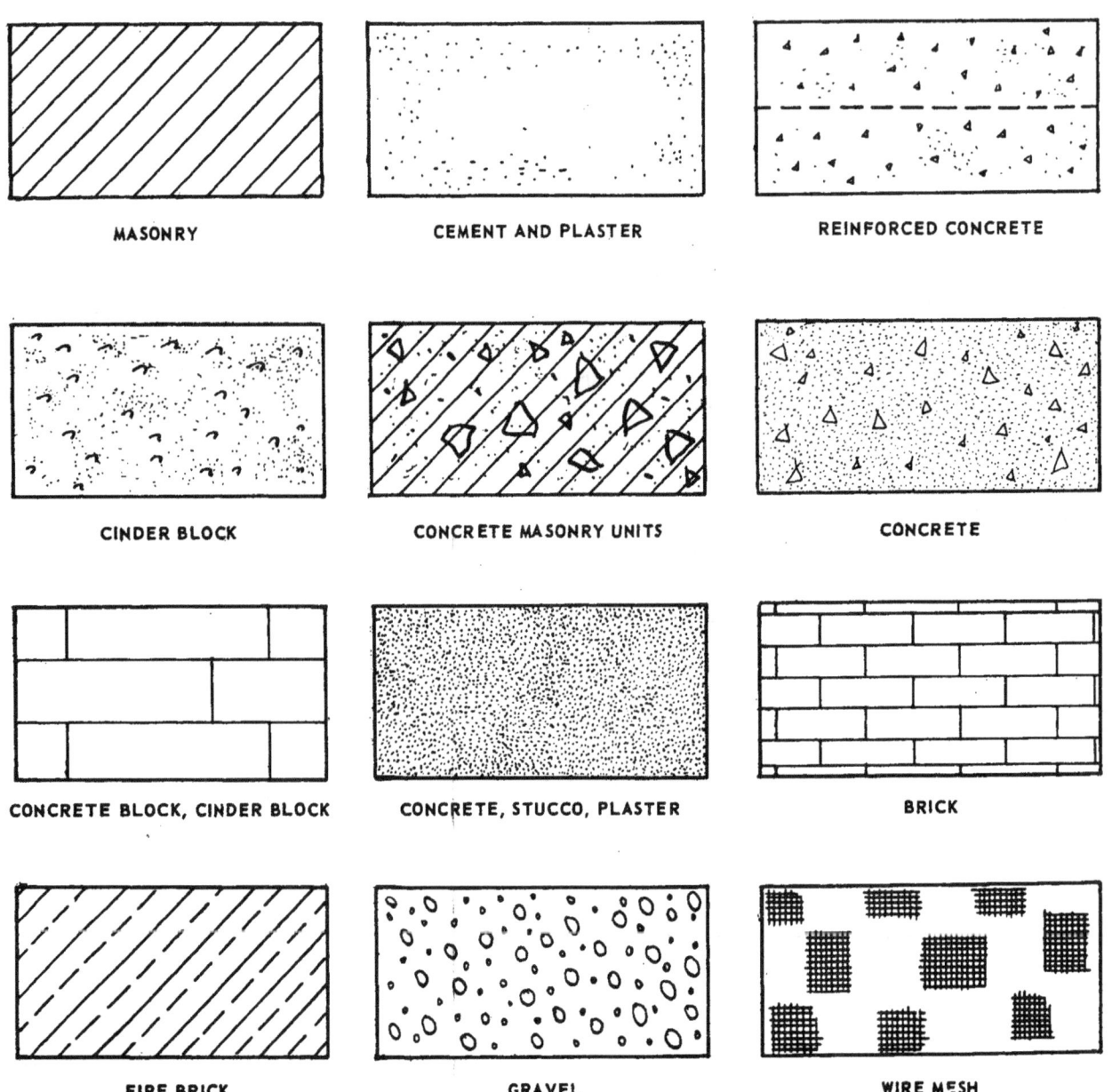

Figure 1.—Material symbols.

first floor. Upper floor columns usually are located directly over lower floor columns.

A PIER in building construction might be called a short column. It may rest directly on a footing, or it may be simply set or driven in the ground. Building piers usually support the lowermost horizontal structural members.

In bridge construction a pier is a vertical member which provides intermediate support for the bridge superstructure.

The chief vertical structural members in light frame construction are called STUDS. They are supported on horizontal members called SILLS or SOLE PLATES, and are topped by horizontal members called TOP PLATES or RAFTER PLATES. CORNER POSTS are enlarged studs, as it were, located at the building corners. In early FULL-FRAME construction a corner post was usually a solid piece of larger timber. In most modern construction BUILT-UP

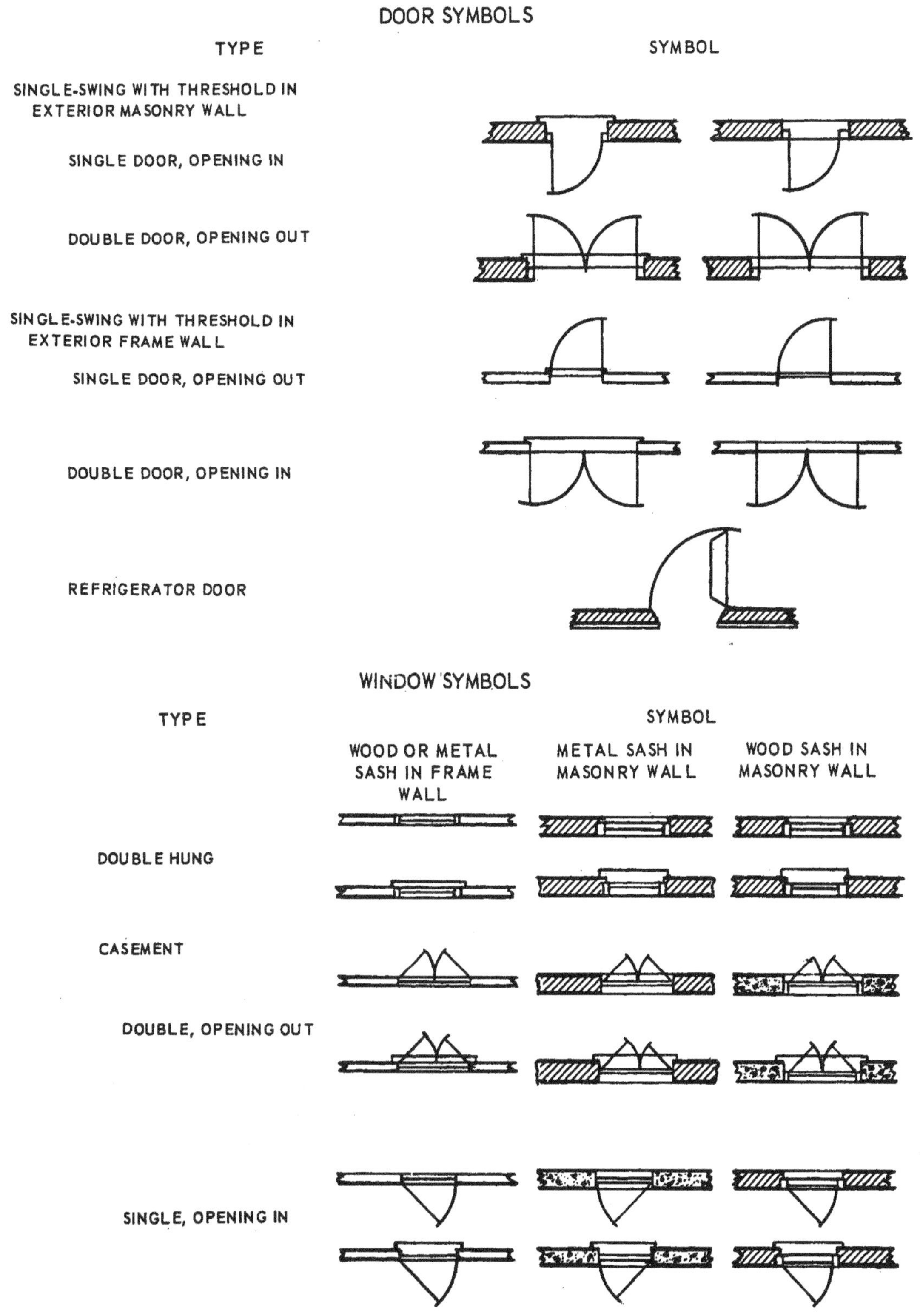

DOOR SYMBOLS

TYPE	SYMBOL
SINGLE-SWING WITH THRESHOLD IN EXTERIOR MASONRY WALL SINGLE DOOR, OPENING IN	
DOUBLE DOOR, OPENING OUT	
SINGLE-SWING WITH THRESHOLD IN EXTERIOR FRAME WALL SINGLE DOOR, OPENING OUT	
DOUBLE DOOR, OPENING IN	
REFRIGERATOR DOOR	

WINDOW SYMBOLS

TYPE	WOOD OR METAL SASH IN FRAME WALL	METAL SASH IN MASONRY WALL	WOOD SASH IN MASONRY WALL
DOUBLE HUNG			
CASEMENT DOUBLE, OPENING OUT			
SINGLE, OPENING IN			

Figure 2 —Architectural symbols (door and windows).

corner posts are used, consisting of various numbers of ordinary studs, nailed together in various ways.

HORIZONTAL STRUCTURAL MEMBERS

In technical terminology, a horizontal load-bearing structural member which spans a space, and which is supported at both ends, is called a BEAM. A member which is FIXED at one end only is called a CANTILEVER. Steel members which consist of solid pieces of the regular structural steel shapes are called beams, but a type of steel member which is actually a light truss is called an OPEN-WEB STEEL JOIST or a BAR STEEL JOIST.

Horizontal structural members which support the ends of floor beams or joists in wood frame construction are called SILLS, GIRTS, or GIRDERS, depending on the type of framing being done and the location of the member in the structure. Horizontal members which support studs are called SILL or SOLE PLATES. Horizontal members which support the wall-ends of rafters are called RAFTER PLATES. Horizontal members which assume the weight of concrete or masonry walls above door and window openings are called LINTELS.

TRUSSES

A beam of given strength, without intermediate supports below, can support a given load over only a certain maximum span. If the span is wider than this maximum, intermediate supports, such as a column must be provided for the beam. Sometimes it is not feasible or possible to install intermediate supports. When such is the case, a TRUSS may be used instead of a beam.

A beam consists of a single horizontal member. A truss, however, is a framework, consisting of two horizontal (or nearly horizontal) members, joined together by a number of vertical and/or inclined members. The horizontal members are called the UPPER and LOWER CHORDS; the vertical and/or inclined members are called the WEB MEMBERS.

ROOF MEMBERS

The horizontal or inclined members which provide support to a roof are called RAFTERS. The lengthwise (right angle to the rafters) member which support the peak ends of the rafters in a roof is called the RIDGE. (The ridge may be called the Ridge board, the Ridge PIECE, or the Ridge pole.) Lengthwise members other than ridges are called PURLINS. In wood frame construction the wall ends of rafters are supported on horizontal members called RAFTER PLATES, which are in turn supported by the outside wall studs. In concrete or masonry wall construction, the wall ends of rafters may be anchored directly on the walls, or on plates bolted to the walls.

II. CONSTRUCTION DRAWINGS

Construction drawings are drawings in which as much construction information as possible is presented GRAPHICALLY, or by means of pictures. Most construction drawings consist of ORTHOGRAPHIC views. GENERAL drawings consist of PLANS AND ELEVATIONS, drawn on a relatively small scale. DETAIL drawings consist of SECTIONS and DETAILS, drawn on a relatively large scale.

PLANS

A PLAN view is, as you know, a view of an object or area as it would appear if projected onto a horizontal plane passed through or held above the object or area. The most common construction plans are PLOT PLANS (also called SITE PLANS), FOUNDATION PLANS, FLOOR PLANS, and FRAMING PLANS.

A PLOT PLAN shows the contours, boundaries, roads, utilities, trees, structures, and any other significant physical features pertaining to or located on the site. The locations of proposed structures are indicated by appropriate outlines or floor plans. By locating the corners of a proposed structure at given distances from a REFERENCE or BASE line (which is shown on the plan and which can be located on the site), the plot plan provides essential data for those who will lay out the building lines. By indicating the elevations of existing and proposed earth surfaces (by means of CONTOUR lines), the plot plan provides essential data for the graders and excavators.

A FOUNDATION PLAN (fig. 3) is a plan view of a structure projected on a horizontal plane passed through (in imagination, of course) at the level of the tops of the foundations. The plan shown in figure 3 tells you that the main foundation of this structure will consist of a rectangular 12-in. concrete block wall, 22 ft

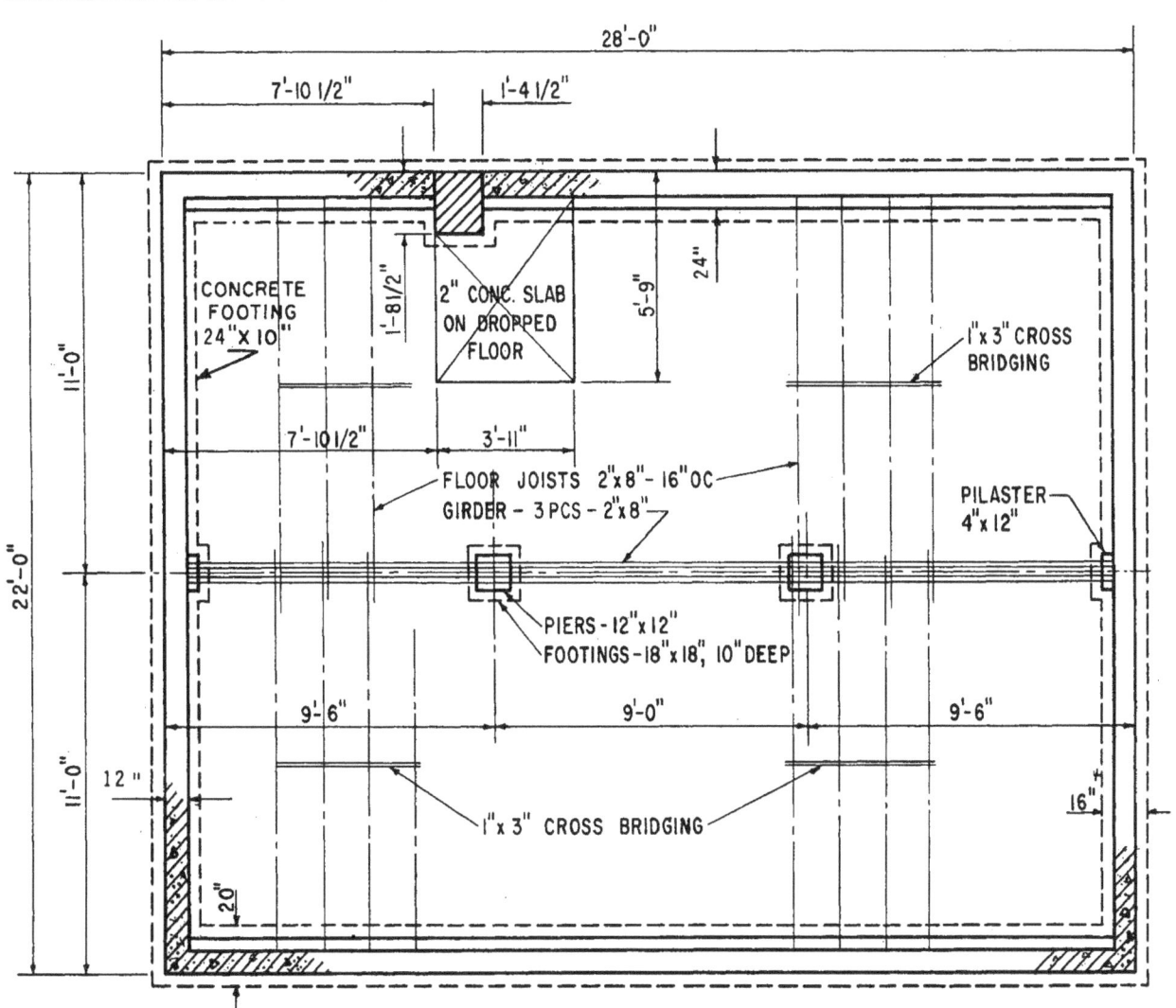

Figure 3.—Foundation plan.

wide by 28 ft long, centered on a concrete footing 24 in. wide. Besides the outside wall and footing, there will be two 12-in. square piers, centered on 18-in. square footings, and located on center 9 ft 6 in. from the end wall building lines. These piers will support a ground floor center-line girder.

A FLOOR PLAN (also called a BUILDING PLAN) is developed as shown in figure 4. Information on a floor plan includes the lengths, thicknesses, and character of the building walls at that particular floor, the widths and locations of door and window openings, the lengths and character of partitions, the number and arrangement of rooms, and the types and locations of utility installations. A typical floor plan is shown in figure 5.

FRAMING PLANS show the dimensions, numbers, and arrangement of structural members in wood frame construction. A simple FLOOR FRAMING PLAN is superimposed on the foundation plan shown in figure 3. From this foundation plan you learn that the ground-floor joists in this structure will consist of 2 x 8's, lapped at the girder, and spaced 16 in. O. C. The plan also shows that each row of joists is to be braced by a row of 1 x 3 cross bridging. For a more complicated floor framing problem, a framing plan like the one shown in figure 2-6 would be required. This plan

  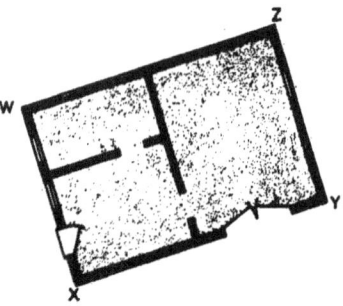

PERSPECTIVE VIEW OF A BUILDING SHOWING CUTTING PLANE WXY

PREVIOUS PERSPECTIVE VIEW AT CUTTING PLANE WXYZ, TOP REMOVED

DEVELOPED FLOOR PLAN WXYZ

Figure 4.—Floor plan development.

shows, among other things, the arrangement of joists and other members around stair wells and other floor openings.

A WALL FRAMING PLAN gives similar information with regard to the studs, corner posts, bracing, sills, plates, and other structural members in the walls. Since it is a view on a vertical plane, a wall framing plan is not a plan in the strict technical sense. However, the practice of calling it a plan has become a general custom. A ROOF FRAMING PLAN gives similar information with regard to the rafters, ridge, purlins, and other structural members in the roof.

A UTILITY PLAN is a floor plan which shows the layout of a heating, electrical, plumbing, or other utility system. Utility plans are used primarily by the ratings responsible for the utilities, but they are important to the Builder as well. Most utility installations require the leaving of openings in walls, floors, and roofs for the admission or installation of utility features. The Builder who is placing a concrete foundation wall must study the utility plans to determine the number, sizes, and locations of the openings he must leave for utilities.

Figure 7 shows a heating plan. Figure 8 shows an electrical plan.

ELEVATIONS

ELEVATIONS show the front, rear, and sides of a structure projected on vertical planes parallel to the planes of the sides. Front, rear, right side, and left side elevations of a small building are shown in figure 9.

As you can see, the elevations give you a number of important vertical dimensions, such as the perpendicular distance from the finish floor to the top of the rafter plate and from the finish floor to the tops of door and window finished openings. They also show the locations and characters of doors and windows. Dimensions of window sash and dimensions and character of lintels, however, are usually set forth in a WINDOW SCHEDULE.

A SECTION view is a view of a cross-section, developed as indicated in figure 10. By general custom, the term is confined to views of cross-sections cut by vertical planes. A floor plan or foundation plan, cut by a horizontal plane, is, technically speaking, a section view as well as a plan view, but it is seldom called a section.

The most important sections are the WALL sections. Figure 11 shows three wall sections for three alternate types of construction for the building shown in figures 3, 5, 7 and 8. The angled arrows marked "A" in figure 5 indicate the location of the cutting plane for the sections.

The wall sections are of primary importance to the supervisors of construction and to the craftsmen who will do the actual building. Take the first wall section, marked "masonry construction," for example. Starting at the bottom, you learn that the footing will be concrete, 2 ft wide and 10 in. high. The vertical distance of the bottom of the footing below FINISHED GRADE (level of the finished earth surface around the house) "varies"—meaning that it will depend on the soil-bearing capacity at the particular site. The foundation wall will consist of

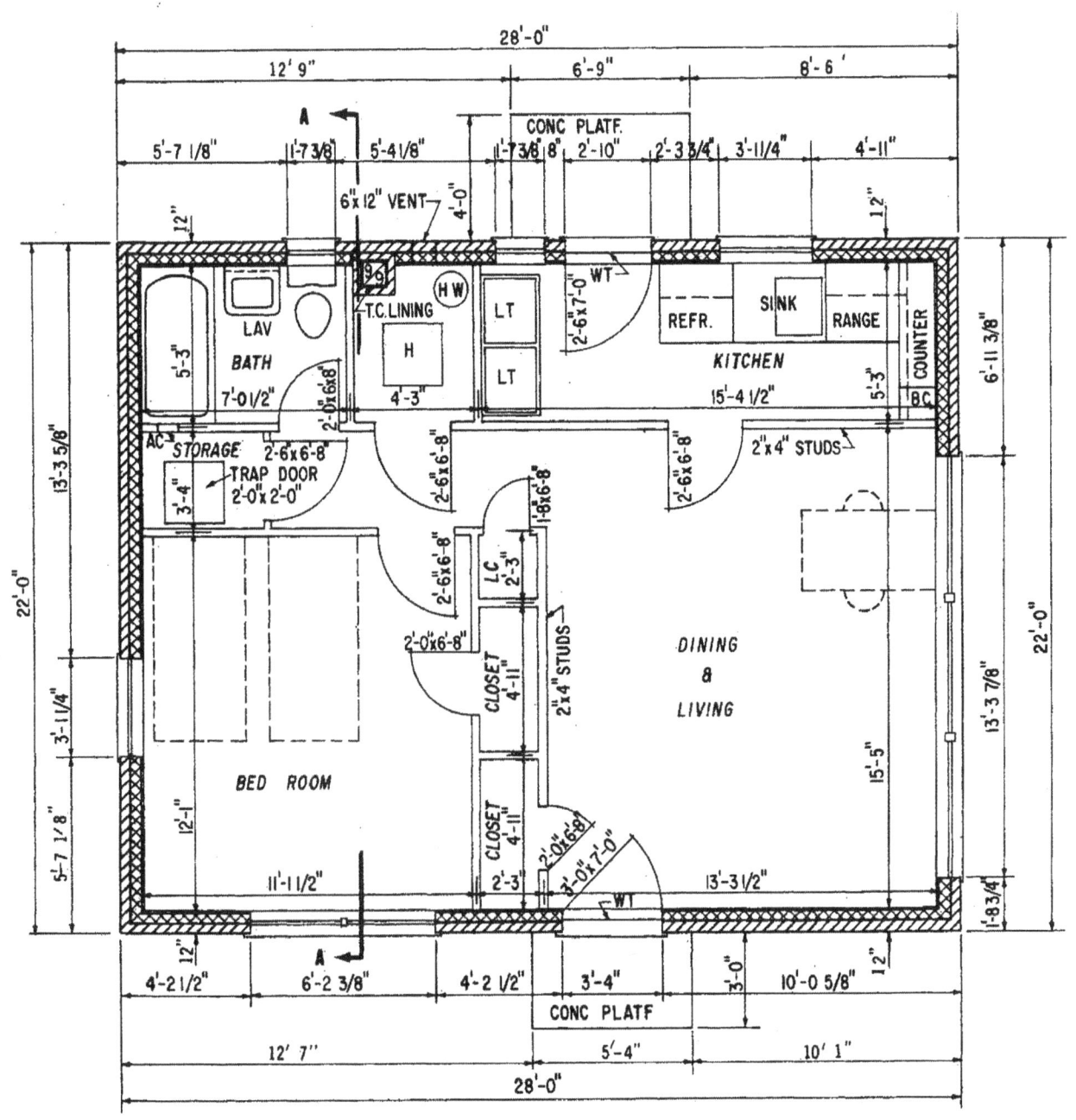

Figure 5.—Floor plan.

12-in. CMU, centered on the footing. Twelve-inch blocks will extend up to an unspecified distance below grade, where a 4-in. brick FACING (dimension indicated in the middle wall section) begins. Above the line of the bottom of the facing, it is obvious that 8-in. instead of 12-in. blocks will be used in the foundation wall.

The building wall above grade will consist of a 4-in. brick FACING TIER, backed by a BACKING TIER of 4-in. cinder blocks. The floor joists, consisting of 2 x 8's placed 16 in. O.C., will be anchored on 2 x 4 sills bolted to the top of the foundation wall. Every third joist will be additionally secured by a 2 x 1/4 STRAP ANCHOR embedded in the cinder block backing tier of the building wall.

The window (window B in the plan front elevation, fig. 9) will have a finished opening

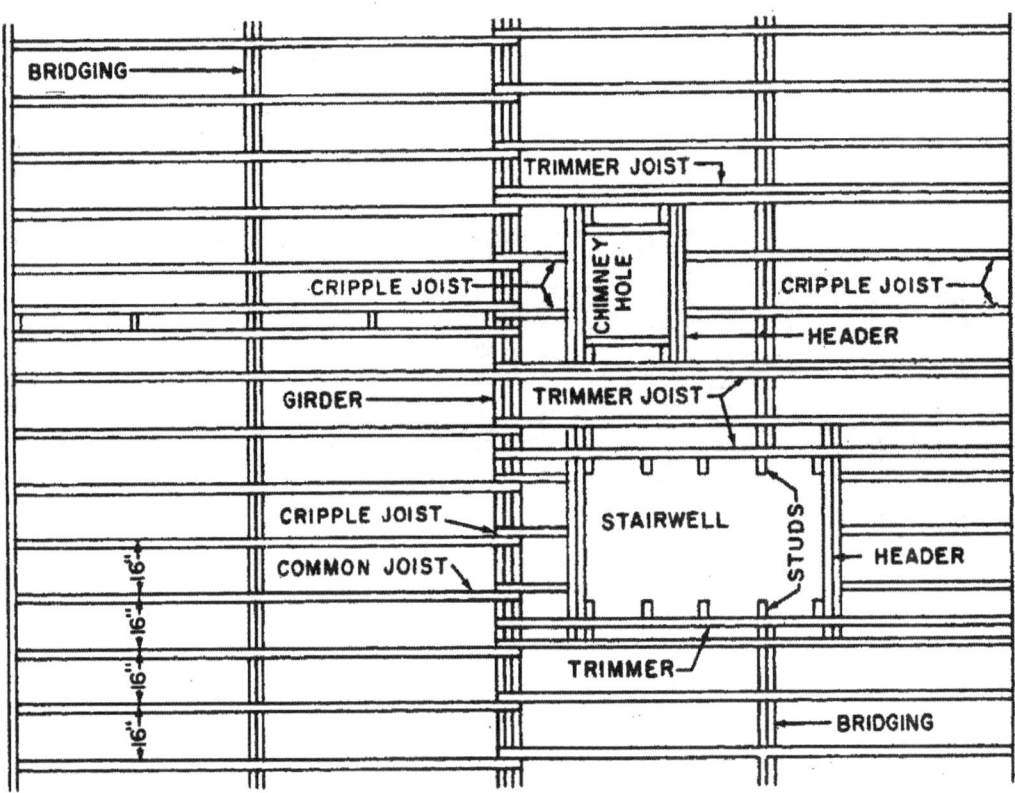

Figure 6.—Floor framing plan.

4 ft 2-5/8 in. high. The bottom of the opening will come 2 ft 11-3/4 in. above the line of the finished floor. As indicated in the wall section, (fig. 11) 13 masonry COURSES (layers of masonry units) above the finished floor line will amount to a vertical distance of 2 ft 11-3/4 in. As also indicated, another 19 courses will amount to the prescribed vertical dimension of the finished window opening.

Window framing details, including the placement and cross-sectional character of the lintel, are shown. The building wall will be carried 10-1/4 in., less the thickness of a 2 x 8 RAFTER PLATE, above the top of the window finished opening. The total vertical distance from the top of the finished floor to the top of the rafter plate will be 8 ft 2-1/4 in. Ceiling joists and rafters will consist of 2 x 6's, and the roof covering will consist of composition shingles laid on wood sheathing.

Flooring will consist of a wood finisher floor laid on a wood subfloor. Inside walls will be finished with plaster on lath (except on masonry wall which would be with or without lath as directed). A minimum of 2 vertical feet of crawl space will extend below the bottoms of the floor joists.

The middle wall section in figure 2-11 gives you similar information for a similar building constructed with wood frame walls and a DOUBLE-HUNG window. The third wall section shown in the figure gives you similar information for a similar building constructed with a steel frame, a casement window, and a concrete floor finished with asphalt tile.

DETAILS

DETAIL drawings are drawings which are done on a larger scale than that of the general drawings, and which show features not appearing at all, or appearing on too small a scale, on the general drawings. The wall sections just described are details as well as sections, since

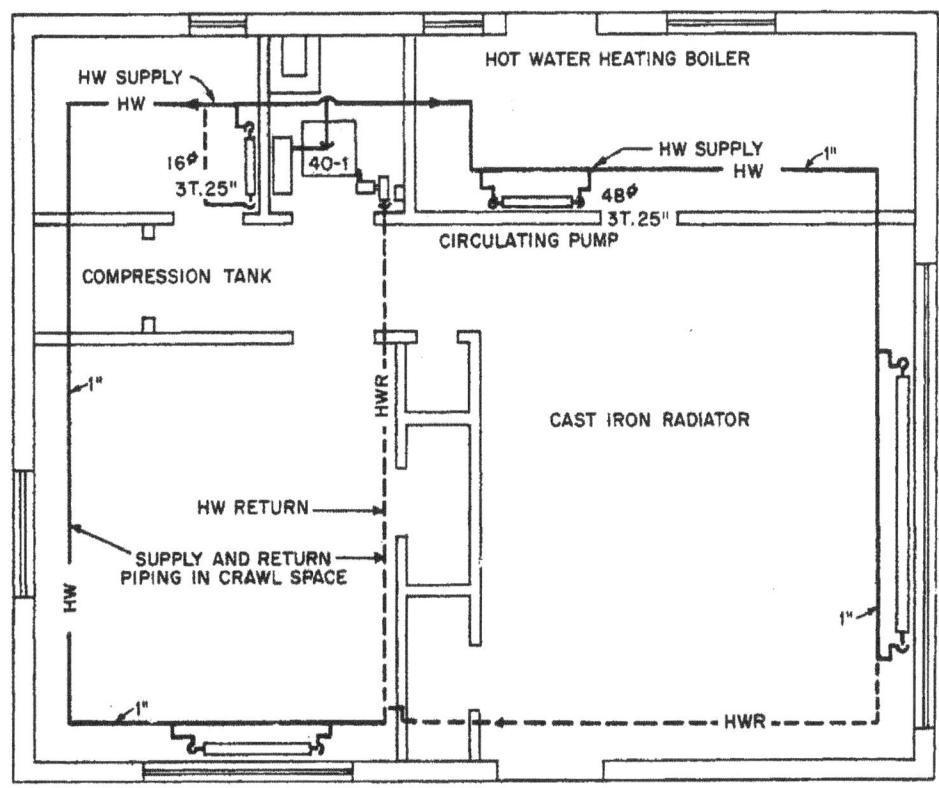

Figure 7.—Heating plan.

they are drawn on a considerable larger scale than the plans and elevations. Framing details at doors, windows, and cornices, which are the most common types of details, are practically always sections.

Details are included whenever the information given in the plans, elevations, and wall sections is not sufficiently "detailed" to guide the craftsmen on the job. Figure 12 shows some typical door and window wood framing details, and an eave detail for a very simple type of CORNICE. You should study these details closely to learn the terminology of framing members.

III. SPECIFICATIONS

The construction drawings contain much of the information about a structure which can be presented GRAPHICALLY (that is, in drawings). A very considerable amount of information can be presented this way, but there is more information which the construction supervisors and artisans must have and which is not adaptable to the graphic form of presentation. Information of this kind includes quality criteria for materials (maximum amounts of aggregate per sack of cement, for example), specified standards of workmanship, prescribed construction methods, and the like.

Information of this kind is presented in a list of written SPECIFICATIONS, familiarly known as the "SPECS." A list of specifications usually begins with a section on GENERAL CONDITIONS. This section starts with a GENERAL DESCRIPTION of the building, including the type of foundation, type or types of windows, character of framing, utilities to be installed, and the like. Next comes a list of DEFINITIONS of terms used in the specs, and next certain routine declarations of responsibility and certain conditions to be maintained on the job.

SPECIFIC CONDITIONS are grouped in sections under headings which describe each of the major construction phases of the job. Separate specifications are written for each phase, and the phases are then combined to more or less follow the usual order of construction sequences on the job. A typical list of sections under "Specific Conditions" follows:

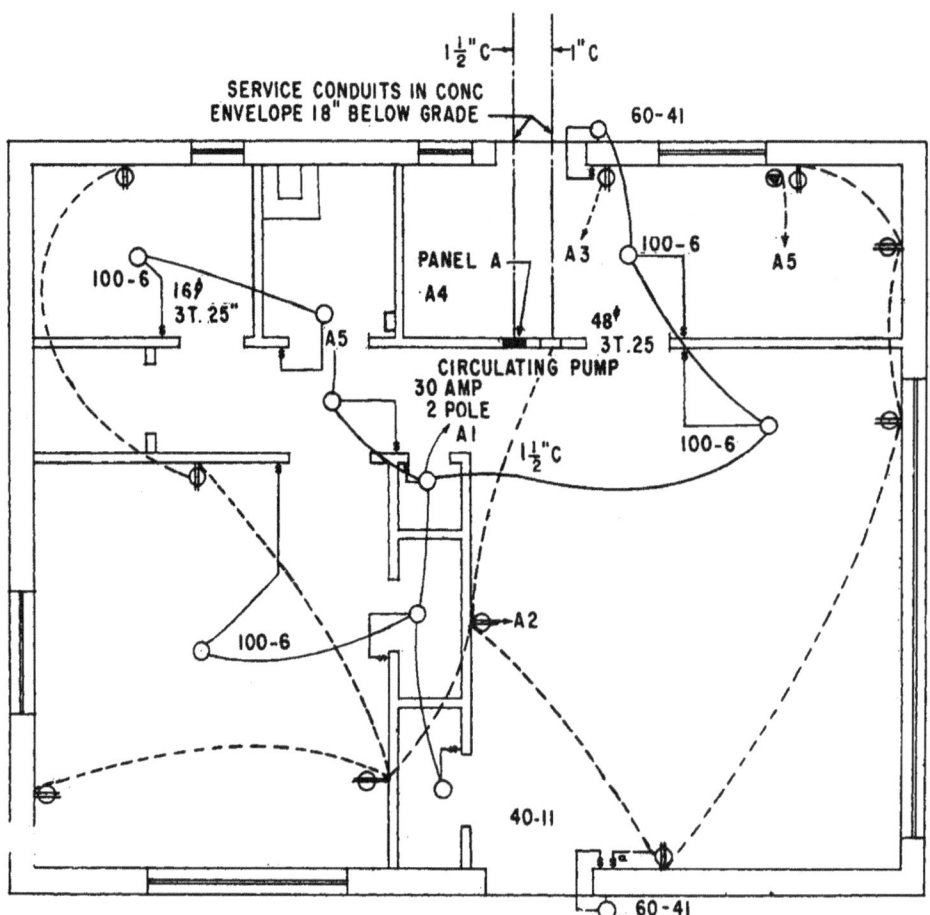

Figure 8.—Electrical plan.

2.—EARTHWORK 3.—CONCRETE 4.—MASONRY 5.—MISCELLANEOUS STEEL AND IRON 6.—CARPENTRY AND JOINERY 7.—LATHING AND PLASTERING 8.—TILE WORK 9.—FINISH FLOORING 10.—GLAZING 11.—FINISHING HARDWARE 12.—PLUMBING 13.—HEATING 14.—ELECTRICAL WORK 15.—FIELD PAINTING.

A section under "Specific Conditions" usually begins with a subsection of GENERAL REQUIREMENTS which apply to the phase of construction being considered. Under Section 6, CARPENTRY AND JOINERY, for example, the first section might go as follows:

6-01. GENERAL REQUIREMENTS. All framing, rough carpentry, and finishing woodwork required for the proper completion of the building shall be provided. All woodwork shall be protected from the weather, and the building shall be thoroughly dry before the finish is placed. All finish shall be dressed, smoothed, and sandpapered at the mill, and in addition shall be hand smoothed and sandpapered at the building where necessary to produce proper finish. Nailing shall be done, as far as practicable, in concealed places, and all nails in finishing work shall be set. All lumber shall be S4S (meaning, "surfaced on 4 sides"); all materials for millwork and finish shall be kiln-dried; all rough and framing lumber shall be air- or kiln-dried. Any cutting, fitting, framing, and blocking necessary for the accommodation of other work shall be provided. All nails, spikes, screws, bolts, plates, clips, and other fastenings and rough hardware necessary for the proper completion of the building shall be provided.

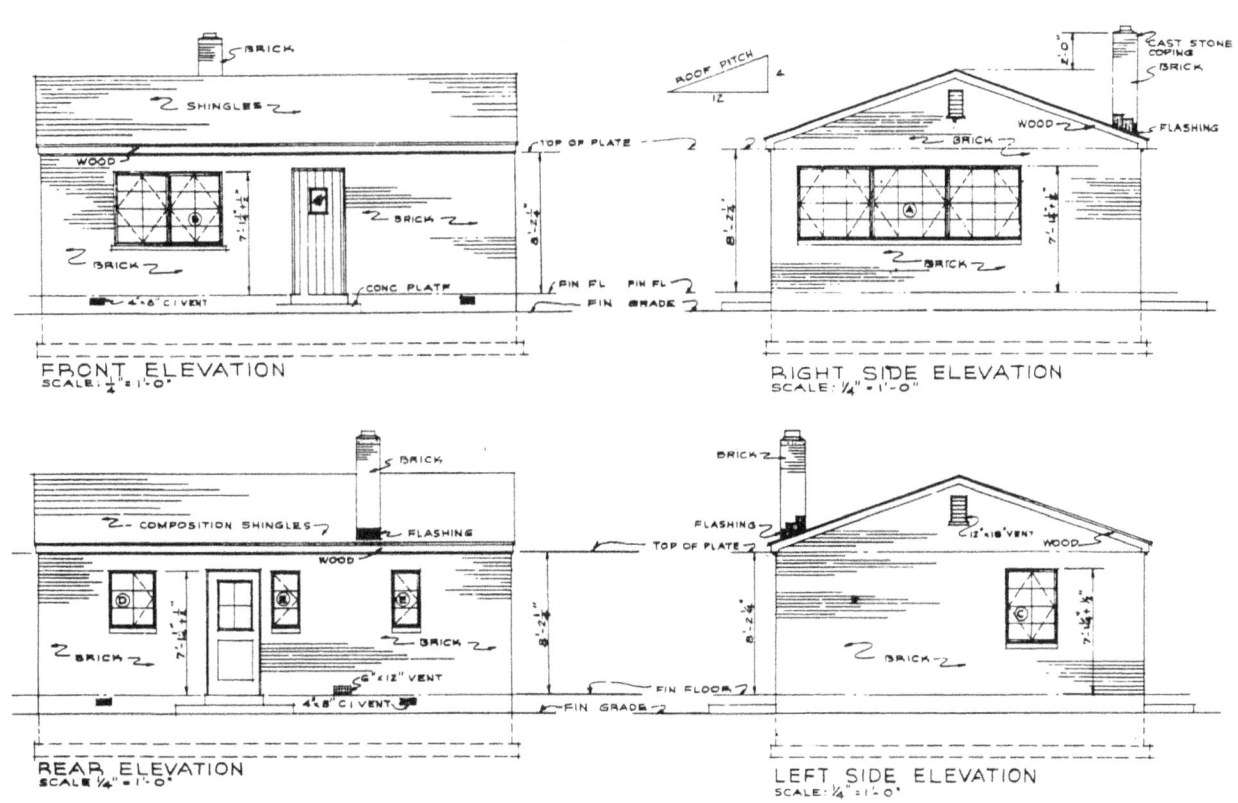

Figure 2-9.—Elevations.

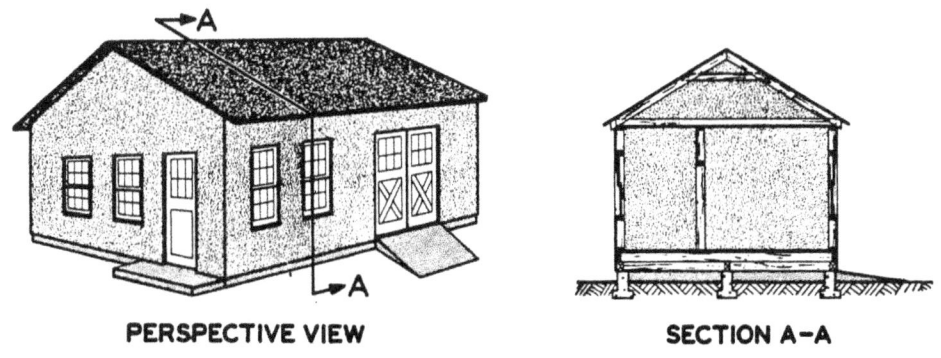

TYPICAL SMALL BUILDING SHOWING CUTTING PLANE A-A AND SECTION DEVELOPED FROM THE CUTTING PLANE

Figure 10.—Development of a section view.

All finishing hardware shall be installed in accordance with the manufacturers' directions. Calking and flashing shall be provided where indicated, or where necessary to provide weathertight construction.

Next after the General Requirements for Carpentry and Joinery, there is generally a subsection on "Grading," in which the kinds and grades of the various woods to be used in the structure are specified. Subsequent subsections

179

DRAWINGS AND SPECIFICATIONS

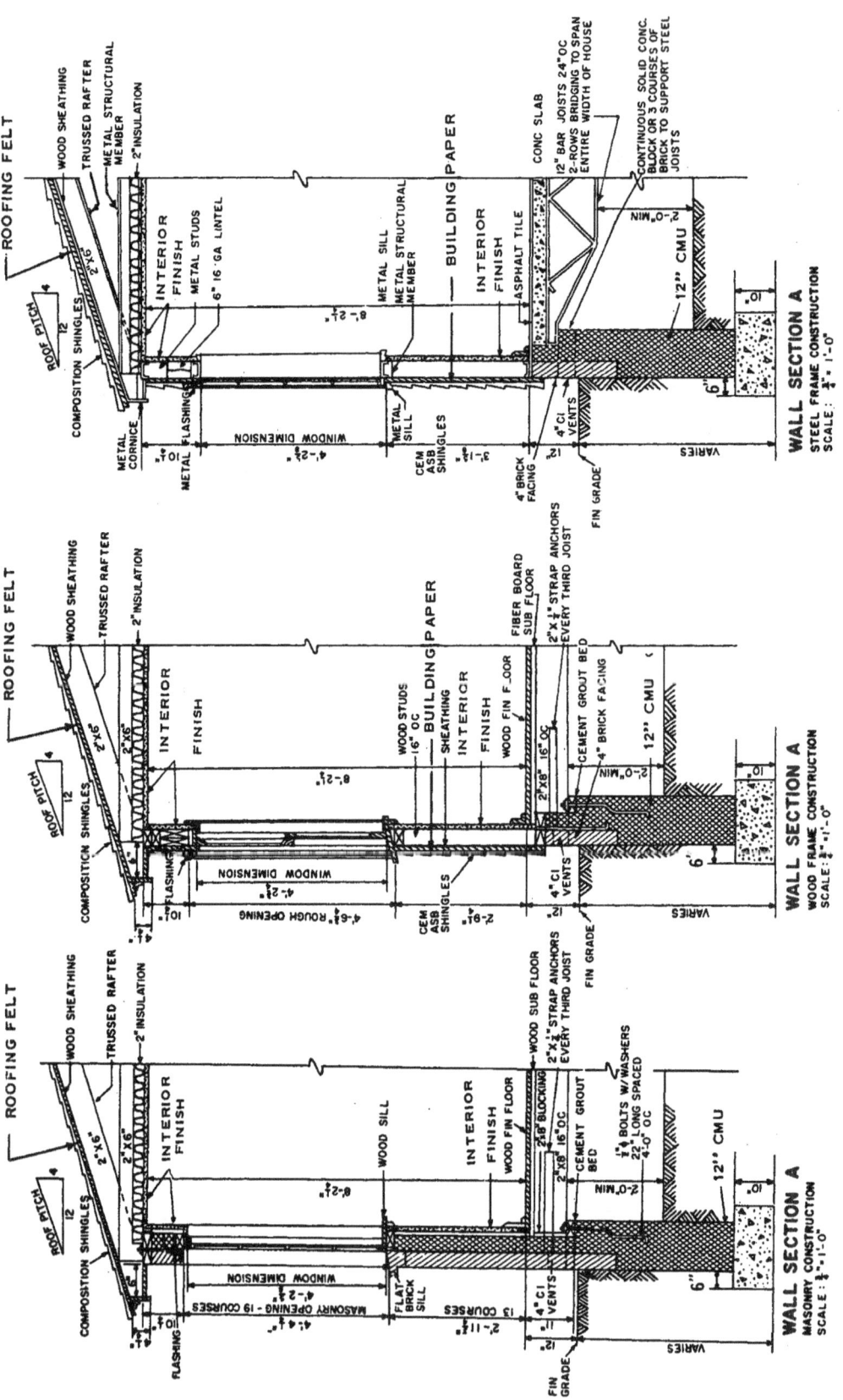

Figure 11.—Wall sections

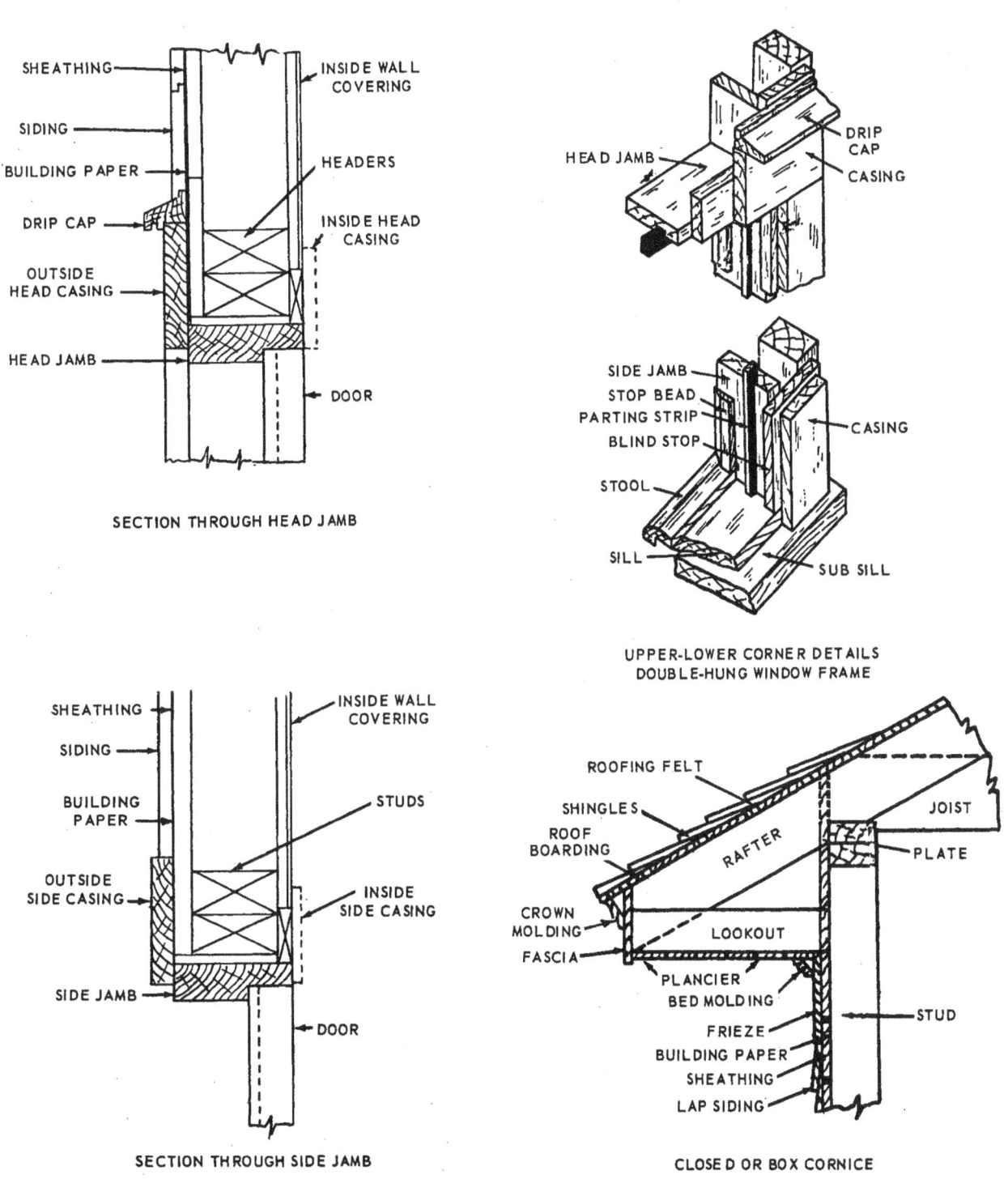

Figure 12.—Door, window and eave details.

specify various quality criteria and standards of workmanship for the various aspects of the rough and finish carpentry work, under such headings as FRAMING; SILLS, PLATES, AND GIRDERS; FLOOR JOISTS AND ROOF RAFTERS; STUDDING; and so on. An example of one of these subsections follows:

>STUDDING for walls and partitions shall have doubled plates and doubled stud caps. Studs shall be set plumb and not to exceed 16-in. centers and in true alignment; they shall be bridged with one row of 2 x 4 pieces, set flatwise, fitted tightly, and nailed securely to each stud. Studding shall be doubled around openings and the heads of openings shall rest on the inner studs. Openings in partitions having widths of 4 ft and over shall be trussed. In wood frame construction, studs shall be trebled at corners to form posts.

From the above samples, you can see that a knowledge of the relevant specifications is as essential to the construction supervisor and the construction artisan as a knowledge of the construction drawings.

It is very important that the proper spec be used to cover the material requested. In cases in which the material is not covered by a Government spec, the ASTM (American Society for Testing Materials) spec or some other approved commercial spec may be used. It is EXTREMELY IMPORTANT in using specifications to cite all amendments, including the latest changes.

As a rule, the specs are provided for each project by the A/E (ARCHITECT-ENGINEERS). These are the OFFICIAL guidelines approved by the chief engineer or his representative for use during construction. These requirements should NOT be deviated from without prior approval from proper authority. This approval is usually obtained by means of a change order. When there is disagreement between the specifications and drawings, the specifications should normally be followed; however, check with higher authority in each case.

IV. BUILDER'S MATHEMATICS

The Builder has many occasions for the employment of the processes of ordinary arithmetic, and he must be thoroughly familiar with the methods of determining the areas and volumes of the various plane and solid geometrical figures. Only a few practical applications and a few practical suggestions, will be given here.

RATIO AND PROPORTION

There are a great many practical applications of ratio and proportion in the construction field. A few examples are as follows:

Some dimensions on construction drawings (such as, for example, distances from base lines and elevations of surfaces) are given in ENGINEER'S instead of CARPENTER's measure. Engineer's measure is measure in feet and decimal parts of a foot, or in inches and decimal parts of an inch, such as 100.15 ft or 11.14 in. Carpenter's measure is measure in yards, feet, inches, and even-denominator fractions of an inch, such as 1/2 in., 1/4 in., 1/16 in., 1/32 in., and 1/64 in.

You must know how to convert an engineer's measure given on a construction drawing to a carpenter's measure. Besides this, it will often happen that calculations you make yourself may produce a result in feet and decimal parts of a foot, which result you will have to convert to carpenter's measure. To convert engineer's to carpenter's measure you can use ratio and proportion as follows:

Let's say that you want to convert 100.14 ft to feet and inches to the nearest 1/16 in. The 100 you don't need to convert, since it is already in feet. What you need to do, first, is to find out how many twelfths of a foot (that is, how many inches) there are in 14/100 ft. Set this up as a proportional equation as follows: $x:12::14:100$.

You know that in a proportional equation the product of the means equals the product of the extremes. Consequently, $100x = (12 \times 14)$, or 168. Then $x = 168/100$, or 1.68 in. Next question is, how many 16ths of an in. are there in 68/100 in.? Set this up, too, as a proportional equation, thus: $x:16::68:100$. Then $100x = 1088$, and $x = 10\ 88/100$ sixteenths. Since 88/100 of a sixteenth is more than one-half of a sixteenth, you ROUND OFF by calling it 11/16. In 100.14 ft, then, there are 100 ft 1 11/16 in. For example:

A.
$$\underbrace{x:12::14:100}_{\text{Extremes}} \quad \text{means}$$

Product of extremes = product of means:

$$100\ x = 168$$
$$x = 1.68 \text{ IN.}$$

B. x:16::68:100

$$100\ x = 1088$$
$$x = 10.88$$
$$x = 10\ \frac{88}{100}\ \text{sixteenths}$$

Rounded off to 11/16

Another way to convert engineer's measurements to carpenter's measurements is to multiply the decimal portion of a foot by 12 to get inches; multiply the decimal by 16 to get the fraction of an inch.

There are many other practical applications of ratio and proportion in the construction field. Suppose, for example, that a table tells you that, for the size and type of brick wall you happen to be laying, 12,321 bricks and 195 cu ft of mortar are required per every 1000 sq ft of wall. How many bricks and how much mortar will be needed for 750 sq ft of the same wall? You simply set up equations as follows; for example:

Brick: x:750::12,321:1000
Mortar: x:750::195:1000

Brick: $\dfrac{X}{750} = \dfrac{12,321}{1000}$ Cross multiply

$$1000\ X = 9,240,750 \quad \text{Divide}$$
$$X = 9,240.75 = 9241 \text{ Brick.}$$

Mortar: $\dfrac{X}{750} = \dfrac{195}{1000}$ Cross multiply

$$1000\ X = 146,250 \quad \text{Divide}$$
$$X = 146.25 = 146\ 1/4 \text{ cu ft}$$

Suppose, for another example, that the ingredient proportions by volume for the type of concrete you are making are 1 cu ft cement to 1.7 cu ft sand to 2.8 cu ft coarse aggregate. Suppose you know as well, by reference to a table, that ingredients combined in the amounts indicated will produce 4.07 cu ft of concrete. How much of each ingredient will be required to make a cu yd of concrete?

Remember here, first, that there are not 9, but 27 (3 ft x 3 ft x 3 ft) cu ft in a cu yd. Your proportional equations will be as follows:

Cement: x:27::1:4.07

Sand: x:27::1.7:4.07

Coarse aggregate: x:27::2.8:4.07

Cement: x:27::1:4.07

$$\frac{x}{27} = \frac{1}{4.07}$$
$$4.07\ x = 27$$
$$x = 6.63 \text{ cu ft Cement}$$

Sand: x:27::1.7:4.07

$$\frac{x}{27} = \frac{1.7}{4.07}$$
$$4.07\ x = 45.9$$
$$x = 11.28 \text{ cu ft Sand}$$

Coarse aggregate: x:27::2.8:407

$$\frac{x}{27} = \frac{2.8}{4.07}$$
$$4.07\ x = 75.6$$
$$x = 18.57 \text{ cu ft Coarse aggregate}$$

ARITHMETICAL OPERATIONS

The formulas for finding the area and volume of geometric figures are expressed in algebraic equations which are called formulas. A few of the more important formulas and their mathematical solutions will be discussed in this section.

DRAWINGS AND SPECIFICATIONS

To get an area, you multiply 2 linear measures together, and to get a volume you multiply 3 linear measures together. The linear measures you multiply together must all be expressed in the SAME UNITS; you cannot, for example, multiply a length in feet by a width in inches to get a result in square feet or in square inches.

Dimensions of a feature on a construction drawing are not always given in the same units. For a concrete wall, for example, the length and height are usually given in feet and the thickness in inches. Furthermore, you may want to get a result in units which are different from any shown on the drawing. Concrete volume, for example, is usually expressed in cubic yards, while the dimensions of concrete work are given on the drawings in feet and inches.

You can save yourself a good many steps in calculating by using fractions to convert the original dimension units into the desired end-result units. Take 1 in., for example. To express 1 in. in feet, you simply put it over 12, thus: 1/12 ft. To express 1 in. in yards, you simply put it over 36, thus: 1/36 yd. In the same manner, to express 1 ft in yards you simply put it over 3, thus 1/3 yd.

Suppose now that you want to calculate the number of cu yd of concrete in a wall 32 ft long by 14 ft high by 8 in. thick. You can express all these in yards and set up your problem thus:

$$\frac{32}{3} \times \frac{14}{3} \times \frac{8}{36}$$

Next you can cancel out, thus:

$$\frac{\cancel{32}^{16}}{3} \times \frac{\cancel{14}}{3} \times \frac{8}{\cancel{36}_{9}} = \frac{896}{81}$$

Dividing 896 by 81, you get 11.06 cu yds of concrete in the wall.

The right triangle is a triangle which contains one right (90°) angle. The following letters will denote the parts of the triangle indicated in figure 2-13—a = altitude, b = base, c = hypotenuse.

In solving a right triangle, the length of any side may be found if the lengths of the other two sides are given. The combinations of 3-4-5 (lengths of sides) or any multiple of these combinations will come out to a whole number. The following examples show the formula for finding

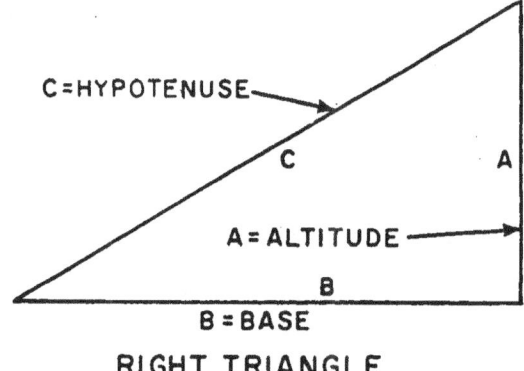

RIGHT TRIANGLE

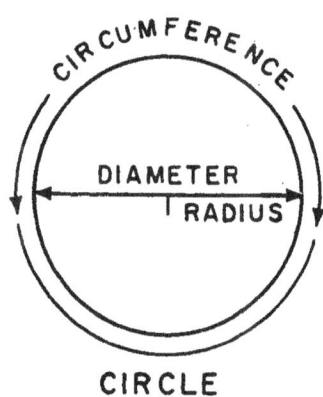

CIRCLE

Figure 13.—Right triangle and circle.

each side. Each of these formulas is derived from the master formula $c^2 = a^2 + b^2$.

(1) Find c when a = 3, and b = 4.

$c = \sqrt{a^2 + b^2} = \sqrt{3^2 + 4^2} = \sqrt{9 + 16} = \sqrt{25} = 5$

(2) Find a when b = 8, and c = 10.

$a = \sqrt{c^2 - b^2} = \sqrt{10^2 - 8^2} = \sqrt{100 - 64} = \sqrt{36} = 6$

(3) Find b when a = 9, and c = 15.

$b = \sqrt{c^2 - a^2} = \sqrt{15^2 - 9^2} = \sqrt{225 - 81} = \sqrt{144} = 12.$

There are tables from which the square roots of numbers may be found; otherwise, they may be found arithmetically as explained later in this chapter.

Areas And Volumes Of Geometric Figures

This section on areas and volumes of geometric figures will be limited to the most commonly used geometric figures. Reference books, such as Mathematics, Vol. 1, are available for additional information if needed. Areas are expressed in square units and volumes in cubic units.

1. A circle is a plane figure bounded by a curved line every point of which is the same distance from the center.
    a. The curved line is called the circumference.
    b. A straight line drawn from the center to any point on the circumference is called a radius. (r = 1/2 the diameter.)
    c. A straight line drawn from one point of the circumference through the center and terminating on the opposite point of the circumference is called a diameter. (d = 2 times the radius.) See figure 2-13.
    d. The area of a circle is found by the following formulas: $A = \pi r^2$ or $A = .7854 d^2$. (π is pronounced pie = 3.1416 or 3 1/7, .7854 is 1/4 of π.) Example: Find the area of a circle whose radius is 7". $A = \pi r^2 = 3\ 1/7 \times 7^2 = 22/7 \times 49 = 154$ sq in. If you use the second formula you obtain the same results.
    e. The circumference of a circle is found by multiplying π times the diameter or 2 times π times the radius. Example: Find the circumference of a circle whose diameter is 56 inches. $C = \pi d = 3.1415 \times 56 = 175.9296$ inches.

2. The area of a right triangle is equal to one-half the product of the base by the altitude. (Area = 1/2 base x altitude.) Example: Find the area of a triangle whose base is 16" and altitude 6". Solution:

$A = 1/2\ bh = 1/2 \times 16 \times 6 = 48$ sq in.

3. The volume of a cylinder is found by multiplying the area of the base times the height. ($V = 3.1416 \times r^2 \times h$). Example: Find the volume of a cylinder which has a radius of 8 in. and a height of 4 ft. Solution:

8 in $= \frac{2}{3}$ ft and $\left(\frac{2}{3}\right)2 = \frac{4}{9}$ sq ft.

$V = 3.1416 \times \frac{4}{9} \times 4 = \frac{50.2656}{9} = 5.59$ cu ft.

4. The volume of a rectangular solid equals the length x width x height. (V = lwh.) Example: Find the volume of a rectangular solid which has a length of 6 ft, a width of 3 ft, and a height of 2 ft. Solution:

$V = lwh = 6 \times 3 \times 2 = 36$ cu ft.

5. The volume of a cone may be found by multiplying one-third times the area of the base times the height.

$$\left(V = \frac{1}{3} \pi r^2 h\right)$$

Example: Find the volume of a cone when the radius of its base is 2 ft and its height is 9 ft. Solution:

$$\pi = 3.1416, r = 2, 2^2 = 4$$

$V = \frac{1}{3} r^2 h = \frac{1}{3} \times 3.1416 \times 4 \times 9 = 37.70$ cu ft.

Powers And Roots

1. Powers—When we multiply several numbers together, as 2 x 3 x 4 = 24, the numbers 2, 3, and 4 are factors and 24 the product. The operation of raising a number to a power is a special case of multiplication in which the factors are all equal. The power of a number is the number of times the number itself is to be taken as a factor. Example: 2^4 is 16. The second power is called the square of the number, as 3^2. The third power of a number is called the cube of the number, as 5^3. The exponent of a number is a number placed to the right and above a base to show how many times the base is used as a factor. Example:

4^3 ← exponent =
   ← base

$4 \times 4 \times 4 = 64.$

2. Roots—To indicate a root, use the sign $\sqrt{\ }$, which is called the radical sign. A small figure, called the index of the root, is placed in the opening of the sign to show which root is to be taken. The square root of a number is one of the two equal factors into which a number is

DRAWINGS AND SPECIFICATIONS

divided. Example: $\sqrt{81} = \sqrt{9 \times 9} = 9$. The cube root is one of the three equal factors into which a number is divided. Example: $\sqrt[3]{125} = \sqrt[3]{5 \times 5 \times 5} = 5$.

Square Root

1. The square root of any number is that number which, when multiplied by itself, will produce the first number. For example; the square root of 121 is 11 because 11 times 11 equals 121.

2. How to extract the square root arithmetically:

```
                       95.
        √9025    √90'25.

                 : -81

        180  :   925
        +5   :  -925

        185  :   000
```

a. Begin at the decimal point and divide the given number into groups of 2 digits each (as far as possible), going from right to left and/or left to right.
b. Find the greatest number (9) whose square is contained in the first or left hand group (90). Square this number (9) and place it under the first pair of digits (90), then subtract.
c. Bring down the next pair of digits (25) and add it to the remainder (9).
d. Multiply the first digit in the root by 20 and use it as a trial divisor (180). This trial divisor (180) will go into the new dividend (925) five times. This number, 5 (second digit in the root), is added back to the trial divisor, obtaining the true divisor (185).
e. The true divisor (185) is multiplied by the second digit (5) and placed under the remainder (925). Subtract and the problem is solved.
f. If there is still a remainder and you want to carry the problem further, add zeros (in pairs) and continue the above process.

Coverage Calculations

You will frequently have occasion to estimate the number of linear feet of boards of a given size, or the number of tiles, asbestos shingles, and the like, required to cover a given area. Let's take the matter of linear feet of boards first.

What you do here is calculate, first, the number of linear feet of board required to cover 1 sq ft. For boards laid edge-to-edge, you base your calculations on the total width of a board. For boards which will lap each other, you base your calculations on the width laid TO THE WEATHER, meaning the total width minus the width of the lap.

Since there are 144 sq in. in a sq ft, linear footage to cover a given area can be calculated as follows. Suppose your boards are to be laid 8 in. to the weather. If you divide 8 in. into 144 sq in., the result (which is 18 in., or 1.5 ft) will be the linear footage required to cover a sq ft. If you have, say, 100 sq ft to cover, the linear footage required will be 100 x 1.5, or 150 ft.

To estimate the number of tiles, asbestos shingles, and the like required to cover a given area, you first calculate the number of units required to cover a sq ft. Suppose, for example, you are dealing with 9 in. x 9 in. asphalt tiles. The area of one of these is 9 in. x 9 in. or 81 sq in. In a sq ft there are 144 sq in. If it takes 1 to cover 81 sq in., how many will it take to cover 144 sq in.? Just set up a proportional equation, as follows.

$$1:81::x:144$$

When you work this out, you will find that it takes 1.77 tiles to cover a sq ft. To find the number of tiles required to cover 100 sq ft, simply multiply by 100. How do you multiply anything by 100? Just move the decimal point 2 places to the right. Consequently, it takes 177 9 x 9 asphalt tiles to cover 100 sq ft of area.

Board Measure

BOARD MEASURE is a method of measuring lumber in which the basic unit is an abstract volume 1 ft long by 1 ft wide by 1 in. thick. This abstract volume or unit is called a BOARD FOOT.

There are several formulas for calculating the number of board feet in a piece of given dimensions. Since lumber dimensions are most frequently indicated by width and thickness in inches and length in feet, the following formula is probably the most practical.

$$\frac{\text{Thickness in in.} \times \text{width in in.} \times \text{length in ft}}{12} = \text{board feet}$$

Suppose you are calculating the number of board feet in a 14-ft length of 2 x 4. Applying the formula, you get:

$$\frac{\overset{1}{\cancel{2}} \times \overset{2}{\cancel{4}} \times 14}{\underset{3}{\cancel{\cancel{12}}}} = \frac{28}{3} = 9\ 1/3 \text{ bd ft}$$

The chief practical use of board measure is in cost calculations, since lumber is bought and sold by the board foot. Any lumber less than 1 in. thick is presumed to be 1 in. thick for board measure purposes. Board measure is calculated on the basis of the NOMINAL, not the ACTUAL, dimensions of lumber.

The actual size of a piece of dimension lumber (such as a 2 x 4, for example) is usually less than the nominal size.

www.ingramcontent.com/pod-product-compliance
Lightning Source LLC
Chambersburg PA
CBHW081814300426
44116CB00014B/2348